Harald Barre
Traditions Can Be Changed

Global and Colonial History | Volume 7

Harald Barre, born in 1984, works at the VolkswagenStiftung in Hannover. He submitted his PhD thesis at the Leibniz Universität Hannover.

Harald Barre
Traditions Can Be Changed
Tanzanian Nationalist Debates around Decolonizing "Race" and Gender, 1960s-1970s

[transcript]

a.t.: Hannover, Univ., Diss., 2020

Bibliographic information published by the Deutsche Nationalbibliothek
The Deutsche Nationalbibliothek lists this publication in the Deutsche Nationalbibliografie; detailed bibliographic data are available in the Internet at http://dnb.d-nb.de

© 2022 transcript Verlag, Bielefeld

All rights reserved. No part of this book may be reprinted or reproduced or utilized in any form or by any electronic, mechanical, or other means, now known or hereafter invented, including photocopying and recording, or in any information storage or retrieval system, without permission in writing from the publisher.

Cover layout: Kordula Röckenhaus, Bielefeld
Printed by Majuskel Medienproduktion GmbH, Wetzlar
Print-ISBN 978-3-8376-5950-4
PDF-ISBN 978-3-8394-5950-8
https://doi.org/10.14361/9783839459508
ISSN of series: 2701-0309
eISSN of series: 2702-9328

Printed on permanent acid-free text paper.

Contents

Acknowledgements 7

Acronyms 9

1. **Debating the Nation**.. 11
1.1 Research Context 15
1.2 Some Theoretical Considerations 19
1.3 Structure... 42

2 **State and Society in the Colonial Era**....................................... 47
2.1 Asian Agency in the Colonial State 50
2.2 African Nationalism – the Evolution of a "Common Sense" 55
2.3 Gender in Colonial Tanganyika 63
2.4 TANU – Seizing the State.. 70
2.5 The Social World and the Public Sphere after Independence 74
2.6 Conclusion: Challenges to Persistent Colonial Structures.................... 80

3 **1964-1966 Search for Unity & Independence** 83
3.1 Racial Relations 84
3.2 Decolonizing Education?... 99
3.3 Decolonizing Gender Roles? 110
3.4 Conclusion: Independence in Crisis 118

4 **1967-1970: African Socialism or African Tradition?**......................... 121
4.1 (Non-) Racialism in Schools 123
4.2 Reforms on the Hill – the Pretext.. 145
4.3 Gender – the Articulation of Women's Critique in the Public Sphere 164
4.4 Conclusion: Debating New Concepts and Struggling with Old Structures 179

5 1971-1974: Achieving Liberation from Colonial World Views? 183
5.1 The Comeback of "Race"? 185
5.2 The University – A Contested Space 201
5.3 Gender – A Struggle Against Colonial Laws and Values 212
5.4 Conclusion: "Race" Demoted and Gender Transformed 228

6 1975-1979: Finding New Arenas in which to Debate 233
6.1 Gender Roles in the Newspaper 238
6.2 New Arenas for Debates on Gender Roles 241
6.3 Conclusion: Uncertainty and Agency 245

7 Conclusion 247
7.1 A Contested National Narrative 248
7.2 Interrelation Between the Public Sphere and Social World 250
7.3 Formative Obscurities 253
7.4 Limitations and Prospects 256

8 Bibliography 259
8.1 Secondary Literature 259
8.2 Sources 268

Acknowledgements

Writing this book was a journey, which I was only able to complete because of the many people who supported and advised me in various ways. Most immediately, I want to thank Brigitte Reinwald for counseling and supporting me. Every conversation we have had was inspiring and led to new ideas and action. In the same vein, I have to thank Mathias Bös, who always readily provided me with theoretical approaches as I laid down my thoughts and ideas for this work.

I discussed this work with my colleagues and fellow PhD students in Hannover. Namely, I want to thank Jana Otto, Daniel Kaune, Christopher Folkens, Susanne Heyn, Mario Peters, Katharina Steffan and Friederike Apelt for their thoughts, ideas and moral support.

This book has come together because of numerous people who advised and helped me in libraries and universities in Europe and in Africa. I feel particularly indebted to my interviewees, who devoted much of their time and who were willing to share their stories with me. Looking at history through the eyes of those who experienced it has always been humbling to me.

Through many of my interviewees, I have learned how privileged one is with a supportive family. I am lucky to be able to say that I have such a family. Specifically, I am grateful that I have never doubted the support of my parents, Bernd and Brigitte Barre. They were there for me whenever I needed them. I also have to thank my father-in-law, Gregory Mertz, who has diligently given me input on the last stretch towards publishing this work.

Last and certainly not least, I want to thank my wife, Katrina Mertz and our children, Liam, Ainsley and Hannah. This book would not have come to be if it was not for you. Beyond support and wisdom, you provided me with perspectives on life. Many of the issues discussed in this book are not unique and part of that human experience. As I have learned from the stories of my interviewees, I have learned from my family.

I have thanked only a fraction of the people I would like to thank. I hope that this book will be a contribution to Africa, to Tanzania, and to its people, wherever they live.

Acronyms

6PAC	Sixth Pan African Congress
ANC	African National Congress
DUSO	Dar es Salaam University Students Organisation
KAR	King's African Rifles
Frelimo	Frente de Libertação de Moçambique
IDS	Institute of Development Studies
NAUTS	National Union of Tanzania Student
PAC	Pan Africanist Congress of South Africa
SNCC	Student Nonviolent Coordinating Committee
TAA	Tanganyika African Association
TAMWA	Tanzania Media Women's Association
TANU	Tanganyika African National Union
TAPA	Tanganyika African Parents Association
TPH	Tanzania Publishing House
TYL	TANU Youth League
SWAPO	South West Africa People's Organisation
UCD	University College Dar es Salaam
UDA	Usafiri Dar es Salaam
UDSM	University of Dar es Salaam
UMATI	Chama cha Uzazi na Malezi Bora Tanzania
UN	United Nations
USARF	University Students African Revolutionary Front
USUD	University Students' Union
UWT	Umoja wa Wanawake
WRDP	Women's Research Documentation Project
ZANU	Zimbabwe African National Union
ZAPU	Zimbabwe African People's Union

1. Debating the Nation

> "And there were young folks, whether they were lecturers [...] students, postgrads, everybody working together, plus all these folks from downtown, pushing, pushing to have more radical changes. At the same time, people were concerned. [...] It was funny: [...] at the time we were quite critical of what was going on, later we had to defend what was going on, because regardless of what mistakes had been made, there were real achievements."[1]

In the 1960s, the unfolding national independencies in Africa harbored a multitude of hopes, fears and expectations. Tanganyika, being the first East African state to gain independence in 1961, was no exception to this. A spectrum of Tanzanians[2] worked devotedly to build a society in a country that had been shaped by the "racial" and gender order as well as economic exploitation of colonialism. During the struggle for liberation, Tanzania's first president Julius Nyerere gained widespread support by making promises of equality irrespective of "race"[3] and gender. On the one side, colonial institutions

---

1 Marjorie Mbilinyi, interview by Harald Barre, March 12, 2018, Café, Dar es Salaam.
2 My research focuses on Tanzania's mainland, Tanganyika. Zanzibar, which formed a union with Tanganyika in 1964, will only be discussed in this work in so far as it became part of the newspaper's readers' debates. While Zanzibar was a frequent topic in the newspapers, it rarely spurred any readers to respond. See e.g. chapters 2.5-3.1, 4.1.
3 Since "race" had been used as a biological category, this work emphasizes that "race" is understood throughout the paper as a social construct by putting it in quotation marks.

were not only the basis for administrative institutions, but also continued to shape the administrative practices of the independent nation.[4] As well, social norms and practices had been shaped in the colonial era.[5] Therefore, on the eve of independence, "racial" and gender backgrounds were essential in defining individual chances of economic security and freedom.

Although some historians, like Schneider, have emphasized that the independent government's authoritarianism was a practice taken from colonialism, the first two decades of independence were shaped by phases of intense controversial debates in the public sphere. Analyzing these debates, this work points out how norms and laws that would characterize the new nation were questioned and transformed by readers, journalists, academics and politicians in the 1960s and 1970s. As the quote above indicates, an intense struggle ensued between varying visions and with uncertain outcomes.

A central problem lay in the aforementioned fact that the independent government was in many ways shaped by the colonial era. Therefore, critiques of regulations and attitudes which were rooted in the colonial era often constituted an implicit government critique. Such critique frequently proved to be delicate, as the Nyerere administration feared the socio-political tensions that arose from colonial fault lines and Cold War antagonism.[6] Hence, the struggle over a national identity independent of structures shaped by colonialism held the potential to spur authoritarian reaction if the administration felt threatened by challenges to its politics.

One arena where these struggles were manifested was in newspapers. In April 1964, just weeks ahead of unification with Zanzibar, the newspaper of the Tanganyika African National Union (TANU), *the Nationalist*, was launched. The long-term narrative of *the Nationalist* and its successor *the Daily News*, which included the weekly *Sunday News*, was characterized by dramatic shifts which reflected various positions in the struggle for an independent nation. While the newspaper attempted to align itself with government views, these views were neither homogenous, and the newspaper positions did change

---

4   See: Leander Schneider, "Colonial Legacies and Postcolonial Authoritarianism in Tanzania: Connects and Disconnects," *African Studies Review* 49, no.1 (2006), accessed March 18, 2018, http://www.jstor.org/stable/20065195.

5   See: Chapter 2 for a more detailed analysis of the evolution of social structures during the colonial era and the colonial state's impact on the process.

6   See: Paul Bjerk, *Building a Peaceful Nation: Julius Nyerere and the Establishment of Sovereignty in Tanzania, 1960-1964*, Rochester Studies in African History and the Diaspora v. 63 (Rochester: University of Rochester Press, 2015).

over time. Even greater diversity was reflected in the correspondence section, where readers from within and outside Tanzania provided their views on the nation. As such, the newspaper fulfilled a crucial role in what Chambi Chachage considers to be Nyerere's legacy: "The ability to generate public debate on issues of importance to the society."[7]

The party newspaper would not only become a platform for the controversies surrounding the struggle to build a nation, but also consciously shaped them, as the first editorial proclaimed: "This newspaper is the baby of the Tanganyika African National Union and for that matter the Government. We will speak authoritatively for Tanganyika, but that does not prevent us making constructive suggestions wherever we deem necessary. [...] We shall reflect modern Africa and the thinking of men and women who are shaping its destiny."[8] The newspaper and its successors would oscillate between their role of representing the government and criticizing the same. In doing so, it reflected Nyerere's own dilemma of striving for an African socialist nation while preserving the peace and stability of a society and administration that was structured by colonialism.

Another place where debate increased was the University of Dar es Salaam. It quickly emerged as a hub for scholars from across the world, and progressive as well as conservative ideas were debated on campus. However, the university was not only an arena of debate, but (higher) education itself became subject and object of the debate of independence. Thus, education as such, particularly at the university level, was caught in the struggle over varying visions of Tanzania's nation building, as well as concerns of the ruling party over politically active students. The university was an ambivalent arena for academics: On the one hand, it offered new perspectives on Tanzania and its place in the world, along with innovative approaches to relate to society, education, and politics, On the other hand, fear of repercussions at the hands of the administration accompanied student activism.

Even though African socialism was the uncontested goal of the participants in these debates, the controversies brought a spectrum of imaginations of the nation to light. While Nyerere had been a stalwart of "non-racialism," the social divisions along "racial" lines surfaced in the newspaper frequently.

---

7   Chambi Chachage, "Mwalimu in our popular imagination: The relevance of Nyerere today | Pambazuka News," Pambazuka News, accessed July 15, 2019, https://www.pambazuka.org/pan-africanism/mwalimu-our-popular-imagination-relevance-nyerere-today.
8   Editor, "Our Policy," *The Nationalist*, April 17, 1964, No. 1.

Only over the course of the years was the category "race" gradually moderated out of the socio-political discourse. This included both "race" as a category of difference, as well as a category of solidarity. The latter was a particularly difficult process, as Nyerere had put pan-African solidarity on Tanzania's banner before independence. Since pan-Africanism had been strongly associated with "racial" solidarity in the country,[9] the notion of "race" quickly emerged to being a defining aspect of pan-Africanism. Only in the late 1960s did the narrative begin to die down, and it was eventually supplemented by a "non-racial" vision of pan-Africanism.

Gender equality was a central aspect to TANU's vision of African socialism, and the party newspaper advocated for its significance to the nation building project from its inception. However, the colonial era had left women in marginal positions, particularly in relation to the modern state. As in most African states, women had no or a limited voice in Tanzania's newspapers.[10] However, as Hunter observed for the newspaper *Komkya* in the 1950s, women began to use the women's page as a forum to critically discuss their experiences of social life.[11] However, women's calls to strengthen gender equality, by dropping regulations from the colonial era, were occasionally supported by editorials and increasingly shaped the general readers' section, as well. This was occasionally contrasted by opinions that argued for a hierarchy between men and women, either against a religious background or against claims to African tradition. Unlike leftist student activists' socio-political critiques, women's critiques appear to have been supported by the party leadership and the newspaper until the mid-1970s, when women's voices quickly faded from the newspaper.

At this point, it should be noted that a great spectrum of people in Tanzania did not actively shape the discourse in either the newspapers or the university. However, a crucial arena through which gender roles and images of "race" were negotiated was the urban music culture. Soul music continued to be played at private parties after it was publicly banned. This constituted a connection to the African American struggle and went beyond the complex academic and political discussions that surrounded it. Likewise, parties

---

9   See: Chapter 2.2.
10 See: Stephanie Newell, "Afterword," in Peterson; Hunter; Newell, *African Print Cultures*, 430.
11 See: Emma Hunter, "*Komkya* and the Convening of a Chagga Public, 1953-1961," in Peterson; Hunter; Newell, *African Print Cultures*, 296-297.

were the space wherein men and women performed the opportunities and restrictions of the new nation through the type of dances and fashion their decided to wear.[12] Such arenas gave individuals, whether literate or illiterate, the chance to communicate and demonstrate their understanding of themselves in a young nation that was shaped by hopes and concerns. Of equal significance were the many ways of contesting and also restricting such self-expression. These expressions were also perceived in the newspapers, where they eventually sparked lively debates.

This work explores how a nation that emerged out of decades of colonialism attempted to restructure itself in independence: How did debates around nation building evolve in newspapers? And how were these debates interrelated to events and agents in the social world? For this purpose, I will be examining contemporary debates in the 1960s and 1970s, as well as retrospective reflections of individuals who considered themselves supportive of Tanzania's reimaging a new community.

1.1 Research Context

Methodologically, this work is inspired by James Brennan's *Taifa* (2012) and Emma Hunter's *Political Thought and the Public Sphere* (2015). Their historiographies take published opinions from newspapers as a central source in reconstructing discourses and highlight their interrelation with socio-political developments. Brennan meticulously illustrates how "race" and gender became not only central aspects of the material conditions in colonial Tanganyika, but also shaped people's world views. Hunter focuses on the era after World War II and highlights that TANU's success as a party of mass recruitment for the Liberation movement was far from inevitable. In contrasting TANU's appeal to the Tanzanian public with that of alternative political organizations, she demonstrates the significance of TANU's promises and visions. Brennan's work is also particularly important in regards to the content of his analysis, which informs the second chapter of this book, the social structures and world views that were shaped in the colonial era. However, their works only touch upon the debates and discussions in independent Tanzania prompting

---

12 See: Kelly Askew, *Performing the Nation: Swahili Music and Cultural Politics in Tanzania* (Chicago, The University of Chicago Press, 2003).

the goal of a detailed study of the evolving debates around Tanzania's nation building project in the 1960s and 1970s.

Even though the continuities, shifts and recurrences of public debates in independent Tanzania have not been studied comprehensively, the two decades after independence in the country have been part of a spectrum of research. While such studies did not examine the evolution of published debates systematically, these works' systematic foci have been crucial in reconstructing events and shifts in the social world during the two decades in question.

Sociologist Ronald Aminzade in his work *Race, Nation, Citizenship* differentiates between the ruling party, TANU, on the one side, and the government bureaucracy, on the other side. Coming from different social backgrounds and being motivated by different political commitments and ideals, he argues that they strove for diverging policies. The former was rather committed to rapid Africanization and empowerment of workers and peasants, whereas the latter pushed for "non-racial" equality and transnational solidarity. He rests his argument on historical studies and surveys, as well as selected newspaper articles. Looking at a longue-durée encompassing the colonial era up to the 2000s, Aminzade demonstrates that power between these poles oscillated. While shifts in small periodical steps are less pronounced, his approach is very helpful in distinguishing the political forces in Tanzania's social world, and therefore supports this work in explaining political interventions, which often alter the public discourse.

Seth Markle's *Motorcycle on Hell Run* also looks at the relations between the African diaspora and Tanzania. Systematically, it adds to research that seeks to understand the development of the significance of "race" in Tanzania as well as the ambivalent interpretations of pan-Africanism. He builds his narrative around the biographies of key agents, mostly from the African diaspora. While he critically uses articles from both Tanzanian English newspapers, *the Standard* and *the Nationalist*, he pays no attention to shifts in the newspapers' narratives. Nonetheless, his work provides valuable insight into the interactions and obstacles between African American and Tanzanian agents, and contextualizes them usefully on both the regional and international levels. For example, he demonstrates TANU's ambivalent role at the Sixth Pan African Congress. TANU was very supportive and hospitable to the African American organizers, but TANU also reasserted its own dominance over the congress and ensured that the political debates did not weaken its own positions. Namely, TANU ensured that "race" did not become a programmatic aspect of the congress, but rather class. His work helps to highlight events, such as the ties between African American activists and Tanzanian politicians, such as Malcolm X and Abdulrahman Babu. Due to Markle, this work can add depth to the analysis of debates in the newspapers and the recollection of Tanzanian time witnesses, as many fundamental events as well as opinions were absent from those sources.

Andrew Ivaska's *Cultured States* focuses on the interplay between culture, politics and society. In contrast to Aminzade, his emphasis lies on tensions along gender and generational groups, and does not examine the educational socialization of certain groups of agents. By focusing on culture, Ivaska is able to point out male attempts to dominate the discourse on national fashion and to utilize fashion as a political tool. As such, not only were women's clothes scrutinized which curtailed women's freedom, but other cultural influences such as African American music were seen as damaging influences and therefore banned. While his historiographical account details the public protests by women in conferences, as well as letters to the editor, he does not discuss other aspects of women's struggle for equality, such as calls for maternity leave or access to education and work without fear of harassment. However, Ivaska's focus is on cultural expressions and their political implications cover a crucial aspect of "race" and gender dynamics. His book is furthermore very helpful as his findings on general tensions among the African population resonate with this work's findings on generational tensions among Tanzania's Indian community.

Emily Callaci's *Street Archives and City Lives* focuses on competing ideologies and daily life strategies in Dar es Salaam. Her analysis revolves around spatial categories, such as housing, work and dancehalls. Working with historical surveys as well as Swahili and English newspapers and interviews, she juxtaposes positions on social life in Dar es Salaam in the 1960s and 1970s. Crucially for this work, her book demonstrates the central role that was attributed to working women by TANU in its nation building vision. She argues that the rise of Christian educated advice givers for working women changed TANU's gender politics, which had earlier been shaped significantly by Muslim women in the 1950s.[13] Her emphasis on the educational background of influential groups of social agents, while similar to Aminzade, helps to qualify and contextualize opinions in newspapers, which will be analyzed in the following chapters. As such, her book is used to explain shifts and turns in the detailed chronological analysis of the work at hand.

---

13 See chapter 2.4.

Luke Melchiorre's *Building Nations, Making Youth*, contrasts the roles and agency of youth activism in the nation building projects of Kenya and Tanzania from the time of independence up to 1990. In his book, he concentrates on the relationship between that of state and university, and points out the deteriorating conditions for leftist student activists. His work is built on interviews with former students, lecturers and administrators, which constitute a very useful addition to the selection of interviewees of this work, as well as to the newspaper narrative. He points out how President Nyerere's concern over the co-option of students by a Western shaped university led to substantial reforms. However, fearing the independence and radicalism demonstrated by the lecturers spearheading the process, TANU moderated the process and obtained increasing control over the university administration. He argues that Nyerere himself had an ambivalent stance towards the students, as he supported the administration in undermining outspoken students, but also asked academics to challenge him and often agreed with their critiques. Nonetheless, independent student activism died down in the 1970s, as the TANU-led administration exerted increasingly restrictive penalties against critics. The spectrum of perspectives of academics, which are examined by Melchiorre, aids this analysis in understanding the campus debates on colonialism and independence. Furthermore, the detailed focus on the campus developments is a useful means to contrast this work's examination of the newspaper debates, which divert from the TANU administration's policy on campus developments in some phases.

While the works above cover fundamental societal parts of Tanzania's nation building project, Paul Bjerk's *Building a Peaceful Nation* analyzes its political dimensions. He argues that Julius Nyerere, as leader of TANU and the president of the country, emphasized the high significance of the internal stability and international independence of the nation. To ensure these vital standards, he was willing to sacrifice internal liberties, but also defied Cold War powers and their allies. His work, mostly informed by interviews and archival materials, helps the reader to grasp the political landscape that surrounded the social discourse on nation building, African socialism, and ultimately independence from colonial structures. It, along with Aminzade's work, has been vital in understanding the instances of government and party intervention in both newspaper discourse and public activism.

The chronological analysis of the debates that revolved around Nyerere's social vision for the Tanzanian nation departs from the works above, as it details continuities, shifts, and breaks in the social discourse surrounding independence. It illustrates which social groups passively and actively became part of the narrative that characterized Tanzania's nation building. Drawing upon the analyses of the works above, this narrative is grounded in multiple developments and events in the social world.

1.2 Some Theoretical Considerations

This work's exploration of Tanzania's attempts to restructure itself after colonialism fits into a larger theoretical frame. Marjorie Mbilinyi's introductory reflections, as well as the *Nationalist's* first editorial, point to the significance these agents attributed to developing a state and society in the name of the new nation. They are characteristic of the programmatic aspect of nationalism, which Berman and Lonsdale describe as "an attempt to gain state power [...], so as to domesticate modernity in the name of an imagined new community."[14] However, the state's power had been shaped fundamentally by colonialism, and therefore the efforts to navigate the program of shaping such a national community were based on a fractured recent history which evolved over time.

Therefore, this analysis of a nation building process, which emphasizes controversies and developments, has to be sensitive to historical background, social perspective and power relations. Hence, while this work embraces Benedict Anderson's assertion that a nation is socially constructed, it heeds the concerns of critics such as Partha Chatterjee, who lament that Anderson's conceptualization fails to grasp the heterogeneity of a nation's society and the uneven changes in historical progression.[15] A particularly direct conceptualization of the interrelation between social structures and historical developments can be found in Pierre Bourdieu's field theory. Its emphasis on the long-term impact of social structures is especially relevant for the analysis of phases that are associated with revolutionary changes, such as Tanzania's independence and nation building project. As Go points out,

---

14 Bruce J. Berman and John M. Lonsdale, "Nationalism in Colonial and Post-Colonial Africa," in *The Oxford Handbook of the History of Nationalism*, ed. John Breuilly, 1. ed. (Oxford: Oxford Univ. Press, 2013), 316–317.

15 See: Benedict Anderson, *Imagined Communities: Reflections on the Origin and Spread of Nationalism*, Rev. and extended ed., 13. impression (London: Verso, 2003), 5–7; Partha Chatterjee, "The nation in heterogeneous time," *Futures* 37, no. 9 (2005): 927–928, https://doi.org/10.1016/j.futures.2005.01.011.

Bourdieu had, prior to developing his field theory, highlighted the difficulty of independent nations to change the social structure that had developed during the colonial period. During colonialism, categories of thought – e.g. "race" or gender, along with pre-existing structures, had defined roles and the socially accepted agency of certain groups of people within the social world of colonial states. As these structures could not be immediately changed with the end of colonialism,[16] the TANU government and citizenry who wanted to revolutionize the independent country were to meet socio-cultural resistance that would be difficult to overcome.

Bourdieu's field theory explains the specific dynamics that contribute to the longevity of historically grown structures. He describes the social world as a historically evolving multi-dimensional field in which social agents and groups of agents are in relative positions to one another, defined by the amount of certain forms of capital acquired by them. The agent's position is not only defined by economic capital, but also by social, cultural and symbolic capital, for example.[17] Within this field, agents who have similar amounts of the same type of capital, are socialized in similar ways, and are likely to have developed similar interests and perceptions. This also results in a higher probability for similar agency. Bourdieu also speaks of structuring structures.[18] Yet, the perception of social reality is varied and is determined by one's position in the social field in an evolving social world. However, people have learned to perceive their world in certain categories. As such, historical structures are reproduced by agents. Against the background of these assumptions, this work will set out to explore the formation of the social structures which shaped the society in Tanzania's mainland today. These structures fundamentally influenced both the formation of social groups as well as concurring world views. "Race" and gender were crucial

---

16 See: Julian Go, "Decolonizing Bourdieu," *Sociological Theory* 31, no. 1 (2013): 62-63, accessed August 9, 2018, https://doi.org/10.1177/0735275113477082.
17 For a definition of these "properties" or "forms of capital," see e.g.: Pierre Bourdieu, "The Forms of Capital," in *Handbook of Theory and Research for the Sociology of Education*, ed. John G. Richardson (New York: Greenwood Press, 1986).
18 See: Pierre Bourdieu, "The Social Space and the Genesis of Groups," *Theory and Society* 14, no. 6 (1985): 724-725, accessed March 29, 2018, http://www.jstor.org/stable/657373; and Pierre Bourdieu, Loïc J. D. Wacquant, and Samar Farage, "Rethinking the State: Genesis and Structure of the Bureaucratic Field," *Sociological Theory* 12, no. 1 (1994): 13, https://doi.org/10.2307/202032.

categories in characterizing social groups, and the colonial state contributed to this dynamic integrally.[19]

Despite the structuration of the colonial era, Tanzanian nationalists' ideas of building a newly imagined community were not doomed in Bourdieu's theoretical framework. Speaking only of likelihoods, Bourdieu does not allege that structures would be reproduced invariably.[20] The now independent state had a vital role in altering structures. While groups within society form around capital that they accumulate, Bourdieu identifies the state as a particularly crucial social agent. According to Bourdieu, it is constituted by *"the culmination of a process of concentration of different species of capital [...] It is this concentration as such which constitutes the state as the holder of a sort of meta-capital granting power over other species of capital and over their holders [...]"*[21] [in italics in original]. Based on these accumulated forms of capital, a state can make successful claims to "the monopoly of the legitimate use of physical and symbolic violence over a definite territory and over the totality of the corresponding population."[22] Bourdieu considers the ability of the state to structure categories of thought, e.g. through schooling, to be so successful that people perceive them as natural and not as given by the state. Yet, as such, these structuring structures reveal the limitations of the state's agency, which has to invest capital to alter these categories of thought.[23] This explains nationalists' goals of gaining state power, but also a dilemma of the independent state in Tanzania: On the one side, it could be impactful and far reaching in re-imagining a new community. However, on the other side, the independent state faced social structures that were for decades shaped by a colonial state which imagined a vastly different community.

The complexity of ambivalent structures is even more pronounced if the focus lies with the historical period at the heart of this book, the phase of national independence. Étienne Balibar helps us to understand the heterogeneity of 'nation' on the one hand, and the conceptual centrality of the state, on the other:

---

19 See chapter 2.
20 See: Bourdieu, "The Social Space," 726.
21 Bourdieu, Wacquant and Farage, "Rethinking the State," 3-4.
22 Ibid. 3-4.
23 See: Ibid. 1-2. Bourdieu exemplifies this dynamic with orthography, mediated through the state, which has become so natural that people act against reform of such codification.

"Every social community reproduced by the functioning of institutions is imaginary, that is to say, it is based on the projection of individual existence into the weft of a collective narrative [...].
In the case of national formations, the imaginary which inscribes itself in the real in this way is that of the 'people.' It is that of a community which recognizes itself, in advance in the institution of the state, which recognizes that state as 'its own' in opposition to other states and, in particular, inscribes its political struggles within the horizon of that state - by, for example, formulating its aspirations for reform and social revolution as projects for the transformation of 'its national state.'"[24]

The quote reiterates the constructed formation of nation and the significance of the state. However, while Bourdieu's 'field' attributes formative power to the state, Balibar's conceptualization asserts the existential role of a heterogeneous society. His term of "a weft of a collective narrative," i.e. a fabric into which a multitude of opinions and perceptions is woven, not only highlights the complex composition of nations, but also the fundamental role of a narrative for the social community. The self-recognition of a social community is constituted by social agents' expressions of views on the social structures and institutions. These expressions may be ambivalent and contradictory. In fact, Vilashini Cooppan describes nations as "fantasmic objects knotted together by ambivalent forces of desire, memory, and forgetting, even as they simultaneously move within, across, and beyond a series of spatial and temporal borders [...]."[25] Her definition underscores the transnational element of nation. Ambivalent contributions to a national narrative do not just come from within national borders, but directly and indirectly from beyond such boundaries. Such movements may come in the shape of ideas as well as physical social agents. These multitudes of perspectives that were shaped in different contexts – in various locations in the social world of colonial Tanzania or even in other countries – came together in Tanzania in the 1960s and 1970s.[26] While

---

24 Étienne Balibar and Immanuel Maurice Wallerstein, *Race, Nation, Class: Ambiguous Identities*, 1. publ. (London et al.: Verso, 1991), 93.
25 Vilashini Cooppan, *Worlds Within: National Narratives and Global Connections in Postcolonial Writing*, (Stanford: Stanford University Press, 2009), accessed: August 16, 2017, http://search.ebscohost.com/login.aspx?direct=true&scope=site&db=nlebk&AN=395793, xvii.
26 As mentioned above, I am focusing on perspectives that were supportive of the idea of an independent and socialist Africa. Other agents left the country around indepen-

the "racial" and gender structures of the colonial society included many obstacles for debates and exchange between the social groups,[27] places like newspapers and also the university enabled such exchanges. In these fields, people coming from various spaces in the social world could interact. Thereby, they contributed to an unfolding national narrative, which was woven into public debates and arguments. By examining the evolution of this narrative and considering which groups contributed to it, this work will illustrate the continuity and change of structures and worldviews which emerged out of the colonial era.

This development did not only take place in reforms and new policies, but such events in the social world were interrelated to public debates. Jeffrey Alexander's *the Civil Sphere* helps to grasp the intersection between ideas and opinions in the public sphere on the one side, and Bourdieu's social world, on the other. He depicts "civil society" as an independent sphere that is located in the time and space of the "real world,"[28] and which is shaped by social actors. Civil society rests on institutions and organizations of communication and regulation – a conceptualization that echoes Balibar's "weft of a collective narrative." Within this sphere, public opinion is a "real, though non-binding force," which is expressed and structured in mass media.[29] This dissertation seeks to show the interrelations between this public sphere and the social world by tracing the published opinions expressed in newspapers as well as recollections of contemporaries. These opinions were "bounded by [...] non-civil spheres, [...] such [...] as state, economy, religion, family, and community."[30] As such, the public sphere can be seen as a field in which opinions and debates can occur somewhat independently of the obstacles of the social world.[31] It is here where Balibar's national narrative is woven in daily exchanges. However, any opinions are crucially structured by the social world. As discussed with help of Bourdieu's field theory, the social groups which expressed themselves were shaped by the social world and likely reproduced the

---

dence, as they were not supportive. See e.g.: Godfrey Mwakikagile, *Life in Tanganyika in the Fifties*, 3rd ed. (Dar es Salaam, Tanzania: New Africa Press, 2009), 234-235.

27   See chapter 2.
28   In this work, I will refer to the 'social world' instead of the 'real world' in order to emphasize that society gives meaning to material conditions that constitute it.
29   Jeffrey C. Alexander, *The Civil Sphere* (Oxford: Oxford Univ. Press, 2006), 3-6.
30   Ibid. 7.
31   See chapter 1.2 for the limits in accessing the newspapers depending on social background.

structures by which they were shaped, on the one hand. On the other hand, the composition of views on the world in the newspapers, as well as explicitly expressed opinions in editorials, impacted the discourse in the public sphere and exerted force on the social world, and thereby had a chance to alter structures, such as the categories of perception.

While the continuity and evolution of structures only become visible in a chronological study, this analysis is focused on evolving public opinions expressed in the English written newspaper of TANU in conjunction with the opinions developed at Dar es Salaam's university; both the university and the newspaper constituted crucial institutions of communication and regulation of public opinion. Bourdieu's concept explains both the longevity of historically grown structures on the one side, and the possibility of historical change, on the other. Hence, the public sphere in independent Tanzania was structured by developments in the social world and the public sphere in the preceding decades. The particular significance of the state as an agent that shapes social structures more than any other agent, particularly due to its ability to shape categories of perception, explains the scope and foundation of this work. The analysis of the structuration of Tanzanian society will begin with the creation of a state in Tanganyika and focus on views and perceptions expressed in government newspapers. However, as acknowledged by Bourdieu, historically grown structures are revisable. As this study will show, debates in the public sphere and developments in the social world altered the significance of such categories.[32]

Empirical Approach: Newspapers

For an exchange in the public sphere, mass media such as newspapers were an important institution of communication. Media not only disseminated ideas in the public sphere, but also constituted a space where opinions were published and discussed. In fact, the English-speaking party newspaper in the 1970s, the *Daily News*, invoked the idea of a physical space for gathering and exchange by naming its readers' contribution page the "People's Forum." As such, newspapers are a crucial source in understanding the public sphere in Tanzania. For the analysis of the changes of colonial categories of thought

---

32   Chapter 2 will examine the evolution of the significance of categories such as "race" and gender.

after independence, the English-speaking TANU newspapers are particularly valuable.

The *Daily News* and its Sunday edition the *Sunday News* had its roots in the TANU newspaper *the Nationalist* and the private newspaper *the Standard*. At independence, TANU began publishing its weekly Swahili newspaper *Uhuru*, which was turned into a daily newspaper in 1964.[33] As a majority of the population spoke Swahili, the newspaper had the potential to reach many citizens, but it was limited due to poor distribution. Cities in the Hinterland received newspapers several days after publication.[34] Furthermore, for many foreigners – expatriates, foreign politicians or members of the Liberation movements – as well as some citizens of Tanzania, English was more familiar.[35] As President Nyerere hoped to reach out to international politicians by publishing an English government newspaper, *the Nationalist* was established in April 1964. In 1970, the government nationalized *the Standard*, which had been the profitable private competitor of *the Nationalist*. It explained the move with the country's policy of non-alignment and self-reliance, which had been enshrined in the 1967 Arusha Declaration. The editor, Frene Ginwala, who was appointed by President Nyerere, was given "full autonomy." While the newspaper was able to print highly critical stories on the abuses of power by the the Zanzibari Government, Ginwala had to leave the newspaper after she took responsibility for an editorial that was diplomatically highly sensitive.[36] The aspect of nationalization and the sacking of Ginwala, demonstrates that there were limits to the freedom of press in Tanzania. Nonetheless, the discourse within Tanzania's public media can provide valuable insight into Tanzania's national narrative, particularly if it is contrasted with other written and oral sources.

---

33 See: Martin Sturmer, *The Media History of Tanzania* (Ndanda via Mtwara: Ndanda Mission Press, 1998), Zugl.: Wien, Univ., Diss., 1998, 104, 108-109.

34 See: G. L. Mytton, "Tanzania: The Problems of Mass Media Development," *International Communication Gazette* 14, no. 2 (1968): 91-92, https://doi.org/10.1177/001654926801400 204.

35 In the English-written newspapers, readers criticized Asians for their inability to speak Swahili. The presence of such a language barrier is also supported by Najma Sachak, who remembered that many Asian families would merely have known certain commands in Swahili. See e.g.: *The Nationalist*, "My dear Fellow Indian…," September 29, 1964, No. 142; Najma Sachak, interview by Harald Barre, September 1, 2018, in her apartment in Lyon.

36 See: Sturmer, *The Media History*, 107-108, 122-123.

For a historiographical reconstruction of the debates on "race" and gender, other media of the time can only be used to a limited extent as a correction to the reporting of the English-language TANU newspaper. This is mostly due to the fact that the range of media and press was severely limited. During the period examined, almost all local newspapers were controlled by the party or the government. Emily Callaci's research shows that journalists in other Swahili-speaking newspapers linked Tanzanian citizenship with "race" and gender much more aggressively, for example by criticizing Tanzanian women who entered into liaisons with sailors from other countries.[37] An unusual perspective for the media on the understanding of individuality, freedom and gender resulted in the *Standard*, which was a non-state newspaper until the second half of the 1960s. Andrew Ivaska's research suggests that the *Standard* published a different range of opinions. While western fashion, for example, was condemned and finally even banned by the TANU, the *Standard* published letters to the editor that criticized this as an inadmissible interference with the personal freedom of citizens.[38] The analysis indicates that to a certain extent the *Nationalist* only published opinions that pointed to contradictions between the practice and rhetoric of the TANU state, however none that contradicted the rhetoric. Therefore, due to the limited informative value of the media, interview-based studies of other arenas in the public sphere, such as that of Callaci, are important in order to make a broader pool of actors visible.

Tanzania's English-written newspapers are particularly interesting due to their scope. The editors of *the Nationalist* and the private-owned *Standard* assumed that they shared the same readership based on language. Condon reasoned that English-speaking readers from Tanzanian backgrounds – about five percent of the population – shared certain social characteristics: they were likely to have a higher degree of education and therefore either stemmed from an urban and / or wealthy context. Having had access to more education, their interest in larger social and political issues would have been higher, and they would have had better access to securely paying jobs in the cities. While the

---

37   See: Emily Callaci, *Street Archives and City Life: Popular Intellectuals in Postcolonial Tanzania*, Radical Perspectives (Durham: Duke University Press, 2017), 55-56, accessed February 16, 2018, http://ebookcentral.proquest.com/lib/tib-hannover/detail.action?docID=5116557.

38   See: Andrew Michael Ivaska, *Cultured States: Youth, Gender, and Modern Style in 1960s Dar es Salaam* (Durham NC u.a.: Duke Univ. Press, 2011), 108–111.

government's emphasis lay on building Swahili as a national language, English remained the language of instruction in higher education. The urban focus of all Tanzanian newspapers was further increased by the fact that they relied on occasional correspondent articles from the countryside up to 1967, but had not established any salaried staff to attend to the hinterland.[39] As the readers of the English newspapers commonly shared these characteristics, they were the ones whose lives took place at the post-colonial frontlines of Tanzania. While the entire country was shaped by the colonial era, it was urban Tanzania where exclusion and prospects were most immediately felt and discussed.

For this work, the continually published English government newspaper will be the crucial source for the analysis of the historical discourse. For, even though *the Nationalist* and its successor only reached a limited section of Tanzania's society directly, their readers were highly involved and representative in the debates about shape and set-up of the independent society. Up to independence, peasants had had little chance for education and accordingly were not competing for employment in the administration – a field where "interracial" competition would be most lamented. And while African women in the countryside had seized on TANU's message of gender equality during the liberation struggle,[40] it was urban women who would experience and protest sexism and gender discrimination in various sections of the state (e.g. education, housing and employment) most immediately. As such, the debates in the English-written newspapers held particular significance for the entire country, as they reflected not only common injustices and aspirations, but also impacted the direction in which the independent nation would embark upon.

While the party newspapers were hubs for opinions in the public sphere, it was not a space that was neutral. Contemporaries look back differently at the newspapers' degree of independence in their coverage.[41] Karim Hirji,

---

39   See: John C. Condon, "Nation Building and Image Building in the Tanzanian Press," *The Journal of Modern African Studies* 5, no. 3 (1967): 337-339, accessed October 18, 2018, https://www.jstor.org/stable/158728.
40   See chapter 2.4.
41   Deborah Bryceson recalled editor Benjamin Mkapa's openness to her article on family planning, whereas Najma Sachak described *the Nationalist* to be a pure mouth piece of the government.

who was part of the student group University Students African Revolutionary Front (USARF), remembered Ginwala allowing independent critics on the left much more opportunity to express their opinions. However, he considered *the Nationalist*, under editor Benjamin Mkapa, as following the party-line and not open to critical views. After the government merged the two papers into *the Daily News* in 1972, Hirji described the newspaper as the mouthpiece of the government that excluded "independent voices from the left."[42] These different views on the newspaper and varying experiences with the editors indicate the complex interplay between developments in the social world and the discourse in the public sphere. While the government supported news and progressive opinions on gender roles, it attempted to confine other political views that were created outside party control. Opinions that originated at the university strove to overcome colonially-grown structures, but were in part, and at certain times, treated differently.

From an internal perspective, the party newspapers seem to have been very independent from interference and not severely driven by ideological conviction. A 1966 survey by Condon gives some contemporary views on the Tanzanian newspapers from the in- and outside. In that study, he dissected readers' views on the newspapers and identified the Asians and expatriates from the business community as opposed to *the Nationalist's* left leaning positions. Curiously, in interviews, *the Nationalist's* editor, Benjamin Mkapa, claimed that he would prefer the newspaper to be less left-leaning and more on aligned with the government's positions. Yet, he felt the need to balance the conservative stance of *the Standard*.[43] The open, sometimes hostile criticism which was uttered in *the Nationalist* against *the Standard's* political background seemed rhetorically dramatic. Godfrey Mwakikagile, then a journalist for *the Standard*, claims that journalists of the two newspapers would meet covering stories without any contempt.[44] Mwakikagile's reminiscence may be tainted by the fact that the employees from the opposing newspapers had become colleagues after the nationalization and merging into *the Daily News*. Yet, journalistic clashes were likely limited to the public sphere and did

---

42 See: Karim F. Hirji, ed., *Cheche: Reminiscences of a Radical Magazine* (Dar es Salaam: Mkuki Na Nyota Publishers, 2010), accessed September 11, 2015, http://site.ebrary.com/lib/academiccompletetitles/home.action, 183.
43 See: Condon, "Nation Building," 353.
44 See: Godfrey Mwakikagile, *Tanzania Under Mwalimu Nyerere: Reflections on an African Statesman* (Dar es Salaam: New Africa Press, 2006), 90.

not extend to the journalists interactions in their social world. For, if antagonism had been deeper, a successful merger seems unlikely. The apparently benign competition is also supported by the editor's claim which suggests that positions in the public sphere were rather professional decisions than ideological convictions.

Furthermore, recollections of journalists suggest that work for the TANU newspapers was not impeded by directives of party leaders; rather, they look back at their work with a high sense of pride. This can for instance be said of Mkapa who was not only editor of *the Nationalist* and later the *Daily News* from 1966 to July 1974.[45] In an interview he recalled the moment of being asked by President Nyerere to head the party newspapers as a crucial turning point in his life even though he had already been working in the government administration for a number of years. Nyerere, Mkapa went on, encouraged him, and in hindsight he thinks as a "good case of advocacy" with the party newspapers.[46] Evidently, he was not concerned that the party newspapers would be perceived negatively by the public, which makes it unlikely that they were seen as authoritarian mouthpieces of the government, even decades after the single party system had ended. However, the term "advocacy" suggests that he considered the newspapers primarily to be a means of communicating messages of the party. This somewhat corroborates the abovementioned recollections of time-witnesses and Sturmer's assertion that the government newspaper under Mkapa was selective in its coverage, even if it was not blindly supportive of Tanzania's government.

This view can be further differentiated by looking at the newspapers' interactions with their readers, and by recollections of former staff. Journalists like Mwakikagile and Philip Ochieng underlined their freedom in writing for the paper. They did not experience or fear interference from editor Mkapa, nor the editor in chief, President Nyerere, who is remembered as having encouraged criticism of the government. Mwakikagile recalled the diversity of the staff and that the journalists disagreed amongst each about culture, indepen-

---

45 See: "Benjamin Mkapa," accessed June 19, 2019, http://www.clubmadrid.org/miembro/benjamin-mkapa/.
46 See: "Meet the Leader: Interview with H.E. Benjamin Mkapa Former President of Tanzania," UONGOZI Institute, accessed June 20, 2019, https://www.youtube.com/watch?v=BKIpQyeV1_k.

dence and non-alignment in a benign and joking manner.[47] Editor Mkapa was remembered as highly educated, socially conscious, but far less radical than alleged by many foreigners.[48] The memory of a friendly but politically very conscious atmosphere underscores that work at the party newspapers was carried out freely and without concerns of interference by leadership. However, Mkapa's above-mentioned recollection in addition to the views from Ochieng, suggest that the education of the readers was part of the concept conceived of by newspaper staff. As such, the newspaper reflected a spectrum of opinions in which they held in common that they supported TANU's African socialist vision.

The reminiscences of former members of staff correspond with the tone in which the newspaper had with its readers. Despite the abovementioned state's interference in the media, and although the Nationalist and the Daily News considered themselves loyal to TANU, they published a spectrum of readers' opinions on the controversially discussed matters of "race" and gender relations. Furthermore, they released articles which critically dealt with the TANU government in regard to those matters. However, as this work will show, the newspapers' positions, and those of the letters they printed, varied over time. Furthermore, it is clear that the newspapers did not publish all the letters to the editor received, titles were freely added to the letters to the editor, and the newspapers also did not refrain from editing the language in those letters. In the early 1970s, a time where new party guidelines called for critical discourse, the Daily News published critiques of readers who considered their views to be distorted by such editing.[49] Beyond these means to direct the discourse in a manner that was subtle to the reader, the editor occasionally commented on readers' opinions. Such interference may have been seen as intimidating, and therefore enforcing limits on the freedom of opinions expressed. However, typically critical comments by the editor did not deter readers from contradicting those interferences, which suggests that the debates occurred in an atmosphere free of fear. As such, the English-written newspapers can be seen as a space in which journalists and readers exchanged opinions on a free,

---

47   See: Godfrey Mwakikagile, *Life under Nyerere*, 2. ed. (Dar es Salaam: New Africa Press, 2006), 50-55, 162-163.
48   See: Philip Ochieng, "Nostalgia and when to be on first name terms," accessed June 20, 2019, https://mobile.nation.co.ke/blogs/Nostalgia-and-when-to-be-on-first-name-terms/1949942-4995042-item-1-hfpdsgz/index.html.
49   See chapter 5.

but not unbiased basis, as support for TANU's African socialism was never questioned per se.

While the particular impact of interference by the editor with views of readers or other journalists cannot be determined exactly, the analysis of the newspapers over a more than a 10 years' span allows us to identify crucial shifts and changes in the scope of articles and the publishing of readers' opinions. As the party newspapers were published continually, they give a unique perspective into the contemporary evolution of debates around African socialism in Tanzania. Letters to the editor are particularly interesting as they corresponded with opinions in the newspapers. Protests against newspaper positions could have been the result of the continuity of categories of thought, or because the journalists' opinions clashed with the experiences of readers in the social world. For instance, the matter of "race" provoked open verbal conflicts during certain phases. These may be explained by the socialization in the colonial "racial" system, which strove for "racial" division between Asians and Africans.[50] However, at the same time, controversial debates could be exacerbated by the experience of continued gaps in the opportunities of Africans and Asians in the social world.

As such, the analysis can reveal interrelations between events in the social world and the public sphere, i.e. if there are breaks or changes in the narrative that are directly or indirectly following social or political incidents. In the same vein, looking at the composition of articles leads one to deduce how readers were presented with a contextualization of local events in regional and global issues and how, in turn, such events were localized.

Empirical Approach: Retrospective Testimonies

The party newspapers' main group of readers, highly educated men and women, had the most immediate chances to partake in the shaping of the independent country by taking up positions in the administration. They were sought after as the country strove to be independent of expatriate skilled personnel. In this work, the historical written sources are contrasted and contextualized with interviews that were conducted among this group of people during research stays in 2018, as well as published interviews and reminiscences of contemporaries. These witnesses add a narrative to the

---

50   See chapter 2.

historical developments which are only uncovered in glimpses by the historical sources – namely publications in newspapers. As products of continued structuration, these recollections are linked to historical events and can reveal fears, enthusiasm as well as ideological convictions, which remain largely obscure, or at best implicit in published historical sources.[51] As such, the interviews add not only context and narrative, but also an emotional dimension[52] which was constitutive for the historical structuration, and accordingly to expressions in the public sphere.

In order to portray a spectrum of opinions of supporters of the African socialist vision of Nyerere's TANU, a heterogeneous group of dedicated but also critical supporters of TANU were interviewed. These interviewees are all connected through networks revolving around academia, journalism and politics. While some are now retired, they were all active in those respective fields, often more than one. All shared a continued interest in the socio-political events in Tanzania during the phase directly following independence. At the time, they were part of the group of highly demanded, well-educated Tanzanians, or they came from abroad to Tanzania, attracted by its reputation for African socialism. In Tanzania, they were active on campus, published articles or pamphlets, supported community work or organized local or international conferences. While they did not form a majority on campus, through their academic work and activism, they became an influential group as the nation debated the achievement of independence.[53]

Today, some live in Europe, while others remain in Tanzania. All of them are still active in social, political or academic spheres, and many of those who have relocated, frequently travel back to Tanzania, which underlines their continued dedication to the country. Despite their shared contemporary support and continued sympathy for the African socialist project in Tanzania,

---

51 See: Reinhard Sieder, "Erzählungen analysieren - Analysen erzählen: Praxeologisches Paradigma, Narrativ biografisches Interview, Textanalyse und Falldarstellung," in *Ethnohistorie: Rekonstruktion, Kulturkritik und Repräsentation; eine Einführung*, ed. Karl R. Wernhart, 4, gänzlich überarb. und erw. Aufl., Forschung (Wien: Promedia-Verl., 2014), 152–155.

52 For a discussion of the prospects of oral history see for instance: Alessandro Portelli, "What makes oral history different," in *The Oral History Reader*, ed. Robert Perks and Alistair Thomson, 2nd ed. (New York: Routledge, 2006).

53 See: Jonathan L. Melchiorre, "Building Nations, Making Youth: Institutional Choice, Nation-State Building and the Politics of Youth Activism in Postcolonial Kenya and Tanzania" (University of Toronto, 2018), 155-157.

their social backgrounds are diverse and give them unique perspectives on the nation building project in Tanzania.

While the interviews were transcribed verbatim, the interviewees had the opportunity to view and edit them. Most made no rendition or merely spelled miss-heard names, while others toned down the language of their responses. As such, only the former interviews could be considered oral history, while the latter can rather be seen as hybrids of life history and expert interviews. In the following chapters, the interviews will be handled carefully. Due to these limitations, the edited interviews will merely be paraphrased and not directly quoted. As far as possible, the quotes are coherent, although non-verbal interjections have been omitted. In some instances, quotes have been merged for the sake of the argument of this thesis. Emotional memories are treated with higher significance than particular factual memories. Hence, in some cases, larger sections of an interview will be quoted in order to demonstrate the atmosphere that was evoked by the memory. Beyond giving the interviewees more agency, extensive quotes will provide readers the opportunity to contrast my interpretations of the material.

Seizing upon Pierre Bourdieu's *Die biographische Illusion*, the interviews are considered to be a peek into the trajectories of the interviewees through the social world.[54] As this work is structured by a chronology and social categories, their trajectories only appear at such cross-sections, and are contrasted with other memories or written sources. Therefore, the life-history of the respondents is not in the foreground of this dissertation. However, in order to be able to analyze and interpret their reminiscences, the following paragraphs will highlight the biographical background of the interviewees and critically evaluate the interviews' significance to this work.

George Hajivayanis and Salha Hamdani are married and were interviewed as a couple. Their daughters were also present at the interview and occasionally asked questions. The interview was a lively conversation in which Salha Hamdani and George Hajivayanis often bounced ideas between and off one another. Occasionally, their memories varied, but more often they were congruent or supplemented each other. The interview, which was edited with regard to inaudible words by the interviewees, provides insight into a family narrative.

Salha Hamdani is from Zanzibar and was in touch with political activism early on. Her brother was active in the communist party and she would help

---

54 Pierre Bourdieu, "Die biographische Illusion," *BIOS*, no. 1 (1990).

print flyers. Her father was a Muslim judge and ensured the education of his children early on. Her older sister, Zakia Meghji, was a member of the Tanzanian parliament, and later became a government minister. Salha Hamdani started her studies in Dar es Salaam in 1974, but had regularly visited the city prior to that and also stayed with her older sister on campus. Her perspective is unique, as she grew up experiencing the contrast between Zanzibar and the Tanzanian mainland.

Her husband George Hajivayanis grew up as the son of a Greek father and a mother of German and African origin in Dodoma. While his mother was strongly engaged in her church community, he remembered being in between various "racial" groups and sub-groups of the colonial society. While Salha Hamdani and George Hajivayanis were fortunate to be able to obtain good education, both were struck by the extreme poverty of African peasants that they witnessed. His social background afforded him a particular perspective on different social communities on the mainland.[55] They were both were conscious and critical of the social strains in the colonially shaped societies early on. As such, they provide a sensitive insight into the class divisions of Tanzania, specifically from the view of students that were supportive of a socialist nation building project.

The interview with Najma Sachak took place during a two-day stay at her and her husband Jean-Charles' home. Additionally, I asked follow-up questions via email correspondence. Najma Sachak was raised in a Muslim family that was part of the Dawoodi Bohra community. Her community played a crucial role in her upbringing, but she remembered that the boundaries between the Hindu and religious community were not strict, with festivities and holidays being celebrated together. Compared to other families, she bore in mind being raised to treat their African servants with respect. For instance, their cook had the right to determine the radio station they were listening to. While she developed a critical perspective on views from within the Asian community, she also witnessed and sometimes shared fears and vulnerabilities felt within the community, providing a rare perspective on the space where the "racial" layers of Tanzanian society integrated.

She did not edit the transcript, but corrected names that had been misheard or misspelled. Her interview provides a unique perspective into the

---

55   In his recollections, Hajivayanis describes his experience growing up with the class and religious divisions within the Asian community. See: George G. Hajivayanis, "Night-Shift Comrades," in: Hirji, *Cheche*.

experiences within the Indian community in Tanzania, as she contrasted her own experiences and emotions with those of other family members.

Walter Bgoya met me in the office of his bookshop in Dar es Salaam. We had little time to talk before the recording, which may have contributed to a more fact-focused interview. However, he vividly remembered the excitement around events of the independence struggle during which he went to school in Mwanza. In late 1961, he was one of the first students who would study abroad in the United States after Tanzania's independence. Back in Tanzania, he began working for the foreign Ministry which he left in 1972 to work in the East African Publishing House. Being enthralled by Nyerere's vision and studying in the U.S. afforded him a particular lens through which to view the world. Furthermore, his expert experiences in various aspects of pan-African and foreign politics contribute greatly to this study.

Fatma Alloo studied journalism in Dar es Salaam in the 1970s and became a crucial figurehead for female perspectives on journalism. She went on to co-found the Tanzania Media Women's Association (TAMWA) in 1987. I met her for an interview in her Dar es Salaam residence, and I also relied on an interview published online by African Woman and Child Feature Service. In those interviews, Fatma Alloo remembered formative experiences at the university in the 1970s, as well as her struggle against existing structures of male dominance. Life-trajectories such as hers illustrate the nexus between the Liberation movements and the Tanzanian women's movement, as she vividly recalled her experience of the Liberation movements in Dar es Salaam, and becoming an advocate and activist struggling against gender discrimination. Overall, her interviews provide context for a spectrum of women who were active against gender discrimination in the past decades in Tanzania. A publication of such voices is discussed below, at the end of section 1.2.2.

Marjorie Mbilinyi came to Tanzania in late 1966 following her then-boyfriend, Simon Mbilinyi. Prior to meeting him, she was strongly engaged in the struggle to ensure voting rights for African Americans in Alabama where she experienced community-based work. During our interview in a café in Dar es Salaam, she also inquired about my project. She lively remembered challenges she faced coming to Tanzania, especially administrative aspects at the university. Being a newcomer to the country, not being raised in the British colonial system, and having been involved in the struggle for "racial" equality in the United States, she was likely immediately sensitive to continuing forms of domination by the former colonial power. She remembered, for example, discriminatory British administrators and regulations.

Her academic career was strongly devoted to research on "race" and gender discrimination, some of which informs this book's historiographical analysis. However, her interview is guided by a narrative that revolved around her personal and professional experiences. Marjorie Mbilinyi also gave an interview that was published on the website of the Review of African Political Economy. That interview took other directions, which included aspects of personal life as well as opinions, which were not mentioned in my interview. Both of her interviews are particularly helpful, as they shed light on the emerging gender research in independent Tanzania, as well as the support and challenges academics met.

Focusing on Tanzania during the 1970s, Deborah Bryceson provides the viewpoint of a female student and scholar who immigrated into the country as the wife of a government official's son. We were in contact via email prior and after to our interview in Oxford, which gave me the chance to clarify and get additional information. Furthermore, she provided me with one of her works from the early 1970s and the proceedings to a 1979 workshop. Similar to Marjorie Mbilinyi, she was particularly conscious of the particularities of Tanzanian society, most specifically at the university, as she came from a contrasting background. Therefore, her perspective on the university as well as her contribution to gender debates in the government newspaper are unique. In the course of the 1970s, she embarked on research projects which helped to dissect the structural challenges that working women faced. In this sense, her personal and professional experiences are useful indicators of the changes and continuities in gender relations in independent Tanzania. Furthermore, due to her practical experience in gender research, her interview shows that the TANU government was, at least in parts, supportive in overcoming gender discrimination.

Yash Tandon came to Tanzania from London in 1973, where he had been in exile from Idi Amin's regime in Uganda. In his capacity as a politically active academic, he was crucially involved in life on campus. His interview, conducted in Oxford, and his edition of academics' articles at the University of Dar es Salaam uniquely depict political life on campus. Furthermore, his interview helps demonstrate the particular appeal of moving to Tanzania. Of the interviewees in this study, he is one of the few immigrants to Tanzania who originally came from elsewhere in East Africa. Therefore, his interview helps contrast the experience in Tanzania from the East African context more generally.

In addition to these interviews, a number of autobiographies, published recollections, as well as edited group-memories are used to contextualize and contrast events, perspectives and experiences. In contrast to the interviews which were largely unedited by the interviewees after transcription, the publications are likely edited in various ways. Therefore, they are somewhat more subject to retrospective reflection and less an immediate expression of recollection. A crucial advantage to both interviews and recollections is that they were recorded and written decades after the events. As such, they are less inhibited by the immediate fears and ideological constraints of the time. In the 1960s and 1970s, Cold War pressures and fears of internal division led in some cases to limitations of civil liberties. Thus, there is a chance that contemporaries did not express every opinion at any one time, although the contemporary publications reflect lively debates, and there rarely appears to be an intervention by authorities. While it is largely unclear why people chose not to write on specific subjects at the time, it may be assumed that decades later, concerns for immediate personal repercussions no longer played a role in limiting one's expression of thought.

Such advantages of autobiographies can be found in Karim F. Hirji's *Growing Up With Tanzania*. He was not available for an interview, but extensively wrote about his personal experiences in several publications. In his book, he expressed ambivalent perspectives on the implementation of African socialism, as he wrote about the prospects and enthusiasm, but also the intimidation and constraints connected with the TANU government. Hirji also edited the book *Cheche*, to which former members of USARF contributed. In a similar vein, TAMWA[56] published an edition in which memories and opinions of members of the organization appear. These group editions are a meaningful way to identify shared memories. By themselves, these memories as such could be the product of retrospective group recollections and therefore have limited value for the discussion of historical developments. However, in relation to the written historical sources, these recollections help to relate the events to an ongoing narrative in the public sphere which extends to the present day.

---

56   The Tanzania Media Women's Association was founded in 1987 by activists in the field of media who struggled against gender discrimination in the country.

The University: An Arena in Relation to the Newspaper

All the interviewees were active at the University of Dar es Salaam at different times and in different roles. For many it was a formative space as students and others who taught there or participated in political events. Furthermore, the university was a corner stone of the independent state's policies as higher education was intended to play a major role in the achievement of the development of TANU's goal of "socialism" in Tanzania.[57] Yet, as this section shows, the university and higher education in general were complex and contested spaces.

At first glance, students in higher education appeared to share one problem: having gone through an unreformed secondary and university system, they were thoroughly socialized in the British educational system, which suggests, returning to Bourdieu, that they were likely to perpetuate values that they internalized during their education. The entire sphere of higher education shared a common problem: the ability to speak English, the language of the colonial administration, was a prerequisite for participation. This required socialization in a British-based school system, which was one of the most potent ways for the state to inscribe its world views on a population.[58] Beyond financial dependency, dependency on personnel from the former colonial power led in some cases to the suspicion that there was an abuse of power from racist backgrounds. Additionally, the university was not only structured by the language of the former colonial power Britain, but also inherited from it academic protocols and procedures.

However, throughout the 1960s and 1970s, the university was subjected to different and changing forms of influence. While the qualification of local personnel was a goal, the building of the university on its current location, "the Hill" was heavily dependent on British finances and conditioned by British interest. As a result of the diplomatic crisis following Britain's inaction on Rhodesia's Unilateral Declaration of Independence, the United States became the most important donor, while Britain froze funds going into Tanzania. Between 1967 and 1970, the University College of Dar es Salaam (UCD) strove for

---

57 See: Olivier Provini, "The University of Dar es Salaam: A Post-Nyerere Institution of Higher Education? Legacies, Continuities and Changes in an Institutional Space (1961-2012)," in *Remembering Julius Nyerere in Tanzania: History, Memory, Legacy*, ed. Marie-Aude Fouéré (Dar es Salaam, Tanzania: Mkuki Na Nyota, 2015), 284.
58 See: Bourdieu, Wacquant and Farage, "Rethinking the State," 1-2.

a more balanced network of donors, reaching out to Scandinavia. The UCD ceased being part of the University of East Africa and eventually became a national university, the University of Dar es Salaam (UDSM). The state of Tanzania, which partially funded the university during the last decade, became its main source of funding. As such, the university became increasingly independent of the former colonial power Britain, as well as the United States, which was the main representative of the Western Block. The concurrently rising financial obligations of the Tanzanian state potentially put more pressure on students and scholars participating in the discourse of the public sphere, as they were at least morally dependent on the financial support of Tanzanian taxpayers.[59] Yet, TANU's success of shifting funds from the former colonial power and then from the United States to Scandinavian states, who were sympathetic to their socialist vision, likely bolstered efforts to create a university free from direct influences of the former colonial power.

Beyond the administrative goal of gaining skilled and educated personnel, the university was to serve cultural and political goals, and evolved into a remarkable center of open debate and activism. The UCD quickly gained and maintained a reputation of being a hub for international scholars and a site for exchange and debate between East African students and international guests ranging from heads of states, intellectuals and activists, to members of the African Liberation movements.[60] As such, the UCD was a crucial geographical site of the public sphere which enabled views and opinions from an international background into the country to an extent that newspapers could not facilitate, albeit the debates reached an even smaller section of the society than the newspapers. The university's particular openness to debate and transnationally-flowing ideas allowed for the opportunity to question and overcome social structures that were shaped by the British university system.

Even more importantly, TANU and President Nyerere sought to use the university as a tool to eradicate differences and stereotypes that originated from the colonial era. During the inauguration of the university, prior to Tanganyika's independence, Nyerere highlighted its significance for his vision for

---

59 See: Bertram B. Mapunda, "Infrastructure," in *In Search of Relevance: A History of the University of Dar es Salaam*, eds. Isaria N. Kimambo, Bertram B. Mapunda and Yusufu Q. Lawi (Dar es Salaam, Tanzania: Dar es Salaam University Press, 2008), 60-79.
60 See e.g.: Ali Mazrui, "Tanzaphilia," *Transition*, no. 31 (1967): 162, https://doi.org/10.2307/2934403; e.g. NN, "Tanzania 'an inspiration', says Angela." *The Daily News*, August 22, 1973.

the country and pointed out that he pushed for its establishment personally. TANU's efforts for the university foundation, preceding the schedule envisioned by the colonial administration, were mostly motivated by the lack of highly qualified local personnel.[61] By 1963, the university, which was initially associated with the University of London, became a member of the University of East Africa.[62] President Nyerere's inauguration speech was a reflection of the discourse on racialism in society:

> "[The university] must help us in regard to the special temptation to prejudice which faces us now in East Africa. It is the easiest to give way to, and it would be wrong to deny that some of our people have already done so. I refer to the most prevalent social disease of the twentieth century-discrimination on grounds of race, colour or caste. [...]"[63]

The explicit naming of racism as a problem to be tackled by the university points to the significance of the problem in Nyerere's opinion and to the hope he connected with the new institution. Nyerere's call appears to have been heeded, as the majority of interviewees recall that racism did not impact academic life on campus. However, a former Tanzanian student of Asian background argued that there was a "veneer of intellectualism" covering racism.[64] The apparent relative success of TANU to decrease "racial" discrimination in the microcosm of the university points to the efficiency of the party, but also to the potential of Tanzanian young people in overcoming "racial" divides of the previous decades. Furthermore, the absence of overt "racism" in the discourse at the university increased the ability of the "Asian" minority to participate in the public sphere, which could further increase dialogue across "racial" lines.

Gender discrimination, however, as Ivaska points out, was a dominant feature at the university, and almost all female interviewees noticed a male-dominated atmosphere accompanied by misogynist structures and policies in

---

61 See: Bertram B. Mapunda, "Infrastructure," in Kimambo; Mapunda; Lawi, *In Search of Relevance*, 62.
62 See: Isaria N. Kimambo, "Evolution of the Administrative Structure," in Kimambo; Mapunda; Lawi, *In Search of Relevance*, 84-85.
63 Julius K. Nyerere, "Inauguration of the University of East Africa," in Nyerere, *Freedom and Unity*, 219.
64 See: Deborah Bryceson, interview by Harald Barre, February 13, 2018, Oxford; Najma Sachak, interview by Harald Barre.

the 1960s and 1970s.[65] This suggests that TANU was less concerned or aware of various aspects of gender discrimination. In this context, participation in the public sphere would have been harder for women at the university, and required outstanding personalities and the adaption of empowering strategies to articulate themselves in the public discourse.

Bearing the changing atmosphere and limitations of research and higher education in mind, the perspectives of highly educated supporters of Tanzania's African socialist nation building project can more consistently reveal the tensions between the colonial structures and the independent government. For the sphere of higher education was most shaped by the educational standards of the colonial government, and at the same time, most intensively exposed to ideas that challenged these standards. In contemporary publications, academics explored and assessed not only the questions revolving around Tanzania's past, present and future, but they lay the foundation for an African historiography that was detached from colonial paradigms and reflected on the challenges and prospects of implementing an egalitarian, "non-racial" society. In some cases, these works informed a larger social discourse, which would also impact newspaper debates. In other cases, the party and the state's administration blocked such debates. In this environment, dedicated academic activists were most aware of the continuity of authoritarian structures as well as alternative, globally circulating models of societies. As such, contextualizing contemporary academic debates and their reception are a helpful contrast to the discourse in the party newspapers. Furthermore, they are an important framework for the interviews, as the interviewees shaped and were shaped by social structures and public discourses on campus. As such, continuity, rebellion and innovation in higher education are vital indicators for the transformation of the discourse in independent Tanzania. Therefore, higher education will, along with the categories of "race" and gender, be one analytical focus of this work.

---

65 See: Marjorie Mbilinyi, interview by Harald Barre; Fatma Alloo, interview by Harald Barre, March 19, 2018, her residence in Dar es Salaam. Deborah Bryceson, interview by Harald Barre; Andrew M. Ivaska, ""Anti-Mini Militants Meet Modern Misses": Urban Style, Gender and the Politics of "National Culture"," *Gender & History* 14, no. 3 (2002): 591–94.

1.3 Structure

This work argues that social categories of solidarity and differentiation, which were shaped in the colonial era, were fundamentally changed in debates after independence. It sets out to demonstrate how "race" and gender evolved to be characterizing features of colonial society and these categories continued to play a critical role into the first years of independence. The main analysis focuses on the evolution of the characteristics in the published debates in the English-written party newspaper between its foundation in April 1964 up to 1974. It will be noted that phases within this time period were characterized by the perspectives of journalists and readers, which often challenged official governmental positions. Women in particular published outspoken critiques, and thereby contributed to a gender discourse departing from colonial values. In 1974, after a decade of debate, "race" had largely been deconstructed. Furthermore, the imminent end of Portuguese colonialism was also portrayed as a victory of the "non-racial" struggle advocated for by Nyerere's TANU. Gender, conversely, remained an important category, but the meaning of gender roles were profoundly transformed, as discriminatory practices from the colonial era were targeted and discussions were held on new legislation in order to ensure equal opportunities. However, after the international women's year in 1975,[66] these debates were replaced by a return to the narrative on gender in the mid-1960s, which was barely influenced by critical female voices. In the second half of the 1970s, women organized and found new arenas to communicate critiques of various forms of gender discrimination.

Chapter 2 shows how "race" was intentionally introduced as a divisive category, and how individuals developed agency as a "racial" group. While "race" was almost always an openly and controversially discussed topic, gender roles were almost exclusively articulated from a male perspective. Gender roles were crucially shaped by the colonial state and the cash crop system, which limited women's agency and freedom of movement. The success of TANU's liberation struggle in the 1950s was in many ways a response to these structures,

---

[66] The international activism of women was shaped by Cold War tensions, which would also essentially and subtly inform the discourse on gender roles in Tanzania. For a reflection on international socialist activism, see e.g.: Kristen Ghodsee, "Revisiting the United Nations Decade for Women: Brief Reflections on Feminism, Capitalism and Cold War Politics in the Early Years of the International Women's Movement," *Women's Studies International Forum* 33, no. 1 (2010), https://doi.org/10.1016/j.wsif.2009.11.008.

as it advocated for gender equality and "non-racialism" in a socialist society. In the immediate years after the TANU government came into power, gender equality did not evolve into a central aspect of the government's agenda. Conversely, Nyerere's vision of "non-racialism" was hotly contested and dominated the political struggle of TANU's government in colonial and independent Tanganyika. His efforts were aided by an increasing presence of socialist ideas that were circulated by international students and gained attention by urban secondary school students. However, while socialist ideas deconstructed the significance of "race," existing stereotypes and fears in the older generation, as well as violent events such as an attempted coup d'état and the Zanzibari revolution in 1964, reinforced the significance of this colonial category.

Chapter 3 identifies the launching of the TANU newspaper, *the Nationalist*, in April 1964 as a turning point, which enabled the party to debate and interact with the highly educated local population, as well as an international readership. This chapter examines the evolution of the debates around "race" and gender in *the Nationalist*, and demonstrates how political events and reforms altered the discourse. The phase until 1966 was characterized by a relatively low but increasingly lively readership debate. Hostility towards "Asians" was rarely published, but the paper was strongly devoted to calls for pan-African unity and solidarity with other African liberation struggles. Mediated by interaction with prominent freedom fighter Malcolm X, even African Americans became part of this "racial" pan-African vision. Whereas "race" was a dominant, albeit complex topic in the newspaper, gender was less contested, although *the Nationalist* portrayed women's roles almost contradictorily: on the one hand, women were seen as a crucial force in implementing a socialist society. On the other hand, women were also frequently reduced to the passive role of a housewife, much as it had been the ideal of the British colonial government beforehand.

The sphere of higher education was strongly influenced by the colonial system, but ideas from the Eastern Bloc began to challenge these world views, even though only on the initiative of individual teachers. Eventually, against the background of heightening Cold War tensions and increasing conflict with the former colonial power of Britain, the TANU government sought to reform the country's higher education system. The events caused a confrontation between students and coincided with sharper criticism of political and social conditions in *the Nationalist's* readers' section. The greater degree of outspokenness and hostility in the newspaper paralleled a slowly accelerating degree of integration between the "race" and gender divide. Time witnesses and contemporary surveys suggest that "racial" tensions decreased among the young generation, and slowly women became able to obtain education up to the secondary level. These events point to the continued significance of structures shaped in the colonial era, but the developments also suggest at the same time that particularly the younger generation began to seize upon the hitherto vague idea of "non-racial" African socialism.

Articulations of an emerging "non-racial" atmosphere observed in integrated schools for example did reach the larger society and public debates. Yet, initially, as Chapter 4 demonstrates, the period from 1967 to 1970 was shaped by an exponential increase of anti-Asian resentments, even though the Arusha Declaration was intended to be a reiteration of "non-racialism" and African socialism. While the racist narrative was at first advanced in editorials, the newspaper began to moderate such debates, and eventually succeeded in shifting the matter of social disparities around the narrative of class exploitation. The declining of "racially" coded tensions in newspaper debates was also discernible through readers' reactions to an Asian mass exodus from Kenya, which illustrated the interrelation between the social world and public sphere.

Almost parallel to this dynamic was a surge of interest in African American politics and activism, which, however, died down within the period, illustrating the decay of "race" as a category in the public discourse. This concurred with the world views of student activists, who did not regard African American activists' focus on "race" as applicable to the independence struggle in Tanzania. However, these developments at the socio-political level did not necessarily coincide with cultural developments, as African American fashion and music appeared to have a broad impact on the society.

As the significance of "race" diminished in the political debates, gender roles became an increasingly and hotly debated topic by the late 1960s. While mostly men continued to debate fashion along the lines of Christian values of "decency" and imaginations of "African" dignity, female journalists began to highlight discriminatory laws and regulations. It is important to note that their contributions did not only focus on legal relics from the colonial era, but they also began to target the actions of men who held positions of power as administrators, employers, and husbands. Through their contributions, they changed the national narrative on gender roles profoundly.

These debates were entwined with research and debates on campus. After the confrontation between students and the Tanzanian government, a substantial reformation of the educational system was envisaged. This so-called

Education for Self-Reliance inspired students and lecturers to reform research and education. Academic activists attempted to revolutionize education and make it immediately relevant to Tanzanian society. The reforms were contested from many angles, but most crucially TANU gained increasing control over the university administration. Therefore, as the university became nationalized in 1970, conservative-leaning sections in the administration were quickly able to curtail students' publications and contributions to the national discourse.

Chapter 5 looks at the new party guidelines (*Mwongozo wa TANU*) that were passed after the shock of Idi Amin's coup d'état in Uganda. As TANU witnessed the overthrow of a long-time partner in East Africa, it fundamentally questioned whether Tanzania was truly independent. This led to ambivalent dynamics: While the newspapers published increasingly critical positions of readers and journalists, the university became progressively restrictive to students whose positions it considered to be dangerous. The chapter argues that discrimination against women became a main avenue to transport social and political critique. In this sense, gender was a pivotal category in national debates. Furthermore, the debates continued to transform the meaning of gender, as inequality and several forms of discrimination were condemned. Furthermore, the narrative around indecency and fashion was no longer tolerated but it was challenged in letters to the editor.

In the social world, divisions along "racial" lines persisted, and fundamental government intervention such as the nationalization of private estate, led to the large-scale emigration of Tanzanian Asians who were disproportionately affected. Yet, in the newspaper debates, "race" no longer played a tangible role. The younger generation especially explained social differences in terms of class, and not "race." This dynamic was aided by developments in the social world. The Amin regime's violence against Ugandan Asians created sympathy and solidarity with Asians. At the same time, the impending victories of the national Liberation movements against Portuguese colonialism were used to vindicate the "non-racial" argument of Nyerere's TANU.

Chapter 6 briefly illustrates that in the second half of the 1970s, "race" became a deconstructed and unimportant category in the newspaper debates, while retaining significance in everyday life in Tanzania. Developments at the university were ambivalent. Although students' political organizing and activism were effectively subdued, academics concerned with gender discrimination were able to organize and institutionalize. Along with journalists and other individuals working in media and other communicative institutions, a consciousness for gender inequality was transported into the larger society. The continuity and expansion of a discourse on gender at the university ran counter to the developments of the discourse that manifested itself in the *Daily News*. In this communicative institution, gender equality was no longer a topic for which was broadly advocated. This chapter argues that the break in this style of reporting, as well as the support women continued to receive in parts the university, points to the agency of individuals in key positions, such as the editor of the newspaper and members of the university administration.

2 State and Society in the Colonial Era

As Bourdieu has argued, national independence was strongly shaped, if not inhibited, by preceding decades of socialization in the colonial era. This chapter will point out how the social world and debate in newspapers were strongly formed during the colonial era. While the colonial state was a crucial agent in shaping Tanganyika, the society was not independent of pre-existing structures. Furthermore, agency was not limited to the colonial state and its representatives, but included the spectrum social agents. Therefore, it is impossible to clearly differentiate the effects of colonialism. However, the character and scope of the impact of colonialism on social structures will be sketched below. These structures in the social world and the public sphere were to greatly influence the nation in the years immediately following the beginning of independence.

The far reaching influence of a state in the social world in Tanganyika and Zanzibar was closely connected with the establishment of colonialism in East Africa. While the territory was connected through overlapping networks of trade, kinship, language and religion, it was the German colonial conquest that forced the population under one state.[1] Susan Geiger's oral history gives a glimpse into the significance of the colonial state's forceful influence. Her 1980s interviews with female political activists reveal that the difficulty in politically motivating the older generation was rooted in their experience during the German colonial wars. The violence inflicted by Germans had caused such strong fear that it paralyzed the older generation decades after the war. The British were seen as an even greater threat since they had defeated the Germans in World War I.[2] However, Mtei's recollection of the suppression of riots

---

1 See: John Iliffe, *A Modern History of Tanganyika*, African Studies Series 25 (Cambridge u.a.: Cambridge Univ. Press, 1979), 318, 90-122.
2 See: Susan Geiger, *TANU Women: Gender and Culture in the Making of Tanganyikan Nationalism, 1955-1965*, Social History of Africa Series (Portsmouth, NH, Oxford, Nairobi, Dar

by the British colonial administration demonstrates that the British displayed active force as well.³ These examples do not give a quantitative impression of how the colonial state used its physical force to have agency, but they show clearly that the exertion of force left a vivid memory on contemporary witnesses. As such, the state established itself lastingly as a powerful agent on the territory's African population's minds.

While the colonial state was able to establish itself as a formative agent, it did not seek to nationalize the population. To the contrary, the British colonial administration tried to avoid the formation of national sentiment among the population by setting up a system of indirect rule. Guided by this goal, it tried to reconstruct a political system in which a pre-colonial society was imagined and integrated into the colonial administrative superstructure.⁴ In doing so, the colonial state attempted to keep the African population divided. Thus, the imagining of an African community was near impossible, as an African press did not exist for decades, and the rural population was divided into "tribes," which were in some cases the product of colonialism and its underlying ideological assumptions. However, the colonial state also structured the social world by forcing its integration into the world economy. The introduction of taxes and cash-crops not only increased farming, but also urbanization.⁵ Migration to urban centers, namely the colonial capital and trading port Dar es

---

es Salaam: Heinemann; James Currey; E.A.E.P; Mkuki Na Nyota, 1997), 51, 60; Feierman captures the same feeling in his interviews among elders of the Shambaa in the 1960s: Steven Feierman, *Peasant Intellectuals: Anthropology and History in Tanzania* (Madison Wis. a.o.: Univ. of Wisconsin Press, 1990), 125.

3   See: Edwin Mtei, *From Goatherd to Governor: The Autobiography of Edwin Mtei* (Dar es Salaam: Mkuki Na Nyota Publishers, 2009), accessed December 13, 2016, http://site.ebrary.com/lib/academiccompletetitles/home.action, 8, 12. Aminzade points out that Mtei was part of a Western oriented fraction in Tanzania's government that supported economic liberalization. His position may explain his positive perspective on colonial force. See: Ronald Aminzade, *Race, Nation, and Citizenship in Postcolonial Africa: The Case of Tanzania*, Cambridge Studies in Contentious Politics (Cambridge: Cambridge University Press, 2013), https://doi.org/10.1017/CBO9781107360259, 158.

4   See: Iliffe, *A Modern History*, 321-324. James L. Giblin, "Some Complexities of Family & State in Colonial Njombe," in Maddox; Giblin, *In Search of a Nation*. Here Giblin demonstrates in the case of Njombe that these reconstructions were biased by the academic postulates. Therefore, the political structures conflicted with the social practices.

5   See: Iliffe, *A Modern History*, 273-274; Iliffe points out that neighborhoods reflected a concentration of African groups with shared geographic background, but that they were overshadowed by racial patterns. See: Iliffe, *A Modern History*, 386.

Salaam, led to a steady growth of an urban African population. The migrants came from various rural backgrounds which were not governable through indirect rule. Therefore, urbanization provided the potential for Africans to develop an African national narrative.

This self-conception of Africans as a group was aided by the colonial state as it set up "race" as opposed to "tribe" as the crucial administrative category in the cities. In Dar es Salaam, the general legal categorization of the population in British Colonial Africa – "native" or "non-native" – structured individuals' rights and obligations. While the German colonial administration had categorized all non-European groups as "natives," the British sought to narrow down who ought to be considered as "native" and classified people with Asian[6] descent along with Europeans as "non-natives."[7] However, despite the bifurcated legal distinction, the German administration established a building code which indirectly set up "racial" segregation among three zones by 1906.[8] When the British took over the administration of the city in the course of World War I, they orientated their regulation based off the German plans, but also established a segregation that was *de iure* based on sanitation codes, while *de facto* limiting Africans to Zone III which had the lowest requirements and were therefore more affordable. The Asian population remained concentrated in the Commercial Zone and Europeans occupied the Residential Zone. The system limited African mobility, but ended up with a degree of permeability, as wealthy Indians could build houses in the Residential Zone if they met the requirements.[9] Furthermore, the administration did not intercede as Indians moved and invested in Zone III.[10] While the German colonialists had supported German settlement in Tanganyika, in 1922 the British were mandated by the League of Nations to protect the land rights of the African

---

6 The terms "Asian" and "Indian" were used interchangeably in Tanganyika and later in Tanzania. As the members of these groups in East Africa often identified themselves in these terms in relation to the state, I will commonly adopt them. However, if a distinction is necessary, e.g. into religious networks, I will highlight this in the text.
7 See: James R. Brennan, *Taifa: Making Nation and Race in Urban Tanzania*, (Athens, Ohio: Ohio University Press, 2012), 23-26.
8 See: James R. Brennan and Andrew Burton, "The Emerging Metropolis: A History of Dar es Salaam, circa 1862-2000," in Brennan; Burton; Lawi, *Dar es Salaam*, 24, 29.
9 See: Brennan, *Taifa*, 29-31.
10 See: James R. Brennan, "Between Segregation and Gentrification: Africans, Indians, and The Struggle for Housing in Dar es Salaam, 1920-1950," in Brennan; Burton; Lawi, *Dar es Salaam*, 122-123.

population. This protection was not only to discourage white settlement, but also to reduce land speculation by Indians. However, the interpretation of this mandate resulted in crippling regulations that made it impossible for "natives" to obtain credit, denying them a chance to build a strong position in commerce in Tanganyika.[11] These regulations of the colonial state structured the colonial society significantly, as they actually increased the chance of the Asian population to obtain economic capital.

The colonial state cemented these economic structures through a tri-partite "racial" education system. Colonial officials reflected explicitly on the divisive effect of keeping schools segregated. By keeping the population divided along racial lines, political unification against the British Empire would be unlikely. The overwhelming majority of the African population received none or only a primary education, with African girls being frequently excluded. The state's funding for education per capita was lowest for Africans, and it decreased as time passed. Therefore, most of the positions in the state's administration went to members of the "racial" minorities, Europeans and Asians. And even though Great Britain had the mandate to prepare Tanganyika for eventual independence, it sought to educate the population into loyal citizens of the Empire who were attached to "Western civic values."[12] Due to its approach in education, the colonial government not only established "race" as a divisive category, but also attempted to socialize the few Africans who had a chance to go to school according to the administration's conception of the world.

2.1 Asian Agency in the Colonial State

While British colonial practices structured Asians into one group, the concepts to make sense of the social world produced from within this group were diverse across time and social space. As this section will show, the heterogeneity of Indians living in Tanganyika opened up certain prospects in bridging the "racial" divides set up by colonialism. At the same time, the "racial" codification of Tanganyika's social world proved to be so significant that the diverse Asian community began to share many socio-cultural perceptions of Africans.

---

11 See: Brennan, *Taifa*, 23, 36.
12 See: Ned Bertz, *Diaspora and Nation in the Indian Ocean: Transnational Histories of Race and Urban Space in Tanzania* (Honolulu: University of Hawai'i Press, 2015), 67-69, 78-81.

East Africa played a vital role in trade networks and was a site for the multi-directional trajectories of migrants in the Indian Ocean region for centuries. With the dawn of British colonialism, the scope of agents from the Indian sub-continent expanded to laborers and service providers in the administration. While they were coming from diverse backgrounds on the Indian sub-continent, this group of Indians was characterized by the maintenance of active ties to India, through marriage, remigration and education.[13] Thus, even though a diverse group, Asians in East Africa shared a similar position in the social world. Contrasted with Africans, they had access to social networks that reached beyond the limits of East Africa in general, and Tanganyika, in particular. Furthermore, being influential in trade networks and occupying more profitable positions in the colonial administration, they generally possessed more economic capital.

In Dar es Salaam in particular, Arab and Indian traders were encouraged to be part of the city's social space when they arrived in significant numbers in the 1860s. After World War I, the city attracted many Hindu immigrants who sought to work as professionals, replacing the previously dominant presence of Shi'a Muslim merchants.[14] Their position in the social world enabled group action, such as a successful strike against the colonial government in 1923. This strike was the most drastic campaign of Asian civil disobedience in Tanganyika. As they demonstrated their power, Indians gained significant representation in the city's administration on the following decades. For example, the Indian community secured representation in the censorship board for the growing film industry in Tanganyika by advocating for their rights as "non-natives."[15] Furthermore, during World War II, Asians secured material privileges for items such as food, which was rationed, because of the influence Asian representatives had on the Economic Control Board.[16] Their group

---

13   See: Sana Aiyar, *Indians in Kenya: The Politics of Diaspora* (Cambridge, Massachusetts: Harvard University Press, 2015), Accessed October 26, 2017, http://search.ebscohost.c om/login.aspx?direct=true&scope=site&db=nlebk&AN=970803, 5, 22–24.

14   See: Brennan Burton, "The Emerging Metropolis," 16; James R. Brennan, "Politics and Business in the Indian Newspapers of Colonial Tanganyika," *Africa: Journal of the International African Institute* 81, no. 1 (2011): 48, accessed July 26, 2017UTC, http://www.jsto r.org/stable/41484965.

15   See: Ned Bertz, "Indian Ocean World Cinema: Viewing the History of Race, Diaspora and Nationalism in Urban Tanzania," *Africa* 81, no. 01 (2011): 73–74, https://doi.org/10.1 017/S0001972010000045.

16   See: Brennan, *Taifa*, 98-99.

advocacy towards the colonial state was a testament to the unquestioned significance of the state for the entire society, and illustrated how "race" became a category through which Asians could negotiate social upward mobility.

However, despite the ability to collaborate as a "racial" group within the colonial system, Asians remained a heterogeneous group. As the background and transnational connections varied, cultural and religious division remained overt, becoming increasingly hostile in the 1940's. The rationing system, for example, treated each sub-group differently and the reception of films divided religious groups and the Indian Nationalist association. The internal division even resulted in physical attacks on parades and Asian public figures.[17] The lines of conflict did not only run between Hindus and Muslims, Shi'as and Sunnis, but also proponents of modernist Islam who challenged the established religious networks.[18] Burton mentions that these collaborations permeated Dar es Salaam's politically quiet Indian community, where traders depended on African hawkers.[19] These examples illustrate the political and religious complexity of the city's Indian community and its influence in Tanganyika.

While Asians successfully coordinated political group action, the diversity of Asian newspapers in Tanganyika was indicative of the significance of sub-groups of the community. Brennan's analysis of the two major Indian newspapers, the *Indian Herald* and the *Indian Opinion* reveals that Indian nationalism had limited relevance for many Asians in Tanganyika. Both papers were strongly connected with first-generation emigrants from India who worked actively with the Indian National Congress across the Indian Ocean. In Tanganyika, the agents from the Indian nationalist movement, however, had to urge the Indian community to overcome communal thinking and lamented the dominance of religion among the local Asian population.[20]

---

17 See: Ibid. And see: Brennan, "Politics and Business," 54-56, 59-60.
18 See: James R. Brennan, "Constructing Arguments and Institutions of Islamic Belonging: M. O. Abbasi, Colonial Tanzania, and the Western Indian Ocean World, 1925-61," *The Journal of African History* 55, no. 02 (2014): 216-217, 220–223, https://doi.org/10.1017/S0021853714000012
19 See: Andrew Burton, *African Underclass: Urbanisation, Crime & Colonial Order in Dar es Salaam*, Eastern African Studies (Oxford: Currey, 2005), http://www.loc.gov/catdir/enhancements/fy0624/2005044921-d.html, 159-161. See: Brennan, *Taifa*, 58 regarding the withdrawal of Indian nationalism in Dar es Salaam.
20 See: Brennan, "Politics and Business," 50-52.

These comments in the public sphere suggest that Tanganyikan Indians remained heterogeneous despite many similarities, and that Indian nationalism never gained relevance for local political initiatives.

In fact, even members who joined the Indian Congress Party did not necessarily do so because they wanted to invest themselves in the building of an Indian nation. Al Noor Kassum, a son of a wealthy Indian family in Dar es Salaam who went on to be a member of the administration after independence, wrote a recollection of a stay in Bombay:

> "I also joined the Indian Congress Party, which was leading the movement for independence from the British, but my motives were not political. Although I have served in many political positions, I have never been a political person. [...] As a young man in India, although I was moved by the seething political atmosphere, I joined Congress only because it was the thing to do for people of my age."[21]

He went on to affirm that this experience heightened his consciousness of Indian culture, but at the same time, he wrote of wearing Indian garments only for certain occasions, and points to the influence of Western culture. In his memoirs as a Tanzanian politician, he may have been inclined to downplay his commitment to Indian Nationalism as a young man. However, a closer look at the quote reveals that Indian Nationalism became a small part of his life at best. Rather, his life remained dominated by family and religious networks by being a Muslim group devoted to its religious leader, the Aga Khan. An Indian state at no point is something he expressed any hopes or aspiration for.[22] Since he wrote about such other transnational allegiances without any hesitation, it seems improbable that he lessened the significance of Indian nationalism in his youth.

The network around the Aga Khan also proved to be of crucial importance to less prominent members. Karim Hirji, who later became a prominent member in academia and student activism, remembered that even poorer Asians benefited from the ability to get credit via their transnational networks and had a chance to build a life on that:

---

21   Al Noor Kassum, *Africa's Winds of Change: Memoirs of an International Tanzanian* (London, New York: I. B. Tauris & Co Ltd, 2007), accessed December 13, 2016, http://search.ebsco host.com/login.aspx?direct=true&scope=site&db=e000xat&AN=216712, 11-12.
22   See: Kassum, *Africa's Winds*, 12-17.

"Father closed his Lindi shop in 1954 (or perhaps 1955), and began work as a lorry driver. [...] After two years, he secured a loan of TSh 10,000 from the Ismaili run Diamond Jubilee Investment Trust. It enabled him to open a retail shop in Bunju. Mohamedali, his younger brother, was his partner and ran the shop. Father's transport work went on but on a more independent footing. Using a part of the loan and his savings, he got a truck of his own [...]."[23]

As such, transnational networks could uplift their Asian members in the social world in Tanzania. While the transnational community remained important, political activism revolved around the Tanganyikan state. While the Aga Khan network materially supported its members, it also undermined the colonial "race"-based education system, as it funded its own schools. Despite doing so, it was able to obtain co-funding by the colonial state, as it also provided spots for African students. The Indian community lost further cohesion when political tension from the Indian subcontinent radiated to East Africa in the 1940s. However, this led to further attempts by the Ismaili community to collaborate with Muslim Africans.[24] The heterogeneity of the Asian community and the increasing inclusion of Africans by the Aga Khan network demonstrated the limitations of the colonial state to impose "racial" division.

However, despite significant divisions in the Asian community, fear of African criminals seemed to be a unifying factor. Indian newspapers frequently printed articles about violence committed by Africans in great detail. Fears in the Asian community rose exponentially when frustrations in the African community resulted in riots in the 1930s and 1950s.[25] Being pushed into a middle-ground of the colonial society, Asians were relatively prosperous. Therefore, despite its diverse backgrounds and cultures, the Asian community was strongly shaped by the "racial" codes of the colonial administration. This became visible in strategic collaboration within the community and, maybe even more fundamentally, the profound concerns of "African" violence which united Indians in the public sphere. This shared, deep-rooted sense of fear also reverberated with shared experiences in the social world. This product of the colonial society would overshadow the prospect of independent majority rule in the country.

---

23   Karim F. Hirji, *Growing up with Tanzania: Memories, Musings and Maths* (Dar es Salaam: Mkuki na Nyota Publishers, 2014), 7, accessed August 2, 2018, http://search.ebscohost.com/login.aspx?direct=true&scope=site&db=e000xat&AN=839171.
24   See: Bertz, *Diaspora and Nation*, 71-72, 84.
25   See: Burton, *African Underclass*, 180-183.

2.2 African Nationalism – the Evolution of a "Common Sense"

Just as the heterogeneous Asian community did not necessarily have to experience "race" as a common denominator, Africans, initially, did not view themselves as belonging to this broad colonial category, but rather developed such a group consciousness later, as the conception of being "African" and social realities intersected. On the one hand, the fragmented Asian community was united in its fear of crime by the impoverished African population. Africans, on the other hand, only came to identify as a group, when they experienced shared discrimination and suffering at the hands of the colonial state and the Asian community. For instance, the 1923 strike by Indian businesses mostly hurt the African population due to it being cut off from the supply chains.[26] Such economic dependency likely affected the image of Asians among the African population. As such, the experience of material conditions in the social world was inscribed in abstract terms of "race" in the public sphere. In published debates, Indians would be stereotypically described as wealthy exploiters.

In the aftermath of World War I, the 1923 strike, and efforts to turn the former German colony into an Indian sub-colony prompted protest of African clerks in the colonial administration, many of whom came from other British colonies. The line of conflict, however, did not only run along "racial" lines, but also within the African community itself. 'European educated' African clerks disdained the majority of the African population whom they regarded as uncivilized. African clerks organized the Tanganyika Territory African Civil Services Association. It promoted social upward mobility through European education, parity with Indians who were privileged in the political system, and unity of African clerks.[27] This can also be seen in debates around censorship of Tanganyika's early cinema screenings, which can be interpreted to be a microcosm of Tanganyikan urban life. Initially, the "educated," African elite accepted the discrimination of "natives" as being in its own category, but fought for their right as educated Africans to attend movies censored as suitable for "non-natives."[28] "Educated" Africans in the city strove not only for privileges based on their "merits," but they also frowned upon poorer, "less

---

26 See: Brennan, *Taifa*, 54-55, 71.
27 See: Iliffe, *A Modern History*, 264-268.
28 See: Bertz, "Indian Ocean World," 74.

educated" and younger rural urban migrants, particularly if they were unemployed and homeless.[29] These African initiatives and the resulting political structures that sought to "uplift" through assimilation to Europeans could be found in other colonies as well as the United States.[30] These developments illustrate that for "educated" Africans, "race" had barely evolved to a category of thought. Rather than challenging the system itself, the educated natives sought ways to side step the regulations that impacted them.

However, parallel to the group formation of African urban elites in Tanganyika, a less class-dominated identity of Africans emerged. By the turn of the century in West Africa, racial uplifting became more attached to distinct racial pride.[31] Given the consciousness for "race" that African clerks had developed, particularly against the Indian population after World War I, it is not surprising that a visit by West African intellectual James Aggrey in 1924 catalyzed "racial" consciousness and pride among Africans in Tanganyika. In fact, Brennan finds in newspapers' responses to Aggrey's visit that comments went beyond prior calls for unity of African clerks or individual pride. Rather, they took up Aggrey's call for being proud of your color as a call for a collective African project.[32] This suggests that at least a part of the small group of European "educated" Africans in Tanganyika started to imagine a community that went beyond their social and local milieu. This was also reflected in the Tanganyika African Association's (TAA)[33] efforts after 1931 to abolish the cinema censorship category of "non-native." This succeeded in 1936, as the colonial administration feared national group formation around this issue. "Race-consciousness" likely further heightened after the success of breaking

---

29   See: Burton, *African Underclass*, 74-75.
30   See: Philip Serge Zachernuk, *Colonial Subjects: An African Intelligentsia and Atlantic ideas* (Charlottesville, Va.: University Press of Virginia, 2000), 42-43; Katja Füllberg-Stolberg, "Amerika in Afrika: Die Rolle der Afroamerikaner in den Beziehungen zwischen den USA und Afrika, 1880 - 1910," ZMO-Studien 17, (Berlin: Schwarz, 2003), 180-182.
31   See: Zachernuk, *Colonial Subjects*, 67.
32   See: Brennan, *Taifa*, 123-124. For a discussion on Aggrey's education in the Gold Coast and the U.S. and career at Washington's Tuskegee Institute see e.g.: Sylvia M. Jacobs, "James Emman Kwegyir Aggrey: An African Intellectual in the United States," *The Journal of Negro History* 81, no. 1 (1996), accessed January 6, 2018, http://www.jstor.org/stable/2717607.
33   The TAA was founded in 1929 and claimed representation for the entire African population and not just a class of Africans. See: Iliffe, *A Modern History*, 406-408.

the legal barrier to cinemas, because well-off Africans experienced discrimination at the hand of the pre-dominantly Indian cinema-owners, and the majority of poor Africans were too poor to afford the admission to most cinemas.[34] Although access to cinemas can at best be interpreted as a symbol of Dar es Salaam's social world, it points to the power of "racial" categories: While poor, illiterate Africans and "educated" Africans with more means were separated in terms of social and cultural capital, they were pushed together as a group by both experiencing exclusion based on "race." However, while the Asian community was able to discuss their commonalities in newspapers since the 1920s, Africans did not have the economic means to establish a newspaper. In order to recognize themselves as a group, Africans needed to begin to discuss how they perceived the social world in a public forum.

African Group Formation

The foundation of Tanganyika's first African owned newspaper, *Kwetu*, in 1937 projected African perspectives in the public sphere.[35] The 1930s illustrated to the African population their continued marginalization in the colonial society. This dynamic would be accelerated country-wide in the following years, as the experience of World War II at home confronted the entire population with the "racial" colonial system. As pointed out earlier in reference to Brennan, the economic dependency of the "native" population on Indians became most dramatic in times of crisis like the aforementioned 1923 strike by Indian businesses. World War II would have a similar effect, as economic strains affected Tanganyika continually. Out of the resulting hardships, needs, and conflicts and a new ability to debate the socio-political conditions in newspapers across Tanganyika, a narrative of Tanganyikan African nationalism was woven.

In addition to dependency on Asian traders, African life was defined by the poor living conditions in Dar es Salaam's Zone III. The meager and dependent living conditions worsened with the outbreak of World War II, as the British government sought to stabilize the pound sterling by prohibiting imports from countries that did not use British currency. This led to massive in-

---

34 See: Bertz, "Indian Ocean World," 75-77.
35 See: James F. Scotton, "Tanganyika's African Press, 1937-1960: A Nearly Forgotten Pre-Independence Forum," *African Studies Review* 21, no. 1 (1978): 1-4, accessed March 18, 2018, http://www.jstor.org/stable/523760.

flation in Tanganyika due to the country's large dependency on imported consumer goods.[36] Furthermore, crucial wool imports from Japan disappeared and could not be substituted, leading to a price increase of 600%. The colonial state attempted to abate the effect of war time inflation through price regulation, but actually remained powerless as price gouging and the black market circumvented these measures. As the situation deteriorated, the administration set up a ration system for food and eventually also for textiles. However, it excluded rural Africans and unemployed urban dwellers. Furthermore, due to the absence of African representation in the state's decision making bodies, the ration system was set up along the colonial state's "racial" lines. Not only did Asians receive greater amounts of food, but their access to ration cards was arranged to their convenience. "Natives," conversely, had to prove their entitlement and renew their cards often in an arduous process.[37] As such, the urban population especially experienced inequality within the social world based on their "racial" background.

Shortly before the war, African migration to Dar es Salaam accelerated. They were met with a neglected urban infrastructure, particularly in the "native" sector of the town, which only reinvested a fraction of its taxes into local areas of concern. Bad harvests increased rural-urban migration in the early 1940s significantly. The colonial state reacted to this phenomenon with increasing exclusion of Africans from the city and began deporting Africans to the countryside. However, the laws created to regulate these dynamics were targeting a broad spectrum of African urbanites.[38] Particularly in the cities, Tanganyika's division of the social world became increasingly visible due to the war. The declining supply of resources highlighted "racial" lines, as it excluded many and discriminated against the rest of the population. Africans became even more stigmatized for being homeless, poorly dressed and suffering from starvation. These developments suggest that "race" had increasingly tangible effects on people's lives and their position in the social world.

The discrepancies became part of public opinions. Even the administration noticed that the circumstances were openly discussed in the African

---

36 See: Nicholas Westcott, "The Impact of the Second World War on Tanganyika, 1939-49," in *Africa and the Second World War*, eds. David Killingray Richard Rathbone (Basingstoke: Macmillan, 1986), 144-145.
37 Brennan, *Taifa*, 93-94, 99-100. Brennan points out that clothing was an important symbol in display of honor.
38 See: Burton, *African Underclass*, 84-89, 107-109.

neighborhoods. Furthermore, the African "elite" became increasingly disillusioned with the lack of prospects.[39] The concerns of the British administration demonstrate that problems of the social world had reached the public sphere, where Africans found the significance of one's "racial" background when discussing their common grievances.

World War II also revealed interwoven lines of conflict with regard to gender and generational relations. Inflation in Tanganyika also impacted bride prices, which was commonly expected to be paid by the groom, making it increasingly hard for young men to marry and start a family.[40] This dynamic continued well beyond the war, and ample letters to the editor in Tanganyikan newspapers reflected the importance of the topic to citizens.[41] Thus, in contrast to previous decades, education was no longer seen as a means to reach a high position in the social world, as "race" overshadowed any academic achievement. On top of that, the power of the older generations seemed cemented, and young men perceived their position in the social world as increasingly unfavorable. The inability of the colonial state to resolve the challenges within the "racially" divided colonial system likely diminished any hope for reform within the colonial state.

World War II impacted Tanganyikan society in yet another way. African soldiers were detached from the structures of Tanganyika's social world when they experienced international travel and war. Contrasting new experiences with the colonial structures in Tanganyika enabled them to create new perspectives on Tanganyika. Changes began with access to commodities and technology, which were out of reach in most recruits' civilian lives. Furthermore, within limits, social upward mobility in the British Army's ranks was possible. In the King's African Rifles (KAR), the colonial regiment composed of East African soldiers, Swahili was the lingua franca. In addition, during their service, soldiers were encouraged to become literate, learn English and become familiar with technologies.[42] Veterans experienced social respect and self-recognition, which would have been reserved for a small group of

---

39 See: Burton, *African Underclass*, 88-93.
40 See: Brennan, *Taifa*, 129.
41 See: Emma Hunter, *Political Thought and the Public Sphere in Tanzania: Freedom, Democracy and Citizenship in the Era of Decolonization*, African Studies v.133 (New York: Cambridge University Press, 2015), http://gbv.eblib.com/patron/FullRecord.aspx?p=2034112, 50-51.
42 See: David Killingray and Martin Plaut, *Fighting for Britain: African Soldiers in the Second World War* (Rochester: James Currey, 2010), 82-93.

male chiefs in Tanganyika. Furthermore, they learned Swahili as the common language in East Africa, opening the path to a common shared discourse.

The war experience not only altered the soldiers' self-perception and skills, but it also shattered the colonial explanations that hitherto had made sense of their social world. Tanganyikan KAR soldiers saw the vulnerability and weaknesses of British and other 'white' troops, as these troops sought shelter with them.[43] These experiences dismantled the image of 'white superiority' and 'white civilization.' The questioning of "racial" hierarchies deprived colonial Tanganyika of its fundamental structures. For East African and Tanganyikan soldiers, the experience in Asia was particularly crucial as the encounters with the local population challenged the colonially alleged supremacy of Asian civilization. Brennan demonstrates that, in Asia, the confrontation with extreme poverty and the contrast between local customs and the breaking of the color bar in sexual relations, "exploded racial hierarchies while cementing "racial" stereotypes."[44]

While sexual relations with women of other "racial" groups eroded soldiers' acceptance of "racial" relations in colonial Tanganyika, they developed particular perspectives on the role of African women. Eventually, *Heshima* started printing an African "back-page girl," who wore a Sunday dress, resembling missionary ideals. According to a British liaison officer, this display of African women was important to the soldiers. Another military newspaper, *Askari*, portrayed African women in their daily work tasks.[45] Soldiers' letters to the editor indicated that the display of 'respectable' roles of African women was appreciated by Tanganyikan soldiers who considered it a sign of progress.[46] However, this concept of progress was shaped by British and Christian values.

Yet, transnational encounters with colonized people also inspired the empowerment of Tanganyikan soldiers. Through military newspapers, soldiers were able to expand their perspectives on the world beyond their personal experiences. For instance, *Heshima* provided an almost exclusive focus on Chi-

---

43   See: Lorne E. Larson, "A History of the Mahenge (Ulanga) District: c 1860-1957" (University of Dar es Salaam, 1976), 329-330.
44   Brennan, *Taifa*, 139-141.
45   See: Katrin Bromber, *Imperiale Propaganda: Die ostafrikanische Militärpresse im Zweiten Weltkrieg*, 1. Aufl., ZMO-Studien 28 (Berlin: Schwarz, 2009), Zugl.: Wien, Univ., Habil.-Schr., 2009, 255-257.
46   See: Hunter, *Political Thought*, 48.

nese troops in its coverage about allied troops, displaying them in training with modern war machinery as well as discussing Chinese civilian life and culture. These articles and pictures often compared Chinese experiences to life in East Africa.[47] Thus, while African soldiers questioned their subordinate status in colonial Africa due to their experiences in South Asia, the images of Chinese culture, the struggle against the Japanese occupation, as well as the seizing of modern technology likely corresponded with soldiers' new perspectives on the world and their role in it. Against the background of their transnational experiences, returning soldiers saw that the social structures in Tanganyika no longer made sense, as the "racial" differentiation ascribed by colonialism did not correspond with the reality they experienced in Asia. The fact that the administration considered itself forced to resort to corporal punishment[48] symbolizes this clash. The significance of these changes would likely have been contained were they not part of a discourse in the public sphere.

However, the soldiers' transnational experiences were not isolated. Westcott points out that only a very small number of Tanganyikans actively participated in the war, and only a minority of them returned to be politically active.[49] Yet, the soldiers in the KAR not only had access to newspapers, but actively corresponded with the press. As Bromber pointed out, amongst the numerous military newspapers, *Heshima* had an outstanding role. While the number of sold copies remained low, probably due to the fact that the newspaper was not free, it enticed high correspondence with its readership. The newspaper engaged in a factual and reciprocal dialogue with its readership and often aligned its topics along their interests.[50] Thus, per design, *Heshima* encouraged its readers to express their own thoughts, to identify common concerns and to debate solutions. Furthermore, soldiers engaged in debates in Tanganyikan newspapers, such as *Mambo Leo*, which enabled discussions between civilians and soldiers.[51] Newspapers functioned as a public sphere

---

47   See: Bromber, *Imperiale Propaganda*, 229, 259-260.
48   See: Larson, "A History of," 331. Larson points to District Commissioner Culwick who quickly resorted to corporal punishment for turning soldiers who he deemed to be unruly.
49   See: Westcott, "The Impact," 154.
50   See: Bromber, *Imperiale Propaganda*, 177-179, 217, 219.
51   See: Ibid. 221.

where common sense was touted. In newspapers, new world views that explained issues within the social world were openly discussed and shaped. Additionally, the unique perspectives of soldiers not only produced new categories of perception within the KAR, but these views were introduced into Tanganyikan society and affecting the perception of the African population. Thus, despite soldiers' small numbers, their experiences may be deemed crucial in pushing African group formation at home and abroad.

The perspectives of soldiers were incompatible with the colonial society, as the deteriorating living conditions in Tanganyika worsened. After the war, the ration system, which had caused strong grievances among Africans, was only temporarily interrupted, and reinstated after environmental crises. Those seeking a place to live in cities met a housing market that was overwhelmed by rural-urban migration and Indian immigration. The government had not been able to invest in housing due to war-time shortages in materials as well as mismanagement.[52] The colonial government reacted to the housing crisis by restricting the rural-urban migration of Africans. The government decided against a passport-system such as in South Africa, but it established harsh criteria for permitting urban residence to Africans, characterizing most of them as "undesirable natives."[53] While both Indians and Africans faced a dire housing market, Indians tended to have more economic capital in order to gain access to housing. Since the segregation system of Dar es Salaam was not based on "race" but on sanitation codes, Indians increasingly moved into the "native" Zone III, where they were treated preferentially by African landlords. Brennan notes that this dynamic did not result in a class conflict between African landlords and evicted African tenants, but it did heighten racial resentment against Indians.[54] This observation can most likely be attributed to a strong sense of African group consciousness. For, conspicuously, landless Africans did not take action against the African landlords' preferential treatment of more well-to-do Indians, and the African elite expressed unease about the deportation of "undesirable natives." At the same time, European and Indian residents of Dar es Salaam approved of the

---

52   See: Brennan, "Between Segregation and Gentrification," 127.
53   See: Burton, *African Underclass*, 109.
54   See: James R. Brennan, "Democratizing Cinema and Censorship in Tanzania, 1920-1980," *The International Journal of African Historical Studies* 38, no. 3 (2005): 127-128, accessed March 18, 2018, http://www.jstor.org/stable/40033967.

measures.⁵⁵ Between Tanganyika's "racial" groups, class was not a significant category of differentiation.

This, however, did not mean that divisions within the groups of Africans went unnoticed. Susan Geiger demonstrates in her interviews with women who were working in the Tanganyika African National Union (TANU) how educated Africans were perceived with suspicion as being exploiters.⁵⁶ And Andrew Burton points out that well-to-do Africans feared poor and homeless Africans.⁵⁷ Yet, in newspapers, "race" dominated the discourse. This can mostly be attributed to the fact that dependence on and dominance of Indians became ever more visible in Tanganyika and in Dar es Salaam in the 1940s due to the direct experiences of the African population and the explicit discussion of these circumstances in newspapers. The discussions in the public sphere of veteran's experiences abroad and Pan African ideology thwarted the legitimacy of the colonial system. However, just as the Asian community embraced "race" to unite for political action, Africans perpetuated this colonial categorization in the 1940s. Furthermore, as the reports of African soldiers' ideals of womanhood suggest, colonial and missionary gender values were shared by at least a part of the population. This observation supports Bourdieu's assumption that the society was significantly shaped and socialized by the colonial administration.

2.3 Gender in Colonial Tanganyika

The depiction of African women along missionaries' ideals in World War II newspapers suggests that gender roles had been strongly impacted by colonialism. Bourdieu acknowledges that a colonized society was not only socialized by the colonial state, but also by pre-colonial practices. It is hard, if not impossible, to reconstruct the pre-colonial gender relations in various social groups in pre-colonial Tanganyika and to distinguish the impact of colonialism on social life. British ethnographic studies from the colonial era seem to be biased, based on British stereotypes. Reinterpretations of such studies indicate that social dynamics between men and women were complex, even

---

55   See: Brennan, *Taifa*, 96-97.
56   See: Geiger, *TANU Women*, 75.
57   See: Burton, *African Underclass*, 74.

within one region.[58] Oral history and archival research indicate that the colonial economy and administration crucially impacted gender roles. This section will outline how gender became a category which pivotally differentiated individuals' opportunities among the African population in Tanganyika.

The main role of women in society was the maintenance of lineage by becoming a wife, bearing children, and maintaining herself and her offspring through subsistence agriculture.[59] Nonetheless, Mbilinyi has argued that "the image of the servile African woman is oversimplified," as women had varying degrees of social and economic autonomy prior to the introduction of cash-crop agriculture. While they commonly had no land rights, they used to be able to sell surplus from their produce as well as manufactured goods for their own profit. Furthermore, their economic roles were more impactful and therefore more valued before the introduction of the cash-crop economy.[60] Thus, even though the roles of women were distinct from that of men and they were equipped with fewer rights, they seem to have had decisive economic power in the family as well as a degree of self-realization and independence in social spheres that did not include men.

Lovett's oral history focusing on gender relations in Buha demonstrates the significance of the cash-crop economy and colonial rule regarding limitations of women's power. While gender relations were marked by the husband's and father's control over socially valued goods such as land and cattle, women experienced a degree of independence in other areas of socio-economic life. However, Lovett emphasizes that women were expected to be subservient and fulfill their husbands' and fathers' will. If women attempted to resist, they had

---

58   See: James L. Giblin, "Some Complexities of Family & State in Colonial Njombe," in Maddox; Giblin, *In Search of a Nation*, 130-135.
59   See: Marjorie J. Mbilinyi, "The State of Women in Tanzania," *Canadian Journal of African Studies* 6, no. 2 (1972): 371-372, accessed March 18, 2018.
60   See: Marjorie J. Mbilinyi, "The 'New Woman' and Traditional Norms in Tanzania," *The Journal of Modern African Studies* 10, no. 1 (1972): 57, 59–60, accessed March 18, 2018, http ://www.jstor.org/stable/159821. Mbilinyi's conclusions regarding inheritance are somewhat contrasted by an experience of Fatma Alloo. In her interview (Appendix 8.1), she mentioned an experience during her work as an educator for a literacy program where a peasant told her that she had inherited land from her father which she worked on by herself as she would have to share the claim if her husband would join her in the work. Hence, regulations on inheritance were somewhat more heterogeneous, or they had changed by the 1970s.

no social and economic power to act against exploitation or abuse.⁶¹ Again, it is difficult to gauge to what degree male-dominated relations were already prevalent in pre-colonial times. As Lovett's respondents reported about experiences during the British colonial administration, it is likely that their social experiences were strongly impacted by the contemporary global economic and political changes in Tanganyika.

Lovett also points to male long-term labor migration as a factor that increased the burden of women who had to stay behind and take over their husbands' role in sustaining the family, thus diminishing their negligible chances of moving up. Young men, conversely, could utilize this new mode of production to earn cash and pay bridewealth on their own and therefore chose entry into adulthood independent of their fathers. Therefore, even prior to World War II, bridewealth rose significantly in an attempt to contain young men's increasing economic capital.⁶² War time inflation and increased fines on adulterers cemented the power of wealthier, older men even further, particularly in patrilineal societies: Generally, the younger, unmarried generation was strongly under the control of the older generation. However, to young men leaving the parental home to earn cash was a viable alternative which women did not have. As they lost control over young men, older men focused on retaining dominance over women as a source of income through bridewealth and as obliging them to work the lands.⁶³ While the inflation of bridewealth was merely a by-product of colonialism, the exclusion of women from cash wages in the colonial economy was a direct imposition of British gender values onto Tanganyikan society.

In addition to being forced into dependence on their parents, women were also likely to be dependent on their husbands. The documents examined by Mbilinyi and Lovett's oral histories reveal that physical violence was a common

---

61 See: Margot Lovett, "On Power and Powerlessness: Marriage and Political Metaphor in Colonial Western Tanzania," *The International Journal of African Historical Studies* 27, no. 2 (1994): 285-291, accessed April 6, 2018, http://www.jstor.org/stable/221026.

62 See: Margot Lovett, "'She Thinks She's like a Man'': Marriage and (De)Constructing Gender Identity in Colonial Buha, Western Tanzania, 1943-1960," *Canadian Journal of African Studies* 30, no. 1 (1996): 54-56, 58-59, accessed April 6, 2018, http://www.jstor.org/stable/486040.

63 See: Marjorie J. Mbilinyi, "Women's Resistance in 'Customary' Marriage: Tanzania's Runaway Wives," in *Forced Labour and Migration: Patterns of Movement within Africa*, ed. Abebe Zegeye, African discourse Series 1 (London: Zell, 1989), 217-218.

threat to women.[64] Indeed, in colonial Tanganyika, gender defined individual agency to a large extent, limiting the spheres of influence for women. Even though the countryside was politically shaped by British indirect rule, which seemingly left the processes in the agency of Africans, the colonial state structured gender relations nonetheless. The British administration expected to find patrilineal societies which were dominated by male elders and therefore situated the colonial government in cooperation with this group.[65] In doing so, the British favored older African men by backing their political and economic capital with colonial symbolic and military power. In fact, in the case of runaway wives, the colonial authorities assisted men to bring back their wives. Generally, the mobility of women was limited as they were obliged to provide a marriage certificate or written permission if they traveled. Women could rarely count on the state's support if they expressed dissatisfaction or fear of their husbands or guardians. Only after being exposed to excessive physical violence, could a wife hope for support from the colonial state.[66] Being in a subjugated position with regard to all social agents, including the state, women were likely particularly aware of the forces that dominated Tanganyika's social world. African women in rural Tanganyika had little chance to act or defy either the colonial state or men in their comparatively privileged roles. However, those women who did escape or were able to build a life in the cities with a sympathetic relative or husband had a chance to reflect and exchange with others their experiences of oppression.

In the colonial export economy in cities, the state provided no role for African women. Yet, effectively, women played major roles in the secondary economy of Dar es Salaam, providing services from beer brewing, to food processing, to renting out houses.[67] As women only had a miniscule chance of getting a job in the formal wage sector, the vast majority had to succeed in the

---

64   See: Lovett, "'She Thinks She,'" 60. Mbilinyi, "Women's Resistance," 219, 223.
65   See: James L. Giblin, "Some Complexities of Family & State in Colonial Njombe," in Maddox; Giblin, *In Search of a Nation*, 130-135.
66   See: Mbilinyi, "Women's Resistance," 227-232.
67   See: Marjorie J. Mbilinyi, "Struggles Concerning Sexuality among Female Youth," *Journal of Eastern African Research & Development* 15 (1985): 89-92. Willis contends that African women's freedom of movement to the cities was less restricted than in Kenya and South Africa and that the reason was less in targeting women but rather in reducing the casual labor population. See: Justin Willis, "Unpretentious Bars: Municipal monopoly and independent drinking in colonial Dar es Salaam," in Brennan; Burton; Lawi, *Dar es Salaam*, 164. However, given Mbilinyi's observations on the restrictions of

niches of the secondary economy. A sizeable minority of African women were able to earn cash to buy property, accounting for 20% of taxpaying African home owners in Dar es Salaam in 1952.[68] Thus, the state as such was less relevant to women, as it offered no direct opportunity, but also remained inefficient in containing women's agency. However, urban spaces provided a chance to escape rural control mechanisms and gave access to social networks as well as potential economic capital.

Yet, even in the cities, young African women were severely constrained in their freedom. In interviews carried out by Susan Geiger, many women recollected having to accept the custom of being locked up in the house as they entered puberty until they were married off by their male guardians. This confinement was likely to continue in marriage. Bibi Titi Mohamed, who played a leading role in TANU's independence struggle, recollected:

> "It is difficult to explain how I felt about this. Since it is our tradition, I had to tolerate it – that is, just get used to being inside. I wasn't tortured, and I wasn't really a prisoner. It was just the same as when a Muslim woman is kept inside [...] after the death of her husband. She has no worries and I had no worries. This is our religion and I knew these were our customs. Being imprisoned is different from being confined inside in this way."[69]

Bibi Titi emphasized that she found abiding the custom tolerable. Yet, the fact that she emphasizes that imprisonment and torture would be worse, imply that the experience did bring up feelings of involuntary confinement and abuse. The similar notions of powerlessness were expressed by Halima Hamisi, who was also a TANU activist:

> "We used to be imprisoned in our houses and therefore we could not engage in anything. It was your problem if your husband was not able to provide for you. You had no right to reply to anything that a man said to you. We women were far behind; we were far behind. We couldn't express our thoughts in front of men. They wouldn't be acceptable."[70]

---

women's mobility in the countryside, the overall suspicion of the colonial state towards female agency seems to have been a clear impediment.
68 See: Brennan, *Taifa*, 110–112.
69 Bibi Titi Mohamed quoted in: Geiger, *TANU Women*, 47.
70 Halima Hamisi quoted in: Geiger, *TANU Women*, 75.

Hamisi's quote not only demonstrates that domination was passed on from a woman's father to her husband, but also that they had little chance to reason with men. In light of this, women were dependent on the luck of either having a sympathetic and empowering father and husband, or having the chance to find a profitable niche after getting a divorce that made them economically independent. Yet to most, only a passive resistance seemed viable. Women maintained their own female sphere, as another recollection of Hamisi suggested:

> "I did not agree with him. You know, in those days women did not easily take men's views at their face value. I did not share his ideas. I left them with him. However, since we have had some comradeship with Bibi Titi since we were young, she followed to explain what Sheneda had told me …. I told her that I had already heard about that organization [TANU] but I did not believe what I had heard since the news was passed on to me by a man."[71]

Hamisi's experience from the early 1950s seems to reflect the independent social spheres Mbilinyi identified as women's empowerment strategies prior to entering the cash-crop economy. The culture of maintaining group cohesion against male influence may be seen as a last resort to prevent domination of women's minds by men, who dominated not only the social world, but also the discourse in the public sphere. In so far as women had the chance to make their views on oppression at the hands of men explicit within these spheres is hard to say. Given their mounted workload, the collaboration between male Africans and colonial authorities, and their likely high exclusion from newspaper discourses due to illiteracy[72], it seems unlikely that African women had developed a countrywide group identity by the late 1940s.

The assumption is supported by the content of the debate in newspapers as analyzed by Brennan. When African group consciousness was articulated in newspapers in the 1940s and 1950s, gender and generational relations became defining categories which were explicitly discussed in newspapers. Brennan points out that male African authors of letters to the editor condemned "inter-racial" relations as a betrayal of their "race," while "racial

---

71 Ibid., 74.
72 Leslie points out that in his survey of Dar es Salaam in 1956, more than four out of five girls above the age of six had not received any education. See: J. A. K. Leslie, *A Survey of Dar es Salaam* (London, New York, Nairobi: Oxford University Press, 1963), 130.

purity" was considered an achievement of civilization. Interestingly, he observes that the hitherto common Swahili term for civilization, *ustaarabu* – which used to equate civilization with Arab culture – was abandoned. Brennan regards the young men who could not obtain the cash necessary to afford the escalated bridewealth and thus were unable to reach an "honorable" adulthood, as the main proponents of this gendered African discourse. Male frustrations, often uttered by veterans, accused African women of acting immoral and pointed to the Tanganyikan "racial" hierarchies that made it impossible for African men to marry women from other "racial" groups. Rare responses from female perspectives criticized men for mistreating their wives and not being able to provide for them.[73] While men's comments reflect their view of not being able to achieve a respected position in the social world, women were concerned with escaping male domination with the help of men who could afford to buy their freedom. However, in the late 1940s, the discourse on gender roles and Africanization barely included female voices and did not concern itself with the lack of freedom of African women vis-à-vis their fathers and husbands.

This absence of women from public debate about gender roles and relations seemed to change in the early 1950s, as sympathetic voices to the plight of women were voiced and female education was viewed as an indicator of progress. As the newspaper *Komkya* in Kilimanjaro launched a page for women to discuss fashion and related issues, women seized the opportunity and discussed a range of socio-political issues such as inheritance laws. Other correspondence focused on the need to educate daughters and sons alike. Crucially, the authors compared the situation in Kilimanjaro with that of other countries' achievement of civilization based on "unity, love and respect."[74] While it is unlikely that these discussions reached far beyond the region at the time, they certainly reflect women's awareness and eagerness to bring about change. Furthermore, women's crucial role in TANU in the 1950s can be interpreted as an indicator for women's consciousness of the discrimination they were experiencing. Had there been less awareness and discontent with their status as a social group, African women would not have seized on TANU's message of equality.[75] However, despite the emerging voices of

---

73 See: Brennan, *Taifa*, 128-129.
74 See: Hunter, *Political Thought*, 49, 51, 59.
75 Susan Geiger points out that TANU was attractive to African women because of its emphasis on equality. See: Susan Geiger, "Engendering & Gendering African Nationalism:

women in the public sphere, in the social world they faced extraordinary challenges to access opportunities, such as education, material independence, or freedom of movement. While the social factors are certainly diverse, the colonial state influenced these limitations significantly and, as the next section will show, also lacked any vision for women beyond that of being a wife.

2.4 TANU – Seizing the State

Up to the post-war years, neither national independence nor challenges to "racialist" thinking or gender discrimination were part of larger debates. As this section will show, the discourse that accompanied the struggle for independence opposed these structures of inequality in many ways, and advocated for "non-racialism" and gender equality. The idea of national independence was conceived as the culmination of discontent was met with post World War II rhetoric. Hunter illustrates that African Tanganyikans embraced the language of freedom and self-government promised in the Atlantic Charter and reaffirmed in the Universal Declaration of Human Rights. The sacrifices made during the war were an additional argument for their cause.[76] In view of the Allied claims in World War II and the experience of national self-determination in Asia, the situation in Tanganyika, and particularly in Dar es Salaam, must have felt utterly wrong. Witnessing or fearing deportation from the city and struggling for access to land against "non-native" Indians was in contrast to the self-perception of Africans, and counter to the rights promised by the League of Nations and the United Nations.

African self-organization was not focused on just TANU, or its predecessor the TAA. In the economically important Kilimanjaro region, Chief Marealle sought to establish a nationalist Chagga movement. However, in contrast to TANU, his political organization was based on the continuation of chieftainship and ultimately failed. Both parties had emphasized the continuation of order and authority, but TANU ended up gaining stronger support, possibly because it was able to embrace a larger social vision based on the resources and revenue of the entire state of Tanganyika. However, TANU's particular strength may be seen in its emphasis on democratic openness and

---

Rethinking the Case of Tanganyika (Tanzania)," in Maddox; Giblin, *In Search of a Nation*, 284.

76 See: Hunter, *Political Thought*, 66-83, 155.

social progress.[77] As such, the party did not only offer the ideal of equality to women, but also gave them the chance to develop the tools necessary to advance its implementation. Organizationally, women performed the crucial task of networking and providing the communicative and logistical infrastructure for TANU's organization.[78] Beyond this, leaders such as Bibi Titi, head of the Party's women's section, continue to impress her contemporaries to this day. Walter Bgoya, who experienced TANU's independence struggle as a student and who would later work in the government administration and the Tanzania Publishing House, reminisced about being inspired with witnessing TANU leaders' appearances:

> "Well, the party started in 1954, TANU started in 1954 and [...] we were in a school. Of course we were not supposed to participate in politics as such but [...] I heard Mwalimu speak, I heard Bibi Titi Mohamed speak – the best two speakers I listened to – [I] read *mwafrika*, the paper that was published by the party[...]. Bibi Titi was an extraordinary woman; put side by side, Nyerere and Bibi Titi, I think she would draw as big a crowd as Nyerere. Fantastic, terrific orator."[79]

Walter Bgoya's recollection of hearing speeches by TANU leaders while being a secondary school student in pre-independence, Mwanza illustrates the significance of the networking described by Geiger. While newspapers certainly shaped the local discourse among higher educated students, the encounter with TANU leaders left a lasting impression. For the mobilization of the larger society, the work was even more crucial, as the vast majority was illiterate and poorly connected. Where newspapers could not reach remote areas, women's networks brought forward discourse and ideas.[80] Equality was embodied in activists such as Bibi Titi. As such, women's networks were the communicative institutions that enabled the discourse of independence.

The British colonial administration's perception of women's roles starkly contrasted with the views, goals and actions of female TANU members. Look-

---

77 Ibid. 151-155, 165, 182-183. Hunter points out that his nation building efforts were revolving around the before mentioned newspaper *Komkya* – an indicator of the significance of the public sphere to the relation between state and society.
78 See: Geiger, *TANU Women*, 66-69, 203-204.
79 Walter Bgoya, interview by Harald Barre, March 8, 2018, in his office, Dar es Salaam.
80 See: Geiger, *TANU Women*, 96-99.

ing back at his recent governorship of Tanganikya, Lord Twining was asked about his perspective on the education of women. He responded that:

> "[T]he education of girls took a very prominent place in the education programme. It was a very important thing. From a social point of view, if you educated the men but there were no educated girls for them to marry, it led to unhappiness and matrimonial disaster. This matter was being looked after within the resources which were available."[81]

His response is a testament to the detached and biased view of his governance over Tanganyika. African women's roles were only considered accessory to Tanganyikan men leading the country to independence. The contrast to Walter Bgoya's reminiscence of women like Bibi Titi engaging crowded political rallies could not be stronger. Furthermore, Twining's insinuation that the administration dedicated significant resources to the education of Africans, let alone female Africans, was a gross distortion. The majority of education was offered through missionary schools and even by the time of independence less than 10 % of Dar es Salaam's African children attended school.[82] While Twining misconstrued educational efforts in the colony and ignored the crucial role of women for the independence movement, he eagerly emphasized the rights of the non-African minority and credited them with the majority of progress in the country.[83] His comments suggest that he was not concerned with the damaging effects of the colonial "racial" system, as he neither acknowledged the dire social middle ground position of the Indian population, nor the desperate and suppressed position of the African population.

Particularly, education for Africans was a major concern for Julius Nyerere, as he emerged as the leader of Tanganyika's independence movement. In 1954, just prior to the formation of TANU, Julius Nyerere criticized the government's exaggerated claims of educational achievements and goals. If the government achieved its own goals, primary education for all children would only be established in the late 1980s. He continued to urge for more technical education, but not at the expense of primary education for Africans.[84] His

---

81   Twining, "The Last Nine Years in Tanganyika," *African Affairs* 58, no. 230 (1959): 24, accessed April 6, 2018, http://www.jstor.org/stable/718045.
82   See: Aminzade, *Race, Nation, and Citizenship*, 46.
83   See: Twining, "The Last Nine," 21.
84   See: Julius K. Nyerere, ed., *Freedom and Unity: A Selection from Writings and Speeches, 1952-1965* (Dar es Salaam: Oxford University Press, 1973), 31-32.

statements, uttered five years before Twining contemplated the situation of Tanganyika, pointed to a crucial concern: Having been denied large scale education, Africans would be highly dependent on foreign skills and know-how in running the country.

This dreaded dependency soon became an unavoidable certainty. While Nyerere reiterated that "indiscriminate immigration" from Asia, Europe or America would be opposed, he pointed out that Europeans and Asians currently residing in the country would be welcome, as well as other foreigners, whose contribution to development would be seen as important.[85] His statements reflected the acceptance of foreign-born residents, and that skilled immigration and investments from outside Africa were considered a necessity. Beyond this dependency, Nyerere faced pressures from Britain that insisted that the rights of businesses owned by Asians and Europeans, and the legislative influences of these groups, would be secured.[86] As such, "racially" coded socio-economic structures were perpetuated as Tanganyika headed towards independence.

The 1958 election was to be held in the colonial tri-partite model, granting each "racial" group equal representation in the legislature.[87] As TANU was able to secure a political majority in the elections by working with candidates from all "racial" groups, it was able to marginalize a European settler party. However, the decision to take part in the elections that were based on a racist system catalyzed African opposition against Nyerere, even within the party. For Nyerere, a "non-racial" society was essential for peace and stability. Accordingly, he pressed for an inclusive citizenship for all residents of Tanganyika.[88] "Ethnic" groups retained significance as cultural institutions, but they were stripped of political influence, as Nyerere feared that the unequal power between groups would lead to conflict.[89] The political demotion of chiefs helped to contain separatist sentiments within the African population. However, his call for "non-racialism" had to address deeply engrained "racial" structures in the social world and the public sphere.

---

85   See: Julius K. Nyerere, "Oral Hearing at the Trusteeship Council, 1955," in Nyerere, *Freedom and Unity*, 37-38.
86   See: Twining, "The Last Nine," 21-22.
87   See: Bjerk, *Building a Peaceful Nation*, 41-43.
88   See: Aminzade, *Race, Nation, and Citizenship*, 71-75.
89   See: Feierman, *Peasant Intellectuals*, 225-226.

After TANU had gained control of the administration, it faced a society that had been significantly shaped by colonial rule. "Race" and "gender" were categories that determined individuals' opportunities, as not only economic and educational backgrounds differed, but also imaginations of the society. As Glassman noted regarding Zanzibar,[90] the perception of the island's society through a "racial" lens had become part and parcel of local discourses. The sections above demonstrate how conceptualizations of "race" were shaped by local agents. Yet, they did not differentiate or demonstrate possible influences of "racial" thought beyond the colonial state. While such influences were likely, the state's impact on the social world and implicitly the public sphere was much more immediate. As such, "race" had become a category that was perceived as natural. While "race" had become a category that had shaped the society not only in its material divisions, but also in the self-perception of the respective "racial" groups, gender had only emerged as a topic of public debate after the war. However, since TANU's success arguably rested on the mobilization of women to a large degree, it may be assumed that women challenged the social structures which surrounded them. Beyond the tensions along lines of "race" and "gender," Tanganyika faced strong dependency in its institutions, its finances, and its access to skilled personnel. The following years would witness an escalation of these structural problems.

2.5 The Social World and the Public Sphere after Independence

Despite the immense challenges to overcome the social structures that had been defined in the colonial era, the independent nation was also exposed to new ideas and concepts that could challenge "racial" structures and gender discrimination. However, the Tanganyikan state under Julius Nyerere's leadership embarked on a pragmatic political agenda serving its own survival. Despite a secret diplomatic mission of the members of parliament Lucy Lameck and Bibi Titi to China, Nyerere emphasized not only non-alignment, and cultivated a strong and public diplomatic relationship with the United States' Kennedy administration. Furthermore, the country remained highly dependent on Western financial aid as well as on British administrative staff.

---

90 See: Jonathon Glassman, "Slower Than a Massacre: The Multiple Sources of Racial Thought in Colonial Africa," *The American Historical Review* 109, no. 3 (2004): 731-735, accessed May 8, 2018, http://www.jstor.org/stable/10.1086/530553.

African independence and unification was part of the national interest defined by the state. Before independence, the TANU government had defined socialism as an internal goal, and non-alignment as an external goal. While Nyerere threatened that British support of the Apartheid regime would lead to Tanganyika's withdrawal from the Commonwealth, his government had to deal with members of parliament who called for a withdrawal from the Commonwealth, in light of British indecisiveness regarding Rhodesia.[91] While diplomatically and symbolically the Tanganyikan government had reiterated its independent and non-aligned stance, materially it remained highly dependent on Western, namely British, funding and expertise. These dependencies point to the far reaching influence of the former colonizer in the administration and higher education.

Despite the continuing impact of the former colonial power, Tanganyikan society could discuss ideas and vision that were alternative to the socio-economic outlook of colonialism. Tanganyika's non-aligned political course allowed literature from the socialist block to permeate into the society. Therefore, the hitherto predominant socialization in colonial values encountered a challenge, at least in Tanganyika's urban social landscape. George Hajivayanis, who would become a student at the University College of Dar es Salaam in the late 1960s, remembered:

> "As a matter of fact [...] you know before independence [...] Tanganyikans or Zanzibaris had only started going to China and the Soviet Union clandestinely because they never had any [...] opportunity for further studies [...] and [...] some of these that came back brought a lot of new ideas, brought in a lot of radical books and at the same time in the 60s a lot of bookshops were opened for example in Dar-es-Salaam and Zanzibar. The Chinese and Soviet Union, they offered free books, we went to collect free books, they were everywhere. There were some book shops who would sell them but at a very cheap price. But my experience is when I was in secondary school, I

---

91 See: Paul Bjerk, "Postcolonial Realism: Tanganyika's Foreign Policy under Nyerere 1960-1963," *The International Journal of African Historical Studies* 44, no. 2 (2011): 217-219, 222, 230, 239-240, 244-245, accessed July 14, 2015, http://www.jstor.org/stable/23046879. In South Africa, Apartheid had been violently enforced and the African political opposition was forced to go underground. Rhodesia's settler population threatened unilateral independence from Great Britain in order to exclude Africans from democratic participation. However, in either scenario, Great Britain did not exert pressure to enforce democratic principles.

met some of these guys who had come back from the Soviet Union. [...] [A]nd my first book was the big book called 'Fundamentals of Marxism-Leninism,' published in the Soviet Union, they were given free. [...] I remember this person called Musa Nchelewa, he had many copies, He gave me a copy and I began to read 63/64 [...]."[92]

This recollection suggests that the ability to learn new perspectives through exposure to international context increased the ability of the people to challenge the social structures that were rooted in the colonial era. It highlights that the significance of Tanganyikan civil society in the formation of a political discourse was crucial and not dependent on the strong influence of Western expatriate staff in the country's administration. This assumption may be supported by Walter Bgoya's recollection of the Cuban Missile Crisis:

"In 1962, there was the Cuban crisis, and I remember very well that I was on the Cuban side. [*Laughing*]. Absolutely with the Cuban side. [...] not very openly because that would have been dangerous, but I was rooting for Cuba. [...] [I]t was a chance of supporting people struggling for liberation, struggling for their national independence, struggling for their self-determination."[93]

Interestingly, in his memory, he explained his support of Cuba not as support of the Eastern Bloc, but rather as solidarity with national independence. This perspective may have been particularly strong due to his personal experience of

threats while studying in the United States.[94] The contrast with Tanganyika's progress and the experience of impactful TANU leaders in the 1950s compared to the terror committed by American white supremacists may have amplified the need to resist U.S. domination. However, his views may also be the product of a discourse on socialism in the public sphere in Tanzania.

The mushrooming of bookshops with communist literature helped popularize socialism as an alternative to the decade-old system of capitalism

---

92 Salha Hamdani and George G. Hajivayanis, interview by Harald Barre, February 14, 2018, Cafeteria of School of Oriental and African Studies, London.
93 Walter Bgoya, interview by Harald Barre.
94 See: Walter Bgoya, "Walter Bgoya. From Tanzania to Kansas and Back Again," in *No Easy Victories: African Liberation and American Activists Over a Half Century, 1950-2000*, ed. William Minter, Gail Hovey and Charles E. Cobb (Trenton, NJ): Africa World Press, 2008), 103.

in Tanganyika. However, these were independently discussed ideas and not part of a clearly articulated vision by TANU. Nonetheless, it seems likely that the students' sympathy for Nyerere's vision of African socialism was boosted by their own discussion of socialist ideas, and finding common ground with other nations that successfully defied Western domination.

While students embraced Nyerere's stance on socialism, the President began to face opposition regarding his "non-racial" politics. Nyerere had advocated since TANU's foundation a "non-racial" stance. However, after independence, "racial" categories remained a dominant category of perception in society. Resentments that had been fostered by decades of legal and material discrimination remained in society and were augmented by the unanswered cry for Africanization. As union leader Christopher Kasanga Tumbo rallied critics of continued discrimination, Nyerere countered that there were not enough qualified African personnel for the majority of posts. However, his argument that the priority was to fill posts with local personnel instead of expatriates did not satisfy the vocal critics. Even from within his own party, Nyerere was only able to overcome opposition by threatening to resign and by pointing out the risk of "racial" and "tribal" conflict.[95] Nyerere's concerns were reflected by fears in the Asian community of African self-rule. Najma Sachak experienced the changes growing up in a family which recognized the religious customs, but was also well-connected to the larger Indian community:

> "[...] [I]t was difficult, because there was a fear of [...] the coming end of the British mandate of Tanzania. [...] What they [the Indian community] wanted for India, they did not want as Indians in a dominantly African country anymore. They feared [...]. And this is what shaped, I guess as I was growing up - child and an early teenager - [...] the vision of things, the fear. Your parents questioning what to do. [...] So at the time, the choice was staying in Tanzania – with the fear as to the future, when the British leave, what will happen. A lot of people, of course, thought the country would just go to the dogs,

---

95   See: Bjerk, *Building a Peaceful Nation*, 68-74. While the political struggle in Tanganyika no longer included strong party opposition, the late 1950s and early 1960s in Zanzibar were shaped by an escalating, vicious confrontation between the Zanzibari National Party and the Afro-Shirazi Party, with the latter having support of TANU. See: Jonathon Glassman, *War of Words, War of Stones: Racial Thought and Violence in Colonial Zanzibar* (Bloomington: Indiana University Press, 2011), accessed August 5, 2018, http://site.ebr ary.com/lib/alltitles/docDetail.action?docID=10448616, 147-176.

because there was this notion, Africans can't govern. [...] It was sort of engrained and that is what ... that is the thing I remember growing up: Sort of some trepidation, some optimism – mixed with some optimism, not quite sure."[96]

Najma Sachak's recollection illustrates the fear and the notion of vulnerability that reverberated among the Asian community. Furthermore, her reminiscence demonstrates that thinking in "racial" categories was present in the Asian community as well. While the end of colonialism was also viewed positively, the prospect of African majority rule marred the picture.

Her recollection is supported by Hirji's memoirs. He mainly viewed his parents' generation as being deeply influenced by the colonial era.[97] She explicitly recollected doubt in Africans' ability to self-rule. However, possibly due to decades of heightened concern about African crime or because of a sense of the harsh racial stratification of the country, there was apparently also a strong concern for safety. The immediate fears were somewhat alleviated by the multi-racial character of the first cabinet. "[S]o, it was almost a relief 'we got some people who represent us.' But in a way you still felt far away."[98] Yet, while the diversity of the cabinet created some relief in the Asian community, it was resented by some African members of parliament.[99] In either case, in contrast to Nyerere's "non-racial" socialist vision, the debate was fed by the realities and imaginations of "racial" discrimination.

The "racially" inscribed fears and resentments would make discourse in the public sphere difficult, as fear would likely have held Asian residents back from speaking out publicly. Such constraints would be exacerbated in the Zanzibari revolution in January 1964. The exact reason of the revolution remains obscure, but the events on the island were marked by large-scale vi-

---

96   Najma Sachak, interview by Harald Barre. Karim Hirji, by contrast, claims to have no recollection of the immediate period around independence. See: Hirji, *Cheche*, 41. This may be explained by the fact that he spent a considerable amount of time with his friends and was thereby possibly not exposed to hopes or concerns of the older generation.
97   See: Hirji, *Growing up*, 24-25.
98   Ibid. 2.
99   See: Aminzade, *Race, Nation, and Citizenship*, 79-80.

olence.[100] The turn of events provided Asian citizens of Tanganyika with a front row seat of the violent potential of "racial" conflict:

"In '64, when I was doing my O-Levels, my Cambridge School Certificate is when the revolution [in Zanzibar] happened. The revolution was a fearful time. [...]. I still remember at most fearing the fear, the hush that settled over Tanga – which is a small town – we felt it had just completely hushed up. 'Cause nobody dared say we are living in an Indian area." "[...]" "[...] there were no African people, neighbors, in those days. Because Indians lived fairly exclusively in Indian areas. [...]

So, this hush I remember very well, because this was now the first fear that became real, ok: 'What is going to happen?' Because [...] reports were coming in about how the, [...], Africans came to revenge their former slave, [...], masters: Were lining up people with sort of the beards and so chopping off a bit of the beard as well the chin, with a Panga. For example, those were the things we heard. Girls were being raped. [...] They were going to be after Indian girls. Indian families left over night in boats and whatever means they could find to vacate Zanzibar. And afterwards [...] I had new classmates, school mates, who suddenly had arrived from Zanzibar in school – overnight! And entered our schools and told these stories of fear as how they left."[101]

For members of the Indian community, the previously underlying fear became tangible and immediate when refugees were able to share their stories. Concerns that had hitherto been predominantly in the public sphere in the form of articles or rumors now affected the social world. Furthermore, as the events unfolded and an attempted coup d'état shook the Tanganyikan Government,[102] the Indian community became acutely aware of the risk of a government overthrow.

---

100 See: Marie-Aude Fouéré, "Recasting Julius Nyerere in Zanzibar: The Revolution, the Union and the Enemy of the Nation," *Journal of Eastern African Studies* 8, no. 3 (2014): 481-482, accessed January 25, 2019, https://doi.org/10.1080/17531055.2014.918313.
101 Najma Sachak, interview by Harald Barre. Karim Hirji confirms Najma Sachak's experience in his reminiscences and considers the revolution in Zanzibar and the mutiny in Tanganyika as triggers of fear and "racial" resentments in the Asian community. See: Hirji, *Cheche*, 80.
102 See: Ibid. 2. Henry Bienen, "National Security in Tanganyika after the Mutiny," *Transition*, no. 21 (1965): 41-42, https://doi.org/10.2307/2934101.

2.6 Conclusion: Challenges to Persistent Colonial Structures

Tanganyikan society was profoundly impacted by the colonial state, which cemented "race" and gender as decisive categories. The continued presence of administrative staff from the former colonizers as well as economic dependencies helped perpetuate this vision. However, more substantially, people's perceptions as well as the material world were shaped through education, the distribution of economic capital and the de facto segregation of urban neighborhoods. Yet, TANU's liberation struggle demonstrated the degree of discontent with discrimination. Women seized upon TANU's message of gender equality and enabled mass-recruitment for the party. Furthermore, the prospect of a better way of life mobilized the African population. However, while Nyerere's politics of "non-racialism" were mostly accepted, the degree of continued imbalance and discrimination to the disadvantage of the African population deepened the severe rift between "racial" groups. While the slow pace of improvement increased discontent among Tanganyika's African citizens, the Indian community, particularly the older generation, was alarmed by the gain of political power by the economically marginalized African majority.

The socio-political tensions also threatened Nyerere's vision for the nation. While the mutiny certainly reflected discontent with the circumstances of the social world, it also demonstrated the lack of means within the society to communicate. Bjerk argues that Nyerere's resignation in 1962 served the purpose of keeping his unifying public image undamaged as discontent remained and the unions were legislatively contained. He was also able to promote his idea of "non-racial" socialism on a grassroots level.[103] The need for this can be seen as a further signifier for the interdependency between the social world and the public discourse. The continued material discrepancies along "racial" lines empowered a "racial" discourse which Nyerere could not overcome. In a country that faced a widely dispersed population, which was not well connected through communication infrastructure, he had to resign and become the spokesperson for the discourse through grass-roots lobbying efforts instead.

Beyond the need to reach the broader population and to facilitate discourse, education was the space in which change could be prompted. Great Britain had attempted to socialize students according to the values of the

---

103 See: Bjerk, *Building a Peaceful Nation*, 78.

British Empire. Meanwhile, Nyerere had made access to education his main critique of the colonial state.[104] Students' reminiscences of their curiosity in alternative ideas for a society supported the potential of youth and education for change. This was true for both "race" and gender discrimination. In light of these deep-rooted tensions, the establishment of daily national newspapers as well as the increased development of a university held the potential to change the discourse by inserting and debating new ideas and perspectives on social relations in the nation.

---

104   See chapter 2 and 2.4.

3 1964-1966 Search for Unity & Independence

The first publication of *the Nationalist* in April 1964 marked a turning point for Tanganyika's nation building project. Contrary to existing private newspapers, such as *the Standard*, it was the first paper that was explicitly sympathetic and supportive of the Tanganyika African National Union (TANU) and Nyerere's "non-racial" socialist vision for Tanzania. Furthermore, it was aimed at the educated, English speaking population, from which the administration wanted to fill government posts. This increasingly influential readership embraced the national narrative in the party newspaper and greatly contributed to it as well. In contrast to the party's Swahili newspaper Uhuru, it enabled a discourse across "racial" lines as well as the input of international readers from Africa and beyond.

When *the Nationalist* was founded, the most dramatic social developments surrounded "racial" relations. Fears, resentments, and socio-economic rifts along "racial" lines, which were fostered by the colonial state, escalated as expectations, political strategies, and reason of state collided after independence. The revolution in Zanzibar demonstrated the destructive potential that Tanganyika narrowly averted. Against this background, the need to identify and bridge social divisions was significant, and the newspaper discourse on "race" reflected an increasingly hostile, but also open debate.

An important strategy to overcome the imprint of "race" was education.[1] However, as Cold War rationales from within the Western Block collided with Tanzania's desire for non-alignment, the debate around education quickly evolved to a more fundamental question: What was education's actual role in perpetuating colonial values? This debate was multifaceted and included generational tensions, along with questions of TANU's political control of higher

---

1   See chapter 1.2.

education, which was detrimental to Tanzania's quest to staff its administrative positions with local personnel.

The establishment of the TANU newspaper, *the Nationalist*, reflects TANU's portrayal of its vision of new gender roles, and at the same time, its own roots in a culture that was shaped by colonial gender norms. These conflicting ideals, as well as the readers' reaction to them, were also embedded in the larger discourse on an independent, non-aligned Tanzania, shaped by watershed events in the social world. It was only the culmination of the Cold War and concurring internal tensions that would stimulate debate in *the Nationalist* by prompting the first female voices in the reader's section, beginning a challenge to the biased male discourse on gender roles.

3.1 Racial Relations

"Racial" relations in *the Nationalist's* coverage included two aspects: On the side, the multifaceted topic of pan-Africanism, and on the other side, the aspect of "racial" minorities, namely Indians. Adhering to Nyerere's "non-racial" vision, the newspaper's coverage was initially nearly silent on the latter aspect of "race." However, in the course of the first three years of publication, *the Nationalist* increasingly published articles aimed at the Asian population in the country. Nonetheless, the topic proved to be controversial, giving voice to Asians and Africans who were frustrated with the enduring material gaps in society. Yet, notably, the topic of fear of physical violence, which had been experienced by Najma Sachak and Karim Hirji, never became a topic in the newspaper. Conversely, pan-African solidarity, particularly towards African Americans became a growingly visible feature in commentaries and editorials. It was here that contacts in the social world would spur a flow of ideas that impacted the public sphere increasingly.

Fear, Resentments and Prospects

The air of fear and uncertainty among the Asian population that both the Zanzibar revolution and the mutiny in Tanganyika had brought must have still been looming over Tanganyika when the first issue of *the Nationalist* reached its readers in April 1964. The events in Tanganyika had shown to the country that the political and rhetorical efforts to weaken racialist opposition could easily be undone. Karim Hirji describes an ambivalent experience.

Firstly, he witnessed his Ismaili family's fear of Africans committing violent crimes. However, on the other side, he also witnessed his African friends at Dar es Salaam's Technical College support and sympathize with riots that targeted Asians.[2] Thus, his experience suggests that the gaps between the races were extreme and included fears and frustrations colliding from both sides of the "racial divide". Yet, the example of his "inter-racial" friendships in school demonstrate that "race" could potentially become a negligible factor.

Initially, the Nationalist published a discourse on "race" which seemed to attempt to bridge the conflicting positions by reassuring its readers of the stability of a state that was committed to a "non-racial," pan-African project. One headline read: "Immediate Federation – call by Kanu [Kenya African National Union]"[3] In this front-page article, the English-written TANU newspaper captured the optimistic mood for an East African Federation, a topic that would dominate interest in the following months. To Tanganyikan readers, this message demonstrated the pan-African support for President Nyerere's vision of an East African Federation – an image of strength and solidarity, which contrasted with the experience of internal rebellion three months earlier. In the newspaper's narrative, this story of success progressed rapidly, as the Nationalist announced successful negotiations for a union with the revolutionary government of Zanzibar only days later.[4] In the meantime, the newspaper sought to demonstrate the president's command of the political situation with the following headline: "19 SOLDIERS ON MUTINY CHARGES – The President orders trial for Monday."[5] Bringing attention to the president's successes and international recognition, and his internal resolve, contrasted with the image of fear and uncertainty. Supporters of the Africanization of posts in the administration may have been particularly pleased with the enthusiasm and apparent progress pan-African unity.

The establishment and – in the case of *Uhuru* – the expansion of a sympathetic press, were developments in the social world that could shift the debate in the public sphere. In the months after the unification between Zanzibar and Tanganyika, the *Nationalist*'s narrative had reassuring messages to the Asian

---

2   See: Hirji, *Growing up*, 80.
3   NN, "Immediate Federation - call by Kanu," *The Nationalist*, April 17, 1964, No. 1.
4   Constantine Kumalija, "Two Presidents hold talks on Zanzibar," *The Nationalist*, April 23, 1964, 6.
5   *The Nationalist*, "19 SOLDIERS ON MUTINY CHARGES: The President orders trial for Monday," April 22, 1964, 5.

minority, for instance claiming that Zanzibar's president Karume condemned "racialism," and that murderers of Arab families in Zanzibar were brought to trial.[6] While the veracity of the reports on the treatment of "racial" minorities by Karume's government cannot be confirmed, the article underlines the efforts of the mainland's government to ease the fears of minorities.

At the same time, it sought to defuse "racial" resentments of Africans. In this vein, the newspaper prominently highlighted efforts from the Asian community to create national unity, overcome socio-economic gaps, and advance Africanization.[7] However, in light of continuing material disparity between different "racial" groups and a wide gap in education, the Africanization debate continued.

While the articles revolving around "racial" relations published in *the Nationalist* had been optimistic regarding the progress in overcoming socio-economic gaps between "racial" groups, the discourse in the newspaper took a strong turn in October. A reader, who according to the editor was "from the Indian community," viciously attacked the Asian community. Notably, the letter to the editor did not criticize socio-economic conditions, but played to stereotypes and ended with a recommendation to leave the country.[8] Unsurprisingly, the publication of the letter spurred lively responses, many of which doubted the writer's background and criticized the newspaper for publishing it.[9] However, one correspondent agreed with the anonymous letter and warned the newspaper:

> "[U]sing your paper as a medium to the "people of the holy land." ... Please don't make yourselves too unpopular."[10]

This exchange marked the first of several opinionated debates on "race" in the newspaper for years to come. While politicians around Nyerere attempted to diffuse the discourse by refraining from "racial" categories,[11] *the Nation-*

---

6   See: *The Nationalist*, "Karume condemns racialisms," May 19, 1964, No. 28; and *The Nationalist*, "Two appear on murder charge in Z'bar," May 15, 1964, No. 25.
7   See: *The Nationalist*, "More Asian Workers Join NUTA," July 28, 1964, No. 88, 2; and: *The Nationalist*, "Traders Launch Bold Plan: Dar Merchants propose more jobs, lunches for workers help in joint enterprises." August 17, 1964, No. 105, 1-2.
8   See: *The Nationalist*, "My dear Fellow," 4.
9   See: SAJJADALL, "Letter to the Editor," *The Nationalist*, October 2, 1964, No. 145, 4; and: Frank Opinion. "Letter to the Editor." *The Nationalist*, October 2, 1964. No. 145
10 Enthusiast, "Letter to the Editor," *The Nationalist*, October 2, 1964, No. 145, 4.
11 See: Bjerk, *Building a Peaceful Nation*, 105.

alist did not only publish racist opinions, but also occasionally highlighted the "racial" background of Asians who were brought to trial.¹² The newspaper's application of colonially established "racial" categories certainly perpetuated resentment of literate Africans against Asians. Concurrently, in the Asian community, fears of being targeted as a "racial" group were probably fed by this type of reporting. Yet, such portrayals remained few prior to 1967. Sporadically, the paper reported on local TANU leaders' critique of Asians:

> "The Regional Commissioner for Kilimanjaro, Mr. Peter Kisumo, has appealed to the Asian community to stop segregating themselves [...]. He said the government did not want to impose its will on the Asian community but it wanted them to realise they also had a responsibility towards the building of this nation. **Mr. Kisumo called on them to change the attitude of "let us wait and see" and reduce their fears by contacting the right authorities for the right answers.** [bold in newspaper]."¹³

The article's critique rather vaguely demanded changes in Asian's attitudes, but did not outline a vision of desired actions. The newspaper's lack of eloquence may be attributed to conflicting positions on "race" and Africanization within TANU, as well as the continuing search for language that embraced Nyerere's "non-racialism" while tackling the socio-economic gaps simultaneously. However, neither the article, nor the commissioner's way of addressing the Asian population was unusual. The style of "preach and exhort" was how the entire population was commonly addressed.¹⁴ In fact, Kisumo's comment almost seems to correspond with Najma Sachak's recollection of fear and seclusion of the Indian community in Tanga: Commissioner Kisumo criticized Asian's withdrawing themselves, but also acknowledged their fears, and seemed to promise the support of the administration.

A much more adamant critique which actively addressed "race" and exploitation occurred in response to a letter to the editor in 1966. A reader, probably of Asian origin, spoke out against curtailing public services in their community. In the letter, Subhash Sampat lamented the closing of the Hindustan program on Radio Tanzania. He argued that the Asian population was contributing greatly to Tanzania's economy, while, radio programming

---

12   *The Nationalist*, "Indian Youth pleads guilty," June 3, 1964, 41.
13   *The Nationalist*, "Stop segregating and join in Nation building Asians told," May 1, 1965, 325.
14   See: Condon, "Nation Building," 352.

for Africans and Europeans remained intact.[15] On the same page, the editor fiercely rejected Mr. Sampat's complaints, accusing "many people of Indian origin in this country" of thinking they could get favors at the expense of the whole nation. Furthermore, he wrote that radio programs were catering to the national language of all Tanzanians, Swahili, and English which is spoken by a large part of the population. Thus, "there is no need for this or that tribe to chauvinistically demand that its language be catered for on Radio Tanzania."[16] The editor's response seized upon the hitherto rather vague definition of Nyerere's Ujamaa.[17] Citizens of Tanzania were supposed to think in "non-racial" classless terms. The correspondent's argument of the government owing the Indian population its own radio programming was turned upside down, interpreted as exploitation and related to colonial dependency.

The exchange reflected the rifts in the experience of the social world. The notion of unrewarded dedication to the nation encountered by members of the Asian community was damaged by measures of the TANU government to equalize a stratified population. In the Asian community, the immediate fear of a coup or radical change in government policies likely decreased in the two years after the mutiny in Tanganyika and the revolution in Zanzibar. However, in theory, the avenue to emigrate was an option, as many had connections to India or possessed the right to settle in Great Britain.[18] In this light, the limitation of public services that benefited the Asian community in particular must have felt like a further set back to them, and the question of leaving the country may have gained more urgency to some members in the Asian communities.

Additionally, the commercially active members of the Asian community probably looked at the economic development of Tanzania with some skepticism. After the union with Zanzibar in April 1964, Tanzania's diplomatic relations with West Germany were strained and resulted in the end of economic assistance by the Federal Republic in 1965.[19] Furthermore, in response

---

15   Subhash H. Sampat, "Letter to the Editor: Hindustani programme," *The Nationalist*, November 26, 1966, 814, 4.
16   Editor, "Change this Attitude," *The Nationalist*, November 26, 1966, 814, 4.
17   See: Priya Lal, *African Socialism in Postcolonial Tanzania: Between the Village and the World* (Cambridge: Cambridge University Press, 2015), https://doi.org/10.1017/CBO9781316221 679, 30–31.
18   Najma Sachak, interview by Harald Barre.
19   See: Ulf Engel, ""I will not recognise East Germany just because Bonn is stupid.": Anerkennungsdiplomatie in Tansania, 1964 bis 1965," in *Kalter Krieg in Ostafrika: Die*

to Great Britain's inaction following Rhodesia's Unilateral Declaration of Independence, Tanzania broke off its diplomatic relations with Great Britain, which in turn cut off its economic aid.[20] Nyerere demonstrated to the world and his citizens that he was committed to non-alignment and pan-African solidarity. Yet, to the pre-dominantly Asian trade community, the economic ruptures and socialist rhetoric were likely alienating. This is supported by views from the community that criticized *the Nationalist* for being "'leftist' in the extreme."[21] Thus, while fear of "racial" physical violence was likely common in Asian communities, it was discontent with socio-economic development and the subsequent increase in regulations that actually spurred more immediate critique. In other words, the government's attempt to deescalate "racial" tension by promoting socialism likely alienated the majority of business-minded readers. These tensions had little chance to ease, as spaces to express differing fears and expectations were scarce. In the social world, contacts between African and Asians were mostly limited to places where economic hierarchies were perpetuated. Africans were hired as servants and employees, and purchased goods in Asian shops; others were tenants in houses, often owned by Asians.

A chance of altering these social structures lay in education, where the independent state could fundamentally challenge the heritage from the colonial era. The potential of creating an even playing field occurred when schools were integrated. Yet, even here, "racial" stereotypes which had festered in the colonial society threatened to prevent progress. Looking back, Najma Sachak mainly remembered fears of the parental generation:

> "This [...] became the Indian parent concern, 'lowering the standards,' [...] bringing in the national exam, removing the overseas exam boards. So that then became the differentiating thing. 'How are our children ever going to progress? We are going to lose the quality of education by democratizing education, because while it was [...] exclusively Indian, we were sure of the standards.' Because Indian parents would impose our standards on the schools, because we were expected to achieve so much. And opening up the schools racially automatically – for them, for us – it was, I would put it like that, it

---

Beziehungen der DDR zu Sansibar und Tansania, ed. Ulrich van der Heyden, Die DDR und die Dritte Welt 8 (Berlin, Münster: Lit, 2009), 19-25.
20 See: Aminzade, *Race, Nation, and Citizenship*, 97-98.
21 Condon, "Nation Building," 353.

was concomitant with falling standards. [...] [B]ecause the other side, the Africans, were not bound to be as good as we were."[22]

This quote not only reflects parents' "racial" stereotypes, but also Indian group perception of being studious and diligent.[23] When school integration was advanced in 1965, parental concerns turned out to be unwarranted, and African students could compete with their Indian peers despite having had fewer resources.[24] While integration would be a crucial means of finally advancing educational opportunities for African students, it also turned out to be a meaningful way to connect interpersonally. Najma Sachak's vivid recollection of integration in her school deserves to be quoted in some lengths, as it illustrates how "racial" boundaries were potentially enforced and bridged:

> "[...] I had a marvelous teacher from Punjab, [...] who declared himself clearly to be – something that Indian people scoffed at – [...] he used to say: 'I am a Communist from the University of Punjab. I'm a Punjabi Communist.' And he was. [...]
>
> [J]ust before school opened, my teacher rang home and asked my mother to send me to school to the staff room to talk to him. He asked me take some "samosas" and "mandazi" [...] and go to the hostel where the girls had arrived from up-country to start their HSC [High School Certificate]. Except for one Indian girl (her community arranged her accommodation in a private home), all my other classmates were going to be African. [H]e asked me specially not to ask my father to take me in the car. He said: 'You should go on your bicycle, with food. Ask your mother to make some. Go and introduce yourself and tell them that you are going to show them where the school was.' [...] Tanga Hotel [...] was turned into the boys' hostel. And

---

22 Najma Sachak, interview by Harald Barre.
23 Hirji, who came from a poorer Asian family, also recollected the emphasis on education in his upbringing. See: Hirji, *Cheche*, 10-11.
24 See: Sachak, 6. This opinion is based on the recollected experience of Najma Sachak and can therefore neither evaluate the impact of integration for the entire country nor is it a quantitative analysis. However, it suggests that in the microcosm of her school, school integration did not disrupt the educational standards. It is somewhat contradicted by Bertz who points to Asian parents' protests against the preferential treatment of African students from entering the limited secondary school spots. See: Bertz, *Diaspora and Nation*, 139. I.e. either Najma Sachak's school had an exceptional composition of African students or the entry tests were not indicative of the actual performance of students in the secondary schools.

the house next door was emptied of the people who lived in it and became the girls' hostel. [...] [W]hen I went to the hostel and knocked and said that we were all going to be going to start in the same class and that I had come to welcome them to Tanga – one girl turned her back and went into her room – and the second girl who came out of her room just stared at me, and only one come forward, took the "kikapu" (basket) from my hands and said that she was going to make tea. She called all the other girls and said 'she brought us samosas and mandazis, we are gonna make tea.' So that is when the ice broke."[25]

Najma Sachak's vivid memory suggests how experiences in the social world had the potential to be transformative and alter structures. The initial reaction of most of her new classmates appears to have been shaped by indifference or even rejection. While this may have been the result of shyness, it may also have been the result of "racial" resentment. Yet, the ostentatious breaking of African stereotypes of Asians (not being driven in a car, not having food prepared by servants) opened up the opportunity for the students to connect. It is noteworthy that integration efforts as such would have placed African students in the same classrooms with Asians.[26] However, stereotypes may have remained for longer as they would have remained unchallenged if the teacher of Najma Sachak had not set up the encounter before classes resumed.[27] His political background as a communist certainly spurred his activism in breaking down barriers between the groups. Yet, he was well informed about what stereotypes to expect. While this may have been the result of astute observation, the publishing of debates in newspapers may have provided further guidance to his plan.

Bearing in mind the experience of fear and insulation that was expressed in remembering the Zanzibari Revolution, the newspaper provided a signif-

---

25 Najma Sachak, interview by Harald Barre. The girl turned out to be Ruth Besha, who would later become professor at the University of Dar es Salaam. Najma Sashak and Ruth Besha would continue to be life-long friends and share important experiences, such as studies in Great Britain.

26 This interpretation is confirmed by Karim Hirji who attributes being exposed to a "multi-racial, multi-religious universe" in Dar es Salaam's Technical College with his ability to overcome "racial" stereotypes quickly, as well. See: Hirji, *Cheche*, 81.

27 Najma Sachak's experience is supported by Bertz, who points out that "race" continued to be a factor but that surveys among teachers in 1966 reported less "interracial" tensions and that friendships between Asian and African students were developing. See: Bertz, *Diaspora and Nation*, 139.

icant prospect: As it printed controversial opinions in its pages, it created a space where an exchange of perspectives was possible. It is interesting to observe that the fear experienced in the Asian communities was not expressed by its members in the newspaper. Only questions surrounding cultural and material conditions were voiced and debated. While these exchanges were limited to literate English-speakers, it had the potential to bridge opinions that remained otherwise insulated in fear or resentment. The significance of these spaces of exchange was highlighted by a survey conducted by Condon, in which readers claimed that the letters to the editor were an important reason to purchase the newspaper.[28] It indicates that experiences in the social world were not only processed and expressed through the media, but that the debates in the public sphere were absorbed by the public, as well.

From East Federation to Pan-African Solidarity

While Nyerere's "non-racial" vision for Tanzania seemed to progress slowly, his pan-African ambition was thwarted. By the beginning of 1965, *the Nationalist* acknowledged that the enthusiasm for an East African Federation had been pre-mature.[29] This setback may have been perceived as particularly dangerous, as the project had likely been seen as prestigious, particularly for the English-speaking African urban population. In light of the slow progress of the Africanization of the administration, this dynamic may have increased the frustration of this relatively unprivileged group. It is therefore not surprising that instead of a formal pan-African federation, the vague concept of pan-African solidarity emerged as a vital topic on the newspaper's pages.

The Nationalist broadly covered the liberation struggles from the get-go, as well as the plight of civil war-torn Congo. The attention devoted to the liberation struggle was high compared to any other Tanzanian newspaper at the time.[30] The motivations behind Tanzania's support for refugees from civil war-torn places and for refugees and fighters from occupied African countries have been interpreted ambivalently by earlier research. Some regarded TANU's solidarity as being driven by humanism, and others emphasized the practical advantages. The support of the Liberation movements further elevated Tanzania's prestige as a pan-African vanguard state, despite

---

28 See: Condon, "Nation Building," 351.
29 See: Editor, "Resolution 1965," *The Nationalist*, January 1, 1965, No. 222, 4.
30 Condon, "Nation Building," 344-345.

very real fear of infiltration and attack from Portuguese colonial forces.³¹ The Liberation movements repaid this support by demonstrating their gratitude and backing TANU's call for African Unity.³² This pan-African political profile served Tanzania not only diplomatically, but also resonated within its population.

When Tanzania gained independence, few African students had the education to consciously grasp the political and geographical dimensions of East Africa. However, Tanzanian radio services brought audiences in touch with music from other African countries.³³ Furthermore, trade connected people across borders, and newspapers brought in images and imaginations of life beyond Tanganyika.³⁴ More fortunate students had the chance to explore East Africa in school trips, gaining unique impressions of the region.³⁵ For the small, but growing group of young, highly educated people, pan-African solidarity became a rallying call:

> "Nyerere was obviously very committed [to African liberation...] Now, [...] this was obviously very attractive to young people; [...]. It was a natural thing for young people to support national liberation."³⁶

The significance of pan-African solidarity is also reflected in an altering coverage of African Americans in *the Nationalist*. In the first months of its inception, the newspaper did not comment on developments in America, and occasionally published reports from international news agencies.³⁷ Cultural affinity to African Americans in terms of "race" was enhanced by the great popularity of Muhammad Ali. Some reports on Ali, then often referred to as Cassius

---

31 See: Charlotte L. Miller, "Who are the "permanent inhabitants" of the state? citizenship policies and border controls in Tanzania, 1920-1980," PhD (Doctor of Philosophy) thesis, University of Iowa, 2011, accessed: September 20, 2018, https://ir.uiowa.edu/etd/4877/, 149–55; and: Paul Bjerk, "African Files in Portuguese Archives," *History in Africa* 31 (2004): 465, accessed July 14, 2015, http://www.jstor.org/stable/4128541.
32 *The Nationalist*, "Liberation fronts greet Tanzanians," January 1, 1965, No. 222.
33 See: Godfrey Mwakikagile, *My Life as an African: Autobiographical Writings*, 1st ed. (Dar es Salaam: New Africa Press, 2009), 35, 46; Najma Sachak remembered that a majority of rural children had little knowledge of Tanzania's geography while she did field research. See: Najma Sachak, interview by Harald Barre.
34 See: Mwakikagile, *Life in Tanganyika*, 104-105, 132.
35 Najma Sachak, interview by Harald Barre.
36 Walter Bgoya, interview by Harald Barre.
37 See e.g.: *The Nationalist*, "Negro detainees protest," April 25, 1964, No. 8.

Clay,[38] critically pointed to the severity of the struggle African Americans had to face.[39] Yet, this cultural affinity did not translate into a political solidarity with African Americans. In contrast to sympathetic reports and editorials on the Liberation movements, the African American struggle seemed detached from the pan-African vision of *the Nationalist*. The tone on "racial" relations in the United States became much more sympathetic when they began to affect East Africans. As experienced by African diplomats and students before them,[40] a group of Kenyan students faced police discrimination during a stay in the US. While an initial report merely presented the official version of events, subsequent articles brought the students' perspectives on the events to light.[41] The situation ended with Kenya's parliament rejecting conditional aid from the U.S.[42] The case illustrates that pan-African solidarity was a dominant feature of debates in the public sphere, despite the stalling prospects of a political federation. The Kenyan students' experience of harassment was one that Tanganyikan students in the U.S. would likely suffer to some degree. The Kenyan case revealed the threats African students faced and thereby highlighted the dangerous persistence of racism in the United States.

If the case of the Kenyan students spurred an emotional shift in the newspaper's narrative, the Africa tour of Malcolm X marked the beginning of new paradigms. Malcolm X was the most prominent African American figure to redefine the relationship between African Americans and the African continent. He advocated seeking alliances with Africans through African American organizations rather than through the Democratic or Republican Party. Between May and July 1964, he established ties to African governments and visited the OAU in Cairo. After sensing a growing understanding among African leaders regarding the plight of African Americans, Malcolm X ended up disappointed by the OAU's unwillingness to embrace his cause. However, in Abdulrahman Babu he found a sympathetic member of Tanzania's Nyerere's cabinet. In a

---

38 See: Condon, "Nation Building," 347. See: *The Nationalist*, "Liberation fronts greet," 347.
39 *The Nationalist*, "Cassius Lashes Out At American Segregation," May 21, 1964, City Edition, No. 30.
40 See: Thomas Borstelmann, *The Cold War and the Color Line: American Race Relations in the Global Arena*, 1. Harvard Univ. Press paperback ed. (2003), 91.
41 *The Nationalist*, "Kenya Students Accused of Assault," June 30, 1964, City Edition, No.64; and: *The Nationalist*, "Arrested Students Give Their version," July 1, 1964, City Edition, No. 65
42 *The Nationalist*, "Kenya MP raps Americans," July 2, 1964, City Edition, No.64.

following visit to Tanzania, Malcolm X was able to connect with other Tanzanian politicians and African American expatriates. While he gave an interview to *the Standard*, his coverage in *the Nationalist* was limited.

Malcolm X's ability to sway the mood in sympathy for the African American struggle can be confirmed by a look in Tanzania's public sphere. Less than two weeks after making his case, the tone in *the Nationalist* on racial relations shifted dramatically. While previous reports on riots sided with the police,[43] now, the newspaper condemned police violence, sympathized with their victims, and spoke no longer of "Negroes," but of "Afro-Americans."[44] Both shifts would be lasting with rare exceptions. The perspectives on African Americans would be additionally clarified in an editorial that denounced the poor living conditions in African American slums:

> "[...] what seemed to be confined to the 'deep South,' as we have often been told, is spreading to the North. [...] the events cannot be treated as isolated incidents. Rather they appear to be a systematic scheme to put the Afro-Americans in their place [...]."[45]

As the editor went on, he compared presidential candidate Senator Barry Goldwater to South Africa's Prime Minister Verwoerd.[46] The following year, *the Nationalist* continued to bring the dramatic events in America to its readers' attention. Occasionally, the newspaper underlined the situation by printing images of police violence.

Not only connecting the African American struggle with African liberation struggles in word, but also through visual materials, possibly illustrated to readers that they had common problems with other people of African descent. The image of African Americans and the literal description of being dragged through the street likely resonated with readers' own experiences of maltreatment at the hands of whites.

While the reports reflected a high degree of sympathy for African Americans, politically they did not advocate the collaboration to which Malcolm

---

43 See e.g.: *The Nationalist*, "Whites-Negroes clash as new law is tested," July 6, 1964, No 69.
44 See: *The Nationalist*, "30 Afro-Americans injured as police stop demonstrations," July 22, 1964, No. 83.
45 Editor, "Racial question in America," *The Nationalist*, July 23, 1964, No. 84, City Edition.
46 Hirji remembered that Radio Tanzania would also run stories on the African American and the African liberation struggles in the same vein, and thereby connected them under a Pan-African umbrella. See: Hirji, *Cheche*, 79.

X had aspired. In fact, successes of integration politics were optimistically described as "a fragrant breeze of change,"[47] which may be contrasted with the "winds of change" that British PM MacMillan had observed in growing national consciousness in Africa.[48] This could be attributed to a lack of individuals promoting and explaining the dynamics of African American politics. One commentary on the newly popularized slogan 'Black Power' cautioned readers not to blindly accept the highly negative media coverage and compared it to what he deemed to be unfairly negative portrayals of Zanzibar in foreign media.[49] The article confirms that there was increasing sympathy for the African Americans' struggle as direct connections to the situation in Tanzania were made. Yet, apparently, the author did not discuss any perspectives from inside the African American community itself.

This vague position of sympathy would gain a further component as another article analyzed the spectrum of African American politics in greater depth, noting the outspoken opposition of the Vietnam War by the Student Nonviolent Coordinating Committee (SNCC).[50] The war had emerged as a critical focus in *the Nationalist's* reporting. By 1966, it unequivocally supported the Vietnamese as a fellow people struggling against foreign domination.[51] With the reputation of the United States declining, the militant positions of African American students became increasingly congruent with the newspaper's own views of the world.

The turn in the coverage of African Americans in *the Nationalist* can likely be connected to Malcolm X's efforts in Cairo. His efforts resonated with a political climate in East Africa that was conscious of "racial" violence in the United States and no longer accepted the myth of marginalized racist elements confined to the U.S. South. In any case, the portrayal in the newspaper depended on relatable experiences to change. The encounter between charismatic activists, Malcolm X and leaders of Tanzania's government, as well as

---

47 Editor, "Fragrant Breeze in the U.S." *The Nationalist*, January 7, 1966, No. 538
48 See: https://www.sahistory.org.za/archive/wind-change-speech-made-south-africa-par liament-3-february-1960-harold-macmillan, accessed 05.11.2018
49 See: *The Nationalist*, "Black Power," July 22, 1966, No. 704. The opinion was expressed in the column Pressman's Commentary which was authored by Babu. (Markle, *A Motorcycle*, 59.) This suggests that in the mid1960s Babu continued to be an important advocate for pan-African relation to African American groups.
50 See: *The Nationalist*, "Black Power in America," September 26, 1966, No. 760.
51 See e.g.: *The Nationalist*, "The Big American Setback in Vietnam," January 1, 1966, No. 523.

the experience of racism against East African students, made the African American struggle personable and relevant. Nonetheless, building relations between African Americans and East Africans would be a challenging endeavor, as African students experienced in the U.S. in the early 1960s.[52] With little direct interaction, African Americans remained on the receiving end of different ideas, ranging from 'fellows in the struggle against oppression' to 'pioneers of a successful integration.'

Conversely, the African Liberation movements developed an increasing presence in Tanzania and Dar es Salaam, and *the Nationalist* devoted space to them frequently. Hence, one may presume that they were more relatable for the population, including the group of readers of the English government newspaper. The majority of articles merely reported on aspects related to the struggle, such as abuses of the African populations carried out by the minority regimes or resolutions of the African Liberation Committee.[53] However, the call for greater unity between the movements was made and cited personal flaws as being the reason behind lagging success. Such suspicion was often eagerly answered by other readers who doubted the liberation fighters' sincerity. These suspicions were keenly picked up by critical readers.[54] Others conflated the Liberation movements and refugees from war-torn areas:

> "They come by thousands. We welcome them, give them land, shelter and other necessities. [...] Are all refugees genuine ones who are really determined to fight for liberation [...]? If the reader decides this evening to pay fact finding visits to several bars you will understand better why these people are undesirable freedom fighters. You will see most of them at the counters and at tables with lots of liquor and undesirable women. [...] You will wonder where these ruined freedom fighters get the money which seems never to desert their purposes. [...]"[55]

---

52 See: Bgoya, "From Tanzania to Kansas," 103.
53 See e.g.: *The Nationalist*, "Life in S. African Jails," July 15, 1965, No. 389; Editor, "Extremely Serious Session: Zapu, Zanu ready to give 'Master Plans'," *The Nationalist*, May 6, 1965, No. 329
54 See e.g.: Editor, "Issues before 'Nine'," *The Nationalist*, February 19, 1965, No. 264; L. Jipula, "The '9' told: Time to re-examine leadership," *The Nationalist*, March 11, 1965, No. 281
55 I.S.A. Mwaipata, "Luxury loving Refugees," *The Nationalist*, July 15, 1965, No. 389.

The letter shows that in view of increasing immigration from Mozambique,[56] critics felt emboldened to speak out against pan-African solidarity. Rhetorically, the author, Mwaipata, stayed within the nation's motive of frugality and coupled it with xenophobia. Miller demonstrates that the introduction of the Refugee Control Act in 1965 was a result of mounting fears of infiltration by a white minority and colonial regimes.[57] However, the legislation likely also served to placate internal critics of the pan-African solidarity. This assumption is strongly supported by an editorial that paraphrased Vice-President Kawawa's speech, introducing the bill to the National Assembly:

> "It has always been the considered policy of Tanzania to help these refugees as much as possible [...]. A great many of the refugees have been accepted and made to feel at home. But there is also a number among them who feel that they should be treated differently, in fact better than any ordinary person in this country."[58]

The debates in the newspaper reflected the friction that occurred in the social world. The refugees had to flee their homes, likely experiencing traumatic scenarios and remained, as potential fighters, the target of the secret services of Portugal and the minority regimes.[59] Furthermore, refugees were in a vulnerable position and prone to falling victim to political infighting in the Liberation movements. Charles Swift a psychiatrist, who arrived in Tanzania in 1966 as an expat consultant, recollected that such freedom fighters would be detained, often suffering from uncertainty and harassment.[60] As such, Tanzania's pan-African solidarity remained a challenge on the continent and beyond. However, after the introduction of the law, the image of freedom fighters' lewd lives vanished from the discourse in *the Nationalist*, and the stories focused on denouncing the white supremacists and supporting the freedom movements' vigor. In fact, some letters to the editor described the support for the Liberation movements as the only purpose of the Organiza-

---

56   See: Miller, "Who are the 'permanent inhabitants,'" 181-182.
57   See: Ibid. 188-192.
58   Editor, "Refugees' Position," *The Nationalist*, December 23, 1965, No. 526.
59   See: Ibid. The editor argued that the law would also protect liberation fighters from infiltration.
60   See: C. R. Swift, *Dar Days: The Early Years in Tanzania* (University Press of America, 2002), vii, 43.

tion of African Unity.[61] Furthermore, the newspaper was able to report on the international prestige, Tanzania gained for its support of the refugees.[62] While tensions in the social world likely continued, the discourse in the public sphere emphasized the need for the struggle as well as the larger benefits for the nation. Karim Hirji recollected how a pan-African spirit captured him as Radio Tanzania featured stories on Martin Luther King, Nelson Mandela, Eduardo Mondlane and Malcolm X.[63] As such, Nyerere's emphasis on pan-Africanism can be seen as a stabilizing force against African opposition of his "non-racial" policies as well as an integrative path for people of Asian origin, such as Hirji. In the newspaper discourse, the colonially grown categories "race" were marginalized, while pan-African solidarity emerged as a contentious rallying call.

3.2 Decolonizing Education?

As it entered the third year of independence, Tanganyika was still strongly diplomatically and financially bound to Great Britain. However, particularly within the small but crucial group of higher educated students, a large amount of skepticism of ties to the former colonial power and its Western partners prevailed. Yet, as they were highly educated, the students had been exposed mainly to a British educational system. There was a high demand for this group of Tanganyikans as the country faced a shortage of local skilled personnel and remained dependent on expatriate experts. These peculiar circumstances would bring young academics in the contentious center of Tanzania's struggle to build a truly independent nation.

While Nyerere's goal of African liberation and unity had progressed at different speeds and with varying repercussions domestically, the goal of developing socialism had remained vague in the public sphere. Diplomatically, Tanzania maintained its non-aligned stance and emphasized its independence from states in the Western bloc. At the same time, China emerged as a crucial partner. China had become an important financial pillar for Tanzania for

---

61 See e.g.: Solomon Koma, "Support for Kambona," *The Nationalist*, November 8, 1966, No. 798; *The Nationalist*, "Only Zimbabweans can break Smith's back," November 11, 1966, No. 801.
62 See: *The Nationalist*, "Tanzania's help to refugees praised." October 23, 1966, No. 785.
63 See: Hirji, *Growing up*, 79.

the preceding years, but with the construction of the railway between Tanzania and Zambia, it supported a project symbolic for African liberation.[64] The Chinese would not only impact the diplomatic balance, but also the public at large. George Hajivayanis, at the time a secondary school student, and Salha Hamdani, who was a few years younger than him, both vividly remembered the impact of Mao's views on young students:

> G.: "Mao became a very very important reader. All of us read Mao. There was a red book that was distributed, it went around, that was in 1965, just when the Chinese had come to build the Railway. They brought in Mao literature. And there was a book that every student carried, we also carried. And it was a mission School. [...] a Lutheran School [...] and well you couldn't do anything, you first had to read what Mao said [...]."
> S. [laughing]: "Fashionable."
> G.: "[laughing]: "It was fashionable, but that book was banned in Kenya. [...] So, really these ideas, the radical ideas, the Communist ideas, had begun to come for a long time."[65]

George Hajivayanis' recollection illustrates that the Chinese presence in Tanzania transformed not only the discourse, but also the culture of secondary school students. As Salha Hamdani's interjection shows, Chinese socialist literature was not immediately important for political ideas, but gained symbolical value as it became a popular trend. In this sense, reading Mao shaped students' group cohesion.[66] However, in contrast to the fashionable aspect that surrounded Maoist literature among youth internationally, Chinese literature made particular sense for the academic elite in a former colony. For students such as George Hajivayanis and Salha Hamdani, who had grown up in a "racially" divided society, a non-aligned socialist outlook on society helped make sense of the world as it matched their personal experiences.

---

64 See: Robeson Taj Frazier, *The East is Black: Cold war China in the Black Radical Imagination* (Durham, NC, London: Duke University Press, 2015), 203.
65 Salha Hamdani and George G. Hajivayanis, interview by Harald Barre.
66 This resonates with Condon's observation that the display of English newspapers was a means of demonstrating ones' successful elite status. George Hajivayanis and Salha Hamdani's recollection of Chinese literature becoming a fashion suggests that it helped to denote one's dedication to explore political ideas that originated in the global south. Thus, this group would have considered itself as particularly devoted to the (vague) idea of African socialism.

Their reminiscences show that secondary schools turned out to be vital sites of public discourse. However, the flow of ideas was not free but, as George Hajivayanis remembered, dependent on teachers and clergy who had the potential to be crucial facilitators:

"Then maybe 65/66 there was a priest, Father Patrick Dinya, I was part of the [...] Catholic youth organisation. [...] And he gave us [...] Marx."[67]

Thus, while socialist literature was available in Tanzania, students were able to access the materials through mediators. This aligns with the education of President Nyerere himself, who was exposed to new ideas through a teacher in his mission school. While Molony argues that missionaries' sympathetic and engaging attitudes contrasted with colonial administrators' aloofness,[68] it appears that instructors had to be particularly engaged and dedicated to changing the colonial structures. Najma Sachak called to mind how the teacher, who had already initiated the contact to her new fellow African students, awoke her consciousness for socialism.

"I started a serious reading with my Hindu Punjabi communist teacher. He said: '[...] You have to understand Marxism to understand where this world is going to:'
So I started serious study of Karl Marx. [...] From ten to twelve / one o'clock I would read my Marx and I would think about what we are going to discuss the following day. [...] So I used to cycle down to the King George V. Memory Library. And we would sit outside [...] and he would question me. I did a thorough reading of Marx for eight months. Well, I have got my father into more trouble, I have to say. [...] Just opposite of our library is our town mosque. So on Fridays now, I am sitting [*laughing*] opposite with my school teacher with Karl Marx, Das Kapital, in my hand. And the boys, young men, and the fathers who were going into the mosque to pray and the door is right across. You can see Mr. Sachak's daughter sitting there: 'what is she doing with that teacher?' 'What is that thing about?' You know, my father would say: 'You know, probably she is reading Marx. It's ok, let her do what she wants.' [...] And if I was reading Marx it was quite obvious that I was not praying at home.

---

67   Salha Hamdani and George G. Hajivayanis, interview by Harald Barre.
68   See: Thomas Molony, *Nyerere: The Early Years* (Rochester: James Currey, 2014), 51-53.

[...] [H]e just scoffed at people: 'It is alright, she will come home and pray. [...].' He used to say to people."[69]

It is notable, that in both recollections, singular teachers communicated the concept of socialism to their students. The majority of instructors, secular or religious, did not leave such lasting impressions, which suggests that they were not as apt to engage students or to discuss socialist theories. Thus, it seems that only a few outstanding teachers were actively working to transform social structures that had grown in the preceding decades of colonialism.

Najma Sachak's reminiscence points to other factors. She emphasizes that some members of her religious community were irritated by her studies, particularly since they regarded it to be in conflict with her role and place as a woman in the community. As indicated in Mr. Mwaipata's quote in the previous section, such conservative religious views on women transcended the "racial" communities of Tanzania. It appears as though a degree of open-mindedness by the parental generation was necessary for new ideas to enter discourse on the self-perception of Tanzanians. With such support, some students had the chance to question existing social structures and alter the discourse on shaping an independent nation.

Education Versus Administration?

Already by the mid-1960s, it became clear that students were particularly engaged in the struggle against colonial dependencies. This revolutionary role of higher education also seemed to reflect president Nyerere's vision, as he had emphasized the significance of the university's independent thinking in overcoming racial tensions in 1962. However, by the mid-1960s the administration's concerns were in conflict with students' ideas and activism. This tension was the result of local and regional socio-political developments as well as an escalating debate around the meaning of independence.

After Ian Smith's minority regime declared Rhodesia unilaterally independent from Great Britain, students from the University College attacked the British High Commission leading to property damage and the burning of the British flag. After being rounded up by Tanzanian police, they were sent to apologize. According to *the Nationalist* "[t]hey, however, made it quite clear

---

69 Najma Sachak, interview by Harald Barre.

to [High Commissioner] Mr. Fowler that they were sorry only for the damages done but not for the demonstration itself."⁷⁰ An editorial in the same issue drew lines between students, whose emotional reactions it considered wrong, but understandable. Conversely, it accused the student leadership of having failed in its responsibility to control the students, but hoped that the authorities would not use the incident to ban future peaceful demonstrations. Above these lines of conflict was "Mwalimu Julius Nyerere [who], like the old teacher, had to summon the University students and counsel them."⁷¹ Interestingly, the editorial publicly juxtaposed a restrictive administration with a caring and thoughtful president. Yet, the authorities remained an obscure force that was not explicitly connected with TANU or the government. This dichotomy in the public sphere reflected developments in the social world, where conservative members of the administration restricted party leaders' social visions.⁷² The editorial can be seen as an active attempt to mediate between students and a conservative administration, as it criticized both sides and merely reiterated president Nyerere' righteousness.

Despite the editorial's critique, students felt largely vindicated. Letters to the editor, most likely from students, praised *the Nationalist* for its unbiased editorial and contrasted it to the privately-owned *Sunday News*. Students wrote in support of Nyerere's rhetoric of independence and rebuked concerns of losing important financial support of Great Britain.⁷³ The correspondence suggests that students considered themselves as the vanguard, which was backed up by a revolutionary government. Outspokenness against foreign domination was not only in line with the President's public opinion, but may also have been a response to lecturers who were skeptical of Britain's politics in Africa.⁷⁴ However, the episode illustrated that Nyerere did not want

---

70 *The Nationalist*, "Government warns of severe action on rioters," November 15, 1965, No 494.
71 Editor, "Students' protest," *The Nationalist*, November 15, 1965, No. 494.
72 See: Aminzade, *Race, Nation, and Citizenship*, 12.
73 See: *The Nationalist*, "Biased Editorial," November 18, 1965, No. 497; Disappointed, "Students' Protest," *The Nationalist*, November 18, 1965, No. 497.
74 McCracken recollected that he and his colleagues from the university were summoned by the British High Commissioner and accused of having instigated the demonstration. He remembers that Terrance Ranger, the head of the Department of History, retorted the students would have done a more thorough job had he been responsible. See: John McCracken, "Terry Ranger: A Personal Appreciation," *Journal of Southern African Studies* 23, no. 2 (1997): 181, accessed January 21, 2019, https://www.jstor.org/stable/2637616

diplomacy taken out of his control, possibly because of the presence of conservative forces in the administration, to which the editor of *the Nationalist* had alluded.

Only months later, the students' image shifted significantly as the newspaper no longer described them as unruly, revolutionary youth, but as colonially educated elitists. In 1963, a National Service was introduced. Young people from across the country were to work together on construction projects and receive military education. However, the government grew increasingly wary of the low participation of highly educated students, fearing a damaging social divide between the economic elite and the remaining population. In late 1965, plans emerged to make the National Service compulsory for graduates of higher education, including a month-long period of obligatory income donations. The subsequent months were marked by heated exchanges in the newspapers, with student leaders accusing their critics being elitist bureaucrats themselves. In other letters, some students seemed to fulfill the government's concern over elitism as they lamented the unsuitable and poor living conditions in the National Service camps.[75] However, much like the confrontation with the British High Commission, the escalating debate was related to the crucial role of higher education to drive Tanzania's politics of independence.

The accusation of elitism was not unfounded, as the university remained largely under foreign funding and expatriate administration,[76] and hence gained a reputation of being luxurious. Even after the Arusha Declaration downscaled opulent services at the university when George Hajivayanis and Salha Hamdani did their studies in Dar es Salaam, the elitist environment left a lasting impression on them:

> S.: "[W]e stayed on the campus. [...] The university was quite big. During my time, during his time, the university was really like a hotel [...]."
> H.: "Which time was that when did you actually start?" [...]
> G.: "For me 69 [...]. For her 74." [...]
> S.: "Those who went even earlier, they had like, I don't know."
> G.: "They had chicken [...] from Norway." [...]
> S.: "This is an American University."

---

75 See: Andrew Michael Ivaska, *Cultured States*, 135–138.
76 See: Ivaska, *Cultured States*, 131; regarding the expatriates' power, see: Mahmood Mamdani, "The African University," *The London Review of Books* 40, no. 14 (2018), accessed November 19, 2018, https://www.lrb.co.uk/v40/n14/mahmood-mamdani/the-african-university.

G.: "It was not paid by the government. It was paid by [...] Americans and so on."
S.: "[...] [D]uring my time, I shared a room with another girl. [...] [W]e used to do our own beds [...]."
G.: "[During] my time there was somebody coming to [...] do my room..."
S.: "Exactly. [...] Before his time, I remember I would visit my sister..."
G.: "...They even washed your clothes..."
S.: "[W]hen I visited my sister, they had white bed sheets on the beds. These cleaners would come and change the white bed sheets, pillows everything, clean, do everything and even the clothes were washed, laundried." [...]
S.: "Yes, and then [...] going to eat. [...] [W]hen we go to cafeteria for example [...] early in the morning so [...] you rush. But during the night you know you have dinner even during our times. When you have dinner [...] you are already back from laboratories or whatever, you're washed, you are clean and you're going now for your dinner. Even during our times."
G.: "With etiquette."
S.: "YES you have to dress up to kill. You comb your hair, your nice dress. And you go [...] to the cafeteria – and women of course are very few 10% or something – so you enter there and everybody in the hall, they all know, 'aha what she has put on!'" [...]
S.: "The type of food. [...] [M]eat of all types. [...] You got there you take [...] this big tray, [...] 'You want this one?' 'No.' 'this one?' 'No.' 'this one?' 'Ok.' 'What about eggs?' 'Just one.' [...]"[77]

The conversation illustrates how awed the interviewees were by the preferential treatment of university students. Even decades later, they vividly recall their experiences in the dormitories and cafeteria, which suggests how much the standards of living on campus contrasted with life prior to entering the university. It is noteworthy that they knew of the even higher living standards of graduates preceding them due to the foreign funding of the university.[78] Therefore, the university's living standard became an embodiment of foreign domination, despite students' protest against the British High Commissioner a few months earlier.

---

77 Najma Sachak, interview by Harald Barre.
78 George Hajivayanis and Salha Hamdani's critical views on the university being foreign-owned was likely the product this ongoing debate.

The heightened sensitivity towards new forms of foreign domination corresponded with further observations of the continued dominance of the colonial power. The presence of expatriate, particularly British, staff was increasingly seen as a perpetuation of colonialism, even by some other expatriate experts. In his biography, American psychiatrist Charles Swift, who worked in the Dar es Salaam Medical School, described arriving in Dar es Salaam in September 1966:

> "I spotted a white man working his way through the crowd. He had his eye on us all right, though I hoped I was mistaken. He fitted the image of the British colonial perfectly: [...]. After introducing himself pompously as the hospital administrator [...] he proceeded to discharge his duty with practiced efficiency. I stood by, embarrassed and impotent as he badgered the Tanzanian custom officials with a patronizing mix of Swahili and British English. [...] [W]e were given a colonial's welcome [...] 'how the natives live,' the small industrial area which 'the British still run at a profit' and then Dar es Salaam itself, 'not half the city Nairobi is.'"[79]

It is remarkable, that Swift, as a newcomer, clearly perceived the British administrative presence as pervasive colonial remnants. Nonetheless, *the Nationalist* did not criticize British expatriates in Tanzania. Rather, the stirring debates in the newspaper began to articulate students' perceived elitism with the threat of foreign domination. In *the Nationalist*, calls for students to commit to physical national building coincided with the increasingly strained British-Tanzanian relations.[80] The diplomatic ties to Great Britain, and along with its funding for the university, were severed after the governments' disagreement over the handling of the Unilateral Declaration of Independence of Ian Smith's government.[81] The concurrently growing concerns over students' lack of commitment to the National Service reflected the concern that the highly educated part of the society was indeed socialized by social structures associated with colonialism and the Western Bloc.

---

79 Swift, *Dar Days*, 1-2.
80 See: Nationalist Reporter, "Isle students to spend holidays working," *The Nationalist*, November 1, 1965, 482; Editor, "Rhodesian crisis," *The Nationalist*, November 1, 1965, 482; Editor, "Role of youth," *The Nationalist*, November 2, 1965, 483.
81 See: Bertram B. Mapunda, "Infrastructure," in Kimambo; Mapunda; Lawi, *In Search of Relevance*, 76.

The conflict between students and the administration was partly driven by access to employment opportunities that were hampered by generational differences.[82] However, the blurred lines of conflict in the debates preceding the strike suggest that the conflict went beyond a generational conflict. One correspondent decried the support of a Member of Parliament – most likely not a young person – who had rendered support to the disobedient students.[83] Another denounced the students for being detached from Tanzania. Yet, the "concerned citizen" argued that responsibility for the curriculum lay not with the students, but rather the university administration and the governing body.[84] Thus, as the editorial in the wake of the embassy riots in 1965 had indicated already, the lines did not only divide students and politicians, but more specifically allegedly elitist students and detached bureaucrats, both of whom were associated with colonialism.

Furthermore, students were by no means united. In May 1966, in response to a letter to a local newspaper by leader of the University Students' Union of Dar es Salaam (USUD), Kimulson, the author angrily rejected his allegation that university students befriend professors in order to get better marks and rise to student leaders:

> "No lecturer interferes with the campaigns. Mr. Kimulson is the president of the University Students Union – he knows how I with a few others campaigned for him. Mr. Kimulson was later suspended by his "cabinet" – We fought hard and reinstated him constitutionally as the rightful president, suspended the "cabinet" and gave him almost dictatorial powers. [...] Mr. Kimulson seemed to be haunted with the idea that he is always being spied on – that is why he talks of political stooges within the University walls. By stooges, I think, he means members of the secret service (C.I.D.)."[85]

The letter explicitly detailed rifts within student leadership and suggests that political life on campus was characterized by intense struggle and suspicion.

---

82 See e.g.: Andrew M. Ivaska, "Of Students, '"Nizers,' and a Struggle over Youth: Tanzania's 1966 National Service Crisis," *Africa Today* 51, no. 3 (2005), https://doi.org/10.1353/at.200 5.0022.
83 Socialist Student, "What is wrong with the Hill?," *The Nationalist*, October 15, 1966, No. 777.
84 A concerned citizen, "The Hill," *The Nationalist*, October 22, 1966, No. 783.
85 A.A.F. Massawe, "'A disgrace to our University'," *The Nationalist*, May 17, 1966, 647.

The allegation that the secret service was active on campus infers that students considered the university to be of existential importance to Tanzania and illustrates the pressure they felt in opposing the state. Furthermore, if the suspicion of the secret service's involvement was proven to be correct, it would indeed show how much significance the government attributed to the university and how vulnerable students felt on campus.

The fact that a purported ally of Kimulson publicly dismantled the President of the USUD suggests that his position was questioned, as does a vote of confidence that challenged him later that summer. It appears as though the university administration utilized this climate to neuter USUD's leadership and dispose of Kimulson.[86] As USUD's role marginalized, the National Union of Tanzania Student (NAUTS) took the leading role in the opposition to compulsory National Service. While the discussions in newspapers revolved around mutual accusations of elitism, George Hajivayanis experienced the debate as less pronounced. Looking back at the time he was a secondary school student, he said:

> "But in Tanzania in the mainland there was one student movement. [...] The head of the hierarchy was in Dar es Salaam. They had branches all over until the primary school. I was part of this in the secondary school. All students were in this. [...] when the leader of the student movement says anything, it's implemented until the primary school. [...] So they participated in it. They participated in all the strikes. The student strike in 1966 [...] [T]hey all went and carried the same thing. They wrote [...], 'colonialism was better.' [...] [T]hey had told the whole Union should do the same thing. So there were strikes all over the secondary schools. The Union had decided. [...] we supported it. We didn't really understand [...] it was kind of student rights. Because we knew we would also go to a National Service."[87]

The statement suggests that secondary school students followed NAUTS' directions without hesitation. Yet, given the popularity of socialism among students, it is notable that NAUTS had greater credibility among students than the government. It is possible that the image of wealthy bureaucrats diminished the administration's reputation, while the union benefited from its network in schools. The display of signs saying "colonialism was better" reaffirms

---

86 See: Ivaska, *Cultured States*, 139-140.
87 Salha Hamdani and George G. Hajivayanis, interview by Harald Barre.

that students viewed the matter in the context of an exploitative administration challenged by a progressive student union. Conversely, the secondary school students appear not to have perceived the power struggles at the university and the concerns over curricula that were dominated by Western countries. Rather, news of international student demonstrations[88] may have made the Tanzanian students more receptive of NAUTS' call for action.

After the demonstrations, President Nyerere attempted to erase the student union's argument of elitism in the administration by cutting his and the cabinet's salary and expelling the majority of demonstrators from the university.[89] This reaction highlights that he was concerned with the public image of his administration. Combatting exploitation by the administration and the provision of services had been the foundation of TANU's success in the 1950s. Therefore, the party could ill-afford accusations of being in line with the colonial government. At the same time, the union's power, not only as a voice in the public sphere, but also as an organizer of large crowds, likely concerned the President who had just overcome challenges from labor union leaders in recent years.

Furthermore, some newspaper correspondents voiced the fear that a class of graduates of higher education, who were mostly driven by personal gain and who were socialized in a university system of the former colonial power, had been created. This concern was not unfounded. As such, the events propelled Tanzania's socio-economic re-orientation in the Arusha Declaration.[90] Preliminarily, however, the expulsion of students was the main action taken against the elitism at the university. The paternalistic rhetoric around this move seems to distract from the underlying fear of foreign domination. This symbolic act had consequences in the social world, where due to the expulsion, classrooms were not filled.[91] It was a drastic step not only for individual students and their families, but also for a country that was struggling to find the financial resources to educate skilled local personnel in order to become independent from expatriate staff.

---

88 See: Ivaska, *Cultured States*, 143.
89 See: Ibid. 144-145.
90 See: Aminzade, *Race, Nation, and Citizenship*, 152-153. See chapter 4 on the implications of the Arusha Declaration on the debates, 1967-1970.
91 See: Swift, *Dar Days*, 15-16. Swift describes losing many students in his clinic after the expulsion.

Markle's conclusion that the expulsion was widely applauded[92] cannot be confirmed. Numerous readers' responses in *the Nationalist* were cautiously skeptic about the expulsion. At the university, Karim Hirji, who was supportive of the National Service, remembered the fear among students following the move.[93] However, despite the initially mixed reaction, Nyerere's move to assert TANU's control over the conflict was effective. His repression of the conflict reiterated that ultimately TANU would define what structures were still colonial and what factors signified independence. Yet, as the discussion on students' alienation from African socialism suggests, he may have been motivated by a fear of students' ideological dependency on Western values. In this sense, it may be assumed that Nyerere viewed the university and the growing influence of Western ideology as the frontline in the post-colonial and Cold War scenario; it would lead to the perpetuation of social attitudes that he considered harmful to his socialist vision for the country, whereas the tensions with expatriate personnel would be limited.

3.3 Decolonizing Gender Roles?

Women were portrayed as having a crucial role in Tanzania's nation building project. As indicated earlier, African women were pictured idyllically in the newspapers read by African soldiers during World War II. In those photos, men projected their varying visions of modernity on women's bodies, but by the 1950's women also carved out own roles and agency by arguing for the sake of national progress in letters to the editor. While Callaci identifies the "working girl" as a "key subject of [this] political imagination" in the years from 1967 to 1974,[94] the era from 1964 to 1966 was leading up to a phase where working women were defined as a critical feature of national identity. This section outlines the newspaper's often contradictory discussion of this narrative, and shows that the role of women in society became a publicly contested topic in 1966.

---

92 See: Markle, *A Motorcycle*, 80.
93 Hirji, *Growing up*, 96-97; E. Z. Lyimo, "'Write letter to President'," *The Nationalist*, November 8, 1966, 798; Editor, "Premature Pleas," *The Nationalist*, November 18, 1966, No. 897. Furthermore expatriate staff in higher education was also appalled by TANU's repression of the students' protest, see e.g.: Melchiorre, "Building Nations," 152–53; Swift, *Dar Days*, 15-17.
94 See: Emily Callaci, *Street Archives and City Life*, 64-65.

The question of gender roles had been a frequent topic since the newspaper's inception, although it was portrayed somewhat paradoxically. Already shortly after its foundation, *the Nationalist* devoted a page to women and presented topics that the editors apparently perceived as feminine, e.g. hair styling or cooking. By June 1964, this page became a frequent, usually weekly, feature of the newspaper.[95] Interestingly, in these pages – varyingly called e.g. "women's page" or "mainly for women" – the government newspaper continued sexist views of African women that former British Governor Twining had expressed shortly before independence, namely that women were an accessory to men and confined to the domestic sphere.[96] The promotion may have been fostered by a conservative ideal of modernity, or it may also have been driven by religious ideals of gender roles. As the following chapters will show, religion would start to play a bigger role in public and published discussions around the role of (young) women in the city.

Despite the conservative bent of the "women's page", these pages were a stark contrast to other articles in the newspaper that underscored the crucial role of women in nation building. These articles covered a large spectrum of roles, the most prominent being motherhood. Women were frequently urged to educate themselves in order to raise healthy children.[97] At the same time, and somewhat conflicting with many "domestic" topics on the "women's page," *the Nationalist* urged women to play a role beyond the household, e.g. in the police force.[98] The promotion of women's activism in such institutions of the state indicates that the government attempted to overcome the gender gaps which had emerged out of the colonial era. The newspaper supported this by pointing out women's achievements in other, mainly socialist, nations.[99] Additionally, very early on, the achievements of individual Tanzanian women and the careers they chose were portrayed in a positive light. A Tanzanian woman who was in London to train for secretarial work was asked by the interviewer:

---

95 See e.g.: *The Nationalist*, "Choosing a bathing suit: Have a 'minimum' style," June 23, 1964, 59; *The Nationalist*, "Delicious Nigerian recipes," November 3, 1965, 484.
96 See chapter 2.4.
97 See e.g.: *The Nationalist*, "Women must take part in more affairs of community," June 29, 1964, 63; *The Nationalist*, "Women told: attend courses and apply knowledge," February 17, 1965, 262.
98 See e.g.: *The Nationalist*. "Police call for women recruits." December 29, 1964. 219.
99 *The Nationalist*, "Women pilots," October 26, 1964, No. 165.

"'And when you are married and have a family,' I queried, 'will that be the end of your careers? Will you want to stop working and just stay at home?' On my left, Miss Hassan of Singida, who had been rather shy and silent during the earlier discussion suddenly, spoke out firmly. 'Certainly not,' she said 'we are training to do jobs that will be of benefit not only to ourselves but to our people as well.'"[100]

Ms. Hassan's response seemed to fit ideally with the socialist vision that Nyerere had for the country, and contrasts with the accusation of elitism against university students two years later. However, as she was able to acquire the funding for such training abroad, Ms. Hassan was indeed an exception. Despite the continued evocation of colonial ideals of womanhood, the newspaper clearly began to articulate a narrative that diverted from such ideals.

Furthermore, the newspaper directly challenged the obstacles which most women faced. *The Nationalist* published calls to husbands to allow their wives to join adult education, as well as an appeal by Bibi Titi Mohamed to not confine daughters beginning at puberty until they were married.[101] Many women had but a marginal chance to participate in education or a have career. Only women who were fortunate enough to have their parents' and husbands' support could start a career. Beyond such immediate obstacles, cultural expectations determined the women's options. In 1965, an editorial mentioned the complaints of the principal of the teachers' college that a majority of his female students either left school early or did not acquire a job after graduation because of marriage. The editor continued to acknowledge that early marriage was commonplace a generation ago, but that the "economic and, perhaps, social climate is now generally favorable for late marriage."[102] In order to take on the problem, he argued, the administration needed to create flexible opportunities for employment of single women, re-employment of married women, and to end colonial practices and attitudes:

> "It is necessary also to adopt a wholly different attitude to the question from the one that prevailed during the colonial period, when marriage was regarded as virtually the end of a woman teacher's career, or when a break

---

100 Audrey Barry. "Tanganyika girls learn secretarial work." *The Nationalist*, March 19, 1964. 28.
101 See: *The Nationalist*, "Allow wives to join classes: Men urged," January 20, 1965, 238; *The Nationalist*, "Give up these old customs: Bibi Titi," November 3, 1964, 172.
102 Editor, "Teacher Troubles," *The Nationalist*, August 19, 1965, No. 419.

in service for maternal purposes was literally a break in service – such that when, and if, the teacher returned, she had to start at the bottom again!"[103]

It is noteworthy that the author explicitly connected the employment styles and gender roles as heavily impacted by the colonial era. Just like the quote from the secretarial trainee, Ms. Hassan, his critique of the discrimination against female teachers was not rendered in terms of the lack of equality, but in terms a waste of resources for the nation. As such, the discourse of socialism did not impact gender relations explicitly yet, but many of the structural problems underlying gender discrimination were discussed.

While the problem of marriage played an important role in that editorial, the newspaper kept idolizing these very roles. Within the same month of this editorial, the "women's corner" featured two stories that largely invoked the ideal of a wife as a non-working accessory to a husband.[104] Although the story on hair styling mentioned a potential career path for women, it largely focused on the comfort bestowed on wives. In frequently displaying articles such as these, the newspaper reaffirmed gender roles that, according to its editor, had been inherited from the colonial era. The impact of such images on the public sphere is probably considerable, as the newspaper was read by the class of people that could afford to live according to these ideals: Urban men and women, with education and chances for employment in the urban job sectors. It seems likely their perception of gender roles were shaped by these articles.

The contradictory style of messages on gender roles may have been caused by TANU's ongoing search for the meaning of Ujamaa socialism. More likely, it reflected the evolution of the newspaper itself, which was seeking to establish its reputation to a paying audience of possibly wealthy, unemployed wives and their husbands. Moreover, the TANU women that were strongly involved in the mass organization of the party in the 1950s were now in politics. Therefore, it was up to young journalists, many of them untrained, to bring together these varying messages and portray them in the newspaper. It is noteworthy that an article on "African hair style" was reported by Hannah Kassambala, whose later efforts in the paper would focus on gender roles and the need for equality. This supports the assumption that journalists, female journalists, in

---

103 Editor, "Teacher Troubles."
104 *The Nationalist*, "Hair care and styling," August 19, 1965, No. 418; *The Nationalist*, "Lady, even YOU can slim," August 25, 1965, No. 424.

particular, were merely in the evolutionary process of determining the problem of gender relations in the independent nation, and gaining the support of the editorial board to articulate their concerns.

Overall, *the Nationalist*, took steps to advocate for a change in gender roles. Remarkably, it not only called for women to enter into job sectors dominated by men, but also for men to pursue careers in jobs hitherto considered as feminine:

> "[...] [T]he government could well consider [...] encouraging more men to take up work with first graders. There is a danger that we are still excessively hidebound in our notions of what kinds of work are best discharged as by men or women. Many jobs that were once regarded as masculine preserves are now successfully held by women. Is it not possible to move in the opposite direction? If a man can be a satisfactory cook (as well as a baby-sitter!) or an adequate hospital nurse – and there are countless examples of both – why should he not be able to teach young children?"[105]

Despite such remarkable comments, and although *the Nationalist* published more substantial critiques of structural gender discrimination, the newspaper's editorials remained largely superficial when emphasizing women's importance in Tanzania's nation building. One editorial re-emphasized the significance of women obtaining high skill-levels in all job sectors. Noting the progress Tanzania and other African nations had made regarding political equality and participation, one editorial continued:

> "This trend should be, and is, encouraged by our government; but the good ladies of Tanzania need to be a little more aggressive in this onslaught on men's bastions. They seem to be satisfied with positions which are only slightly better or higher than those traditionally occupied by women in Western countries a generation ago. [...] The development plans [...] demand as of necessity that we mobilize all our available resources to the full – and this includes women – but if they do not come forward for training, on whom will they lay the blame? [...]"[106]

The comment illustrates the crucial role women were supposed to have in the independent nation. However, it is noteworthy that this editorial did not acknowledge the social constraints women faced, such as parental dominance,

---

105 Editor, "Teacher Troubles."
106 Editor, "Onward, women," *The Nationalist*, August 28, 1965, No. 427.

discriminatory regulations, and oppressive husbands. Furthermore, the urban space, which offered such opportunities, was restrictive, as another article about a conference of African, Asian and Latin American women's organizations showed. The Tanzanian delegate noted that people should only go to the city once they had employment.[107] Yet, newspaper debates in the upcoming years would show that women faced stereotypes and harassment in trying to gain employment. Hence, although women may have found ways to enter the city despite such obstacles, it remained, as in colonial times, a space in which they were viewed with suspicion. Thus, while the political and public debates around gender roles lamented women's underrepresentation in the workforce, it seemed to be blind to the obstacles they were facing. The absence of female readers' voices on the challenges of women in the first years of *the Nationalist* probably exacerbated this problem.

This, however, changed in 1966, when gender roles suddenly became a hotly debated topic when the crisis around National Service for graduates of higher education reached its peak. In October 1966, a letter to the editor targeted the party's women's organization Umoja wa Wanawake (UWT) and accused its leadership of simply being wives of important politicians. The letter went on to assert that they were detached from the majority of women, and only focused on fashion that made them appear non-African.[108] This viewpoint was supported in a letter by Donald Morwatshewa:

"[...] [T]he leadership of U.W.T. [...] is lead [SIC] by big bourgeois wives among whom are wives of Ministers. Their reactionary tendencies have manifested in many occasions. The leadership of this women organization stands for high dresses, the use of lip-sticks, the conversion of their hair. They don't appreciate the African natural way of doing things."[109]

Both letters' underlying critique is focused on that of an elitist, conservative administration. Since they were written while students were criticizing the government for being elitist, their main target may have been the party. In this context, U.W.T. likely presented itself as a promising weak point, as the overt message of acting un-African was in line with Nyerere's emphasis on

---

107 *The Nationalist*, "Employment, a must before moving to towns - seminar," December 9, 1964, No. 203.
108 See: P. Bigilwa, "UWT Leadership," *The Nationalist*, October 12, 1966, No. 774.
109 Donald Morwatshewa, "The task for U.W.T." *The Nationalist*, October 18, 1966, No. 779.

"African traditions."[110] The fact that the readers apparently did not criticize *the Nationalist* for its ambivalent coverage of women and their roles suggests that they intentionally focused on the politically delicate UWT leadership, and not the socially delicate aspect of fashion. Accordingly, the response of UWT focused on defending leadership:

> "[...] [O]ur membership consists of Tanu mamas, many of who are chairmen at village, district and regional level – Bibi Titi, President of the U.W.T., is herself a Tanu mama! So it is a gross misconception to make such inferences that the U.W.T. belongs to the upper classes, and is led by wives of Ministers and Regional Heads!"[111]

Ms. Lupembe's response firmly rebuked UWT as being associated with an upper class of government officials. This may suggest that the administration had a negative reputation in the society. More importantly, by distancing UWT from the administration, she emphasized agency of UWT's leadership. She rejected the accusation of being accessories to their husbands. Women's agency, in her view, was independent of a husband's social position. The defiant tone in her letter suggests that she was used to fighting against marginalizing perceptions of women.

Yet her opinion on the aspect of non-African fashion suggests that the protection of UWT was indeed her main concern:

> "On the safe-guarding of culture in our country, it is childish to blame the women's organization for any extremes in dress or hair-styles worn by young women, which is inevitable in this fast changing world! All the U.W.T. fashion shows have encouraged the wearing of our national dress, and we will continue to advocate in favour of retaining the African personality."[112]

It is conspicuous that Lupembe drew a line between "Tanu mamas" and "young women." It is likely that this reflected the social world itself, where an established guard of TANU women veterans had struggled for independence and equal rights, while the next generation was seen as distinct. Deflecting the blame on young women suggests that UWT did not consider such women as part of their sphere and, maybe even used young women as a convenient scapegoat to protect UWT's reputation. This dynamic would not remain un-

---

110 See: Ivaska, *Cultured States*, 3.
111 L. Lupembe, "U.W.T. Leadership," *The Nationalist*, October 22, 1966, No. 783
112 Ibid.

challenged when young women began articulating their views on social and cultural obstacles in the newspaper in the following years.[113]

An article that *the Nationalist* printed an article on youth and gender in Kenya demonstrated that these concerns were not limited to Tanzania. Somewhat in line with *the Nationalist's* reports on women's fashion, it defended fashionable youth as a sign of true independence. African men, the article continued, were themselves to blame for African women following European trends, as they were eager to "hunt" European women.[114] This perspective was supported by Tanzanian readers:

> "While I feel suspicious of women who go the whole hog to look like whites, I, however, understand and accept the reasons behind the African women's burning wish to appear "whitey." The reasons therefore are as clear as day: the African woman is instigated by the African male to affect her colour, the gait and the appearance of her counterpart the modern European woman. [...] Taking the case in Tanzania, how many men have availed themselves of the chances of wearing a simple national dress – the Kitenge? Only a handful."[115]

The preceding view of women and non-African fashion offer a first corrective glance on the ambivalent gender roles portrayed in the newspaper. Their contributions explicitly integrated fashion in the nation building project, and pointed out men's hypocrisy in the question of Africanization of fashion. The quote above indicates the power men held in the social dynamics of urban life, and that fashion was a key to navigate this landscape. Here, the newspaper's role as a platform for a public debate becomes highly visible. Men and women experienced the social world very differently, and women in particular were subjected to a number of preconceived notions. By the end of 1966, they were beginning to seize the newspaper as a space to communicate their perspectives and contest the monopoly of men's opinions in this part of the public sphere.

---

113 See chapters 4.3, 5.3, 6.2, 6.3.
114 See: Barbara Kimenye, "Are African Men Hypocrites?," *The Nationalist*, November 30, 1966, No. 817.
115 W.K.N. Mungal, "Bourgeois cultural influence," *The Nationalist*, December 7, 1966, No. 823.

3.4 Conclusion: Independence in Crisis

The mid-1960s in Tanzania were characterized by social tensions which were rooted in the structures of the colonial society. These conflicts revolved around "race" and gender, and surfaced in *the Nationalist* during the course of a month-long exchange between university students and the administration in 1966. The fact that the conflict with the students and the increasing debate in the newspaper occurred after the diplomatic crisis between Great Britain and Tanzania indicates that this development, along with the fears of secret services from colonial states, increased readers' concern over independence, exploitation, and associated behaviors.

TANU did not confront the perceived threats in an unvaried manner. On the one side, the conflict with students culminated with the expelling of students in higher education in an authoritarian move. On the other side, as shown in chapter 3.2, the state seized upon the integration of schools as a bottom-up development in order to relieve the persistent "racial" tension in the country. Furthermore, the English-written party newspaper became the arena of increasingly critical and controversial debates.

The Nationalist's coverage of issues revolving around gender roles can be interpreted as outstanding insofar as it emphasized the crucial role women had in TANU's nation building project. This is particularly evident if the coverage is contrasted with the view of Condon's study. Despite Condon's detailed analysis of the newspaper's coverage in October 1966, he neither mentioned the appearance of gender issues nor the regularly published section, 'women's corner.'[116] However, it was not until 1966 that *the Nationalist* published an article that featured a woman in the byline, which suggests that women were partly portrayed through a male lens.

While women were important symbols in the nation building project, they were covered ambivalently in the newspapers. In the national narrative that was woven, the TANU newspaper portrayed women as socialist role models, but also viewed them in terms of colonial and Western values of fashion. While the latter turned women into symbols of progress, much like in the World War II military newspaper *Heshima*, the former called for their agency in nation building. Women began to seize upon the opportunity to contribute to the narrative that the newspaper wove, as they openly criticized men for their attitudes towards "race" and "gender" for the first time in late 1966. These

---

116 See: Condon, "Nation Building."

comments would be the beginning of a discourse on men and women's roles in the socialist nation, which would erupt over the following years and highlight the many shortcomings of the relationship between state and society.

Similar to the topic of gender, "race" was mostly covered from the perspective of journalists or TANU politicians in *the Nationalist* until 1966. "Race" had been a category which had accompanied colonialism and the struggle for national independence from its inception. However, until 1966, *the Nationalist* largely focused on "race" in the sense of pan-African solidarity. After abandoning the goal of a political East African Federation, *the Nationalist* emphasized Tanzania's importance in all African struggles against white supremacy, and developed strong sympathy for the African American liberation movement. In this context, the breaking of ties with Great Britain may be seen as a symbolic climax of Tanzania's dedication to African national self-determination.

Likewise, "race" did not play a significant role until 1966. Relations with the Asian community had been portrayed as imperfect, but improvable. The image accompanying the 'women's corner' article on "hair care and styling", displayed the portrait of a woman from each "racial" group suggesting harmony. However, in late 1966, the Asian community became the explicit target of African resentment, particularly in the readers' sections.

In contrast to women and students who began to express their viewpoints in the readers' section, Asians no longer contributed their opinions as such. In the aftermath of the editorial on Mr. Sampat's call for the Hindustani radio program, no further responses from self-declared Asian citizens arose.[117] This may be seen as a sign that fears in the Asian community, particularly its business community, were surmounting, and this lead to their withdrawal from the newspapers as an arena of public exchange. Conversely, open discussion may very well have helped to create a consciousness despite the background of resentment and fear, and would have enabled participants and observers of the debate to contemplate change.

This was particularly true for the younger generation. Najma Sachak's experience of integration in her school exemplifies the prospects education could bring about: Her fellow African students not only had the chance to gain the educational background necessary to fill responsible posts that would have otherwise been occupied by expatriates, but they benefitted from the initiative

---

117　It is possible that Asians continued to write letters to the editor under non-revealing pseudonyms, or that the editor chose not to publish their views, as an article in the early 1970s suggests. See chapter 5.1.

her teacher took to enable students from different backgrounds to connect on a level playing field, and not along socio-economic hierarchies inherited from colonialism. In this regard, the potential to change categories of perception from the colonial era became most visible in the younger generation.

Overall, the mixed messaging regarding "race" and gender suggests that TANU had not adopted a common perspective. The crisis underlying the student demonstration in 1966 illustrated the need to respond to conflicting perceptions and values that had characterized the meaning of "race" and gender. However, as the following chapter will show, TANU's attempts to boost national confidence and independence were manifold, and even contradictory.

4   1967-1970: African Socialism or African Tradition?

The mid-1960s were not only characterized by Tanzania's assertion of its diplomatic independence, but also open discussion on the continuity of dependence in the form of colonially shaped social structures and attitudes. The 1966 student demonstration turned out to be a climatic manifestation of these public debates. It is attributed with having been a driving force for the development of the Arusha Declaration of 1966.[1] This declaration of the Tanganyika African National Union (TANU) was a conscious attempt to advance independence from colonially shaped structures by defining the hitherto rather vague term of African Socialism by articulating principles and guidelines:

"[...] WHEREAS TANU believes:-
(a) That all human beings are equal;
(b) That every individual has a right to dignity and respect;
(c) That every citizen is an integral part of the Nation and has the right to take an equal part in Government at local, regional and national level;
(d) That every citizen has the right to freedom of expression, of movement, of religious belief and of association within the context of the law; [...]"[2]

The *TANU Creed* seemed to be a direct response to the debates surrounding "racial" and gender relations, and asserted the universal rights of individuals living in Tanzania. In fact, the fundamental *TANU creed* did not even differentiate in further categorizations such as 'men,' 'women' or 'citizen,' and generally acknowledged everyone's right to equality and dignified treatment. This generalization may reflect Tanzania's pan-African position as African

---
1   See: Aminzade, *Race, Nation, and Citizenship*, 152-153.
2   Arusha Declaration, TANU, Publicity Section 1 at 1 (1967), accessed November 26, 2018, https://www.fes.de/suche/?id=84&q=arusha.

American despair in the United States became more visible. African American groups had growing hopes for a closer connection to Africa.[3] What is more likely though is that it was an overture to those Asians that had not yet claimed Tanganyikan citizenship, as well as the large numbers of African freedom fighters and refugees that were facing open challenges in the public sphere. TANU's reiteration of their human rights rejected nationalist correspondents who were hostile towards these groups based on their foreign or "racial" background. Yet, the business community likely had mixed feelings towards the declaration, as it promised to protect property "according to law," and announced:

> "That it is the responsibility of the State to intervene actively in the economic life of the Nation so as to ensure the well-being of all citizens and so as to prevent the exploitation of one person by another or one group by another, and so as to prevent the accumulation of wealth to an extent which is inconsistent with the existence of a classless society."[4]

Thus, while the individual's existence was confirmed, economic rights and independence were officially in jeopardy. Being faced with increasing discontent in the public sphere about elitism and exploitation, the party announced its intention to enforce a greater degree of economic equilibrium into society. Those with some material comfort likely regarded this as a threat. Furthermore, in the declaration, TANU explained that it sought to decrease the country's dependency on money. While this was explicitly aimed at foreign aid, implicitly it weakened the position of the Asian business community, which had prided itself with its financial contributions to Tanzania. Thus, using financial contributions as leverage, as mentioned in the letter to the editor a few years earlier, was certainly not an option for wealthier Asians.[5]

Point d) of the *TANU Creed* seemed directly address the open contest between the administration and students. However, it only superficially clarified the positions. For, on the one side, it confirmed freedom of expression and

---

3   See: Fanon C. Wilkins, "The Making of Black Internationalists: SNCC and Africa before the Launching of Black Power, 1960-1965," *The Journal of African American History* 92, 4, New Black Power Studies: National, International, and Transnational Perspectives (2007): 479-483; see: Seth M. Markle, *'We Are Not Tourists': The Black Power Movement and the Making of Socialist Tanzania 1960-1974* (New York, 2011), A dissertation submitted in partial fulfillment of the requirement for the degree of Doctor of Philosophy, 24.
4   *Arusha Declaration*, 1.
5   See chapter 3.1.

association. However, it limited these rights by "the law," which of course left space for interpretation, and could also be subject to changes and amendments. In this way, academia was not facing direct limitations for now, but the state cemented its right in the future to enact such constraints.

Gender roles also played a crucial role in the entire declaration. While they were implicit in the general rights expressed in the "TANU Creed," they were an explicit part of the declaration's discussion on 'self-reliance':

> "The truth is that in the villages the women work very hard. At times they work for 12 or 14 hours a day. They even work on Sundays and public holidays. Women who live in the villages work harder than anybody else in Tanzania. But the men who live in villages (and some of the women in towns) are on leave for half of their life. The energies of the millions of men in the villages and thousands of women in the towns which are at present wasted in gossip, dancing and drinking, are a great treasure which could contribute more towards the development of our country than anything we could get from rich nations."[6]

In this paragraph, TANU acknowledged the imbalance of power and contribution between rural Tanzanian men and women, and accused rural men of living at the expense of women. However, in the urban areas, the party claimed that "some of the women" were the antithesis to women in the countryside, spending their energy on "gossip, dancing and drinking."

While the declaration was specific in what it perceived as unproductive exploitation, overall it was rather vague with a lot of room for interpretation. In the public sphere, such specifics were hotly debated. As such, the Arusha Declaration gave crucial impetus in a debate that permitted people to exchange their views on roles and problems encountered in the nation. The following sections will examine how the debates in the public sphere evolved after the Arusha Declaration and detail the interplay between discourse and development in the social world.

4.1 (Non-) Racialism in Schools

"Racial" tensions had been a marginal aspect of public debates in *the Nationalist* until 1966. However, in the social world, "race" continued to define most

---

6   *Arusha Declaration*, 15.

peoples' chances and obstacles. After her own secondary school had been integrated in the mid-1960s, Najma Sachak gained vivid insight into the continuities of these formative structures. After finishing her Higher School Certificate, she was hired as a student teacher at a mission school and recalled the dramatic forms of division, but also attempts to overcome them:

> "We used to refer to it as a government school because mainly civil servant employees and Christian children went there. The only other children who went there were some English, some wealthy Indian children who went to primary there and joined secondary at my school. Sometimes some parents thought that the standard of English would be better at the mission school; [...], they would only send their children straight away abroad for secondary education. Even the Karimjee family, who built our school, used to send their children at first to the mission school and then straight abroad to boarding schools."[7]

The observation that many wealthier parents planned to send their children abroad suggests that they either feared physical or financial harm or that due to deeply held stereotypes, they had no confidence in the success of the Tanzanian education system. As richer Indian families invested in a future outside Tanzania early on, their children had no chance to overcome "racial" barriers. Furthermore, the set-up of the school made an exchange between students from different "racial" groups next to impossible:

> "So those were the types of school intake, the fee-paying missionary schools [...] [and] there was an African intake, [...] non-fee-paying – so there was a main school attached to this nice new cathedral that had been built. [...] I got called and I started working at the school. And one of the things that happened was they said: 'Well you are going to teach in the main part of the school,' which is nice buildings, nice classrooms, nice.' [...] I knew there was an African end of the school. So you went down the main school, crossed the road to the old customs-sort-of area, you walked across the football field and then there were huts. Two corridors, a thatch roof, not even a galvanized iron roof [...] and there was no electricity."[8]

According to this rich memory, the contrast in quality between the fee paying Asian and the non-paying African section must have been extreme. "Racial"

---

7   Najma Sachak, interview by Harald Barre.
8   Ibid.

differences were manifested in the social world, even though de iure "race" was not the distinguishing factor. The choice to segregate was a conscious one:

> [...] And I talked about this to Father Smith. I said: 'How come, you separate the African children so much from the Indian?' And he said: [...] 'my dear - how to explain that. There is a long tradition and it is very hard. The Indian parents would say the standard of the children will drop. We have got to keep them in a separate school, because they have not learned English from Standard I. [...] [W]e started preparing them mainly in Standard VII. So we can't mix up Standards.' But essentially standards were racially defined and poverty defined."[9]

Her memory of the structure of the school points to the high visibility of discrimination. It was, as in the early British colonial planning of spatial segregation, not explicitly racist, but implicit due to income differentiation. In the light of independence and political pressure all over Africa for Africanization, the bleak reality of such continued de facto "racial" discrimination must have been painful to advocates of "non-racial" socialism and a welcome argument for proponents of rapid Africanization. However, Father Smith's apparent unease being put on the spot about the separation suggests that there was at least a degree of consciousness about the negative impact of continuing "racial" discrimination. Furthermore, networking between concerned teachers provided an avenue to increase the opportunities of African children:

> "So Sister Fabian called me and said: 'Now Najma, your teacher says, Mr. Bhuchaar (my communist [...] Punjabi teacher) says that if we ask you to go after four o'clock and go to the other side and teach African children, he said, you might do it, but I think you will do it, right?' [...] So at four o'clock, when I was finished with the main school, I would walk across, and this was my voluntary work. I decided I am going to call this nation building. [...] [The class] was only for African boys and girls; very few girls though, mostly boys. Very few girls, I think there were three girls and 21 African boys. [...] [...] [B]y the time national Standard VII exams had come into operation again. But there the only medium of education was Swahili. When they arrived here

---

9   Ibid.

they had to turn into English. In this short period of time, [...] there was a lot of work to be done."[10]

The quote reaffirms the fact, mentioned previously when discussing the university, that "racial" discrimination was not only maintained due to income-based discrimination, but also language-based discrimination. Children lucky enough to obtain higher education had to learn English as the language of instruction. Therefore, they were limited in their chances to obtain a spot at an institution of higher learning and successfully complete a course of study. Furthermore, African girls appear to have suffered the most from a lack of educational opportunities.[11] Conversely, the lack of English being taught in the lower levels and the pre-dominance of English in higher education created the fear among Indian parents that the education of their children would suffer. Due to these barriers, the educational system re-affirmed mutual prejudice and resentments between Asian and African parents. Yet, despite the materially inferior conditions and a potentially conflictual climate, Najma Sachak remembered the extraordinarily good atmosphere in her class:

> "[...] And they were so motivated, these kids. So motivated. And I used to motivate them. I used to say: 'You want to join that class where those people are in those nice rooms? You know, this is what we are going to do. Later on, you are going to be teaching in those classes, you will see. When you go to Secondary School, things will change. You will not be in different classes like this. You will be in normal classes, all of you together with other children in the Secondary School.'"[12]

Thus, despite the limitations and the continued discrimination along gender lines, schools provided the chance to incrementally bridge gaps in education and, importantly, boost the self-esteem of African students. Yet, being faced with social division and discontent, TANU's Arusha Declaration sought to provide ideas to bridge these gaps. While the Arusha Declaration explicitly banned "racial" discrimination, its economic implication strongly affected

---

10   Ibid.
11   The quote can only suggest this trend, as it is not based on a larger survey of schools. However, taking into account the historically proven discrimination of school girls in the preceding years and the strong impact it seems to have made on Najma Sachak, gender discrimination seems to have been a continued problem.
12   Ibid.

the Asian community and added to the alienation of Asians from Tanzania's African socialist project. In the memory of Najma Sachak, who was just about to embark to study abroad, the impact of the declaration was significant:

> "67 is the Arusha Declaration - dramatic changes overnight: the banking system, everything, alright, nationalizations. Overnight where the Indians left, [...] because of the requirement that they disclose their assets in money and property abroad [...] it was a strange time to be going abroad for study. That I was still able to go is quite an achievement, because it became next to impossible for Indian students to go abroad on a private basis, because all foreign exchange allowances were stopped. At first, foreign exchange for study purposes was permitted, but then it became tough to send your children abroad for higher studies. [T]he Bank of Tanzania would not give permission easily to send money to your convert Tanzanian shillings into pounds or dollars or whatever. [...] [S]o the Indians had to find their ways in sending out through the Hawala system as it were to make sure that – if they wanted to send their children abroad – that they were able to pay for their education."[13]

The state's attempt to control financial resources for the country probably affected the generally wealthier Asian population greatly. The quote suggests the Asian community perceived the measures more as a threat than a step toward an egalitarian society. As a result, Asian families began leaving the country in order to evade financial losses. Moreover, Najma Sachak's experience reflects that freedom of movement beyond the borders was potentially impeded, as available financial resources were tied to staying in the country. Here, the transnational networks many Asian Tanganyikans could rely on turned out to be an advantage. Nonetheless, in the Asian communities, the initial impact of the Arusha Declaration was unsettling, as the state seemed to threaten individual freedom.

"Why Can't We Solve Our Difference?" - De-Escalating "Racial" Tensions in the Public Sphere

The abovementioned changes in the social world stimulated newspaper debates and ultimately led to the re-evaluation of the category "race." While the explicit measures connected with the Arusha Declaration are commonly remembered as a watershed moment, the debates in the public sphere had al-

---

13   Ibid.

ready pointed to a change in the atmosphere in the preceding weeks. In a speech to National Service recruits, Prime Minister Kawawa reiterated the importance of establishing Swahili as a national language. The editor concurred and lamented the widespread usage of English in public spaces.[14] And in a speech commemorating the revolution in Zanzibar, President Nyerere lashed out against capitalist exploitation and was quoted as stating: "We shall never rest until our country is a socialist state."[15] Against the background of the severe rhetoric and the administration's response to the students' demonstration a few months earlier, these articles and quotations in the newspaper signaled action against 'class' disparities.

The developments likely met mixed reception within the Tanzanian population, but the newspaper coverage portrayed them as welcome steps against the Asian community. Despite Nyerere's "non-racial," "class-centered" language, comments against Asians skyrocketed in the public sphere. A reader applauded Kawawa's push for establishing Swahili as a national language. However, in contrast to Kawawa, who had lamented the presence of English, he targeted Asians:

> "[...] our Asian brothers, their forefathers as well as their children were born in this country, but up till now they pretend not to know Swahili. Is it not to despise the nation?"[16]

The quote indicates a high degree of suspicion of what was perceived as – and now officially declared – a foreign culture. While the resentments were somewhat expected against the background of continued inequality, it is remarkable that they were increasingly expressed in response to the nationalist rhetoric of the government. Furthermore, even the editor of *the Nationalist* began using a rhetoric that was not only anti-exploitation, but also "anti-Asian." When the impending adoption of the Arusha Declaration was announced, the next article on the front page announced the expulsion of Asians and Arabs. Visually, the newspaper simultaneously linked the Arusha Declaration with anti-Asian sentiment. For, even though these drastic steps were targeting non-citizen traders, the explicit and prominent exposure of "racial" backgrounds seems to have played into anti-Asian resentments.

---

14   See: Editor, "National Language," *The Nationalist*, January 5, 1967, No. 847.
15   *The Nationalist*, "Nyerere hits at Exploiters: 'We shall not rest until our country is a Socialist State'," January 14, 1967, No. 854.
16   Abdi M. Ntaukile, "Congratulations," *The Nationalist*, January 17, 1967, No. 856.

In an editorial printed soon thereafter, the author emphasized that "[i]t is right that all petty businesses should be placed in the hands of Tanzania citizens at once."¹⁷ While acknowledging the rights of all citizens, he not only completely rejected those Asians who had lived in the country for decades, but left in the wake of independence. The author also declared that he considered non-citizens who continued to live in Tanzania but failed to claim Tanzanian citizenship as undesirable. He dismissed their claim of having lived in the country for 40 years: "Could they not decide whether to become true Tanzanians? Apparently they decided not to be Tanzanians. They should therefore not expect to enjoy similar privileges and opportunities like Tanzanians."¹⁸

The quote reflects a rising frustration over the slow pace of localization, as well as the continued power of "race" as a categorical difference. As the author stressed the purported stereotypes of those who had left the country in the wake of independence, he reinvigorated the "racial" stereotypes that other politicians, namely Julius Nyerere, sought to overcome. Furthermore, the editorial expressed no consideration of fears and concerns from within the Asian community – expatriate and citizens alike. Beyond such fears, mere socialization in the transnational networks likely made it difficult for Asians in Tanzania to revoke ties abroad. Najma Sachak remembered:

> "[...] [W]e kept in touch with changes in India, we used to receive, us as children, I read comics in Gujarati, we received a Gujarati magazine, but it was fairly serious, with stories and so on, puzzles etc., math problems to solve and all sorts of activities and things. And that particular magazine - not a comic, but a kind of a joke magazine – there were two types. The one was 'mad' - equivalent of 'mad' and the other was 'absolutely mad.' [...] We had adapted over time our manner cooking with local products, like using cassava and minced meat curry. I mean it entered in our cooking. And then we used a lot of Swahili words when we spoke etc. [...]"¹⁹

---

17 Editor, "A most welcome step," *The Nationalist*, January 26, 1967, No. 864.
18 Ibid.
19 Najma Sachak, interview by Harald Barre. The significance of India, as well as transnational religious networks, is also emphasized in Hirji's memory of growing up in Tanzania. See: Hirji, *Growing up*, 20-22.

Her recollection suggests that cultural influences from the Indian subcontinent were significant. Languages, as well as leisure activities,[20] were shaped by Indian origins, while some aspects of the language and cuisine adapted to local influences. Thus, Asians' experiences of "home" were more transnational than it can be assumed for most African Tanzanians. Against the background of fear, it does not appear that astonishing that Asians who had maintained ties abroad were hesitant to abandon them altogether.

Nyerere's strictly "non-racial" critique of exploitative relations in Tanzania seems to have been a compromise to change the socio-economic structures of the country and placating the group that was calling for rapid Africanization, while not alienating Asians, whose skills and education could also benefit the entire country. In this regard, the "racially" explicit language of the editor is surprising. His use of "racial" categories from the colonial era may have been a door opener for other readers to air their resentments, as one exchange between correspondents a few months later suggests.

In the late 1960s, the neglected issues in urban areas dating from the colonial period continued to be a challenge. Accusations of owners exploiting prospective tenants by demanding key-money stirred up resentment. One article mentioned the trial of three Asians accused of collecting key-money.[21] The story, which once more explicitly detailed the "racial" background of the alleged wrongdoers, spurred the response of an upset reader, Abdul Kassamali:

> "A few days ago I read with interest the news about the three key-money racketeers [...]. [...] It is an irrefutable fact that most of the Asian Cell leaders are die-hard reactionaries and give lip services to Tanu to achieve their selfish goal of exploitation. They are among those reactionary businessmen who oppose tooth and nail African advancement in business and enterprise. [...] I fully endorse the view expressed by the Coast Regional Commissioner Mr. Songambele that 95% of the Asian citizens are 'PAPER-CITIZENS' [capitalized in newspaper]. Their sole aim is to maintain their exploitation grip and nothing else."[22]

---

20   This would also include the significant aspect of Indian movie screenings, and thereby projecting imaginations from India into Tanzanian society.
21   *The Nationalist*, "The Asians fined in key money case," July 25, 1967, No. 1017.
22   Abdul Kassamali, "Key-money," *The Nationalist*, August 1, 1967, No. 1022.

These assertions suggest that debate turned away not only from Nyerere's "non-racial" language, but even the editor's opinion that citizens of Asian origin should not be bothered. Curiously, the reader's attitude does not seem to be based on personal experience, but on the newspaper reports and the political views of Coast Regional Commissioner Songambele. The latter apparently introduced the term "paper-citizen" into the newspaper debates, discrediting the majority of Tanzanian citizens of Asian origin. This suggests that "racial" stereotypes detached from the social world to some degree and gained a stronger momentum in the public sphere.

Mr. Kassamali's letter was quickly challenged. While supporting the judicial action against exploitation in housing, Ajmal Amdami vehemently opposed the condemnation of the majority of Asians, and considered it as an attack on the unity of loyal Asians, Africans, and Arabs.[23] However, Mr. Kassamali did not accept the argument and pushed on:

> "One regional commissioner who is well aware of the mentality of the Ismailis rightly accused them of being "PAPER CITIZENS" [capitalized in newspaper]. He was right. What is applicable to the Ismailis is also applicable to the rest of the Asians. [...] Why do they not invite the Africans to participate in enterprises?"[24]

Abdul Kassamali's response seemed strongly influenced by "racial" stereotypes from the colonial era. He considered Asians to be economic profiteers and unwilling to share their success. He even addressed Ajmal Andani consistently as "master Ajmal." In doing so, he evoked stereotypes of master-servant relations and implicitly accused him of being aloof.

As "racial" imagery from the colonial era was evoked, *the Nationalist* changed its handling of the debate. Probably in response to the exchange, and possibly in rejection of Regional Commissioner Songambele's "paper citizens" comment, a strong pronouncement was published in the regular "Focus" column. While acknowledging that many Asians had only taken up Tanzanian citizenship to continue their business at the expense of the "nation", the author hastened to add that the problem was not exclusively Asian in nature, but rather an issue of class:

---

23 Ajmal Andani, "Royalty," *The Nationalist*, August 11, 1967, No. 1032.
24 Abdul Kassamali, "Paper Citizens," *The Nationalist*, August 17, 1967, No. 1037.

"The Social [SIC] references of the PAPER CITIZENS (feudal and capitalist) are, undoubtedly, nakedly antagonistic to the Spirit of Arusha. This is essentially so on the question of ending exploitation of labour by capital, and the common ownership of the means of production. To them this is a manifestation of "injustice" rather than "justice." [Bold in the newspaper.]
What some fellow citizens fail to realise is the fact that the struggle of the exploited against the exploiters is not aimed at a certain particular ethnic group of people. It is a struggle against all classes, to whom belong both the indigenous and the non-indigenous, who live by the labour of others (the masses)."[25]

In this text, *the Nationalist* made a first conscious attempt to bridge sometimes contradictory goals of combating economic exploitation and "racial" discrimination. Corresponding with arrests of alleged exploiters in the social world, the comments in the public sphere put pressure on this group, particularly Asians. However, in contrast to Mr. Kassamali, the comment not only pointed out that Africans may very well be exploiters as well, but indirectly accused him of wanting to perpetuate exploitation himself. For, in his letter, Mr. Kassamali had squarely blamed Asians for being exploiters, and at the same time, asked that Africans should control these – still capitalist – businesses.

Nonetheless, the emphasis of "race" in economic relations remained strong, and even shaped a parliamentary debate in the following year. However, the exchange turned out to be a watershed moment for *the Nationalist's* editor who sharply criticized the parliamentarians who conflated "race" with exploitation. After highlighting the Arusha Declaration's emphasis on exploitation as such, the author went on to point out that "[t]here are rooms let by African landlords that are twice the justified rentals under our economic circumstances and the existing law governing the fixation of rents. [...] Similarly, not all wholesalers or dukawallahs are Asian. And not all of them exploit their customers by charging abnormal prices."[26]

The newspaper's explicit departure from playing with "racial" resentments evolved in the one-and-a-half years after the Arusha Declaration. However, it appears likely that this was not just a development in the public sphere alone, but in the social world as well. For instance, the tone of the debate in parliament and the worsening relations in the East African context accelerated this

---

25   *The Nationalist*, "Focus on 'Paper Citizens'," August 28, 1967, No. 1046.
26   Editor, "Exploitation and Race," *The Nationalist*, July 25, 1968, No. 1387.

development crucially. *The Nationalist* increasingly reported about the swelling emigration of Asians from Kenya, [27] which in turn evoked sympathetic responses from readers. While such respondents were critical of economic exploitation, they also expressed their sympathy for Asians who had left East Africa after living here for many generations. Furthermore, they argued that both Asians and Africans had been exploited by the British, and that it would be wrong to pour Asian financial resources in the British economy.[28] One letter ended almost pleadingly: "Why can't we solve our differences."[29] Such perspectives constituted a contrast to views expressed such as by Mr. Kassamali, and point to the division "racial" relations caused. On the one side, Indians were decried as exploiters, while, on the other side, they were seen not only as fellow citizens, but also as victims of colonialism.

At the same time, Asians that were able to enter Great Britain, experienced not only racism, but a steep fall within social hierarchy, as Najma Sachak, who went to the United Kingdom for her studies, recalled:

> "You know, in England, suddenly I went from an upper class as an Indian from Tanzania, to be assimilated as a working class Indian in the U.K, because of my race – being Indian and [...] you could see in the society, you could feel, you heard, that people like you – were being insulted by whites, you know: 'get back to your country', whatever. [...] I was invited to their homes to spend Christmas and so on – but, I mean, after telling them my name, the first thing [after] where I was from, okay, the first thing the parents would ask, is: 'Are you going to go back to your own country?' You see, [...] you always felt that you had to justify your presence, even as a student."[30]

Najma Sachak's daunting encounter of racism in Europe was no singular experience, and reports[31] of racism possibly tempered the eagerness of the Asian population in Tanzania to emigrate. Despite the economic restrictions of the Arusha Declaration, prospects in the country likely seemed less risky than a

---

27 See e.g.: *The Nationalist*, "100 Asians quit Kenya daily," February 5, 1068, No. 1181.
28 See e.g.: A. N. Nderingo, "Africanizing minds of non-Africans," *The Nationalist*, February 8, 1968, No. 1183.
29 Ibins A.J. Mwabawalwa, "Open letter to fleeing Asians," *The Nationalist*, March 1, 1968, No. 1203.
30 Najma Sachak, interview by Harald Barre.
31 See e.g.: Mwabawalwa, "Open letter."

move to Great Britain. Conversely, some African readers may have been affected by the shared experience of British racism, as well.

In *the Nationalist*, a more cautious stance by commentators towards Asians occurred in the wake of escalating events in Kenya. Kenya openly attempted to replace the Asian commercial community with African businesses, which was opposite of what Tanzania attempted to do with the Arusha Declaration. Ultimately, tens of thousands of Asians left Kenya in the late 1960s.[32] Kenya strongly diverged from Tanzania, not only rejecting the idea of "non-racialism," but also socialism. The responses in TANU's English-written newspaper illustrated the immediate impact of developments in East Africa across national borders. The situation in Kenya certainly demonstrated that the heated rhetoric from politicians and readers was a threat to the Arusha Declaration in all its dimensions. The increasingly decisive interventions of the editor of *the Nationalist* reflect the attempt by TANU's leadership to control an escalating debate. Apparently, the intervention was successful, as letters to the editor were significantly toned down in the following years. If articles mentioned "race," it was almost exclusively directed towards non-citizens,[33] and no longer questioned the status of any Tanzanian citizen.

As hostile, "racially" coded language disappeared and attacks on Asian citizens declined in the newspaper, events in Zanzibar even spurred downright solidarity with Asians. The dynamic was outstanding as such, because letters to the editor rarely mentioned the mainland's partner in the Union. This changed after Vice-President Karume announced to enforce inter-marriage in Zanzibar in order to bring about "racial" equality. At a May Day rally, he threatened parents with jail if they were found to have aided their children in escaping the island.[34] Initial reactions of readers ranged from showing sympathy for ending "racial" superiority to expressing cautious criticism of the implicated coercion. Many readers complained about the aloofness and self-segregation of Asians, which they mostly perceived in the older generation. Intermarriage was seen as a useful means to overcome such divides, and thus

---

32 See: Aiyar, *Indians in Kenya*, 261-268.
33 *The Nationalist* followed the court dealings of a Mr. D'Silva from Goa for several months who reportedly refused to rent his apartment to a man because he was "Black." See e.g.: *The Nationalist*, "Expelled Asian abused 'Black Skin'," November 17, 1967, No. 1116; *The Nationalist*, "D'Silva to go at last," June 1, 1968, No. 1281.
34 *The Nationalist*, "It's Time for Inter-Marriages: Superiority has no place in Zanzibar, warns Karume," May 2, 1970, No. 1873.

prevent potential hostilities in the future. While these readers main critique lay with Asian communities who would shun their daughters if they were to marry an African, they emphasized the need for free love.[35] Other readers, however, directly seized upon the political overreach:

> "My personal views about marriage (and this includes inter-marriage) are based on (a) mutual understanding, warmth, affection and love between the couple; (b) a desirable and regulated form of ones [SIC] life under the title 'husband and wife.' [...] Politics cannot be the basis for marriage. One loses freedom of will if one is compelled be the state to marry so and so. [...]"[36]

The range of these responses suggests that there was a high awareness of the prevailing division along "racial" lines in the country, but also an articulate sense of personal freedom. Although it was not the focus of all correspondences, there was an overwhelming notion that the personal freedom to choose a partner for marriage was a prerequisite for any larger social development. While readers problematized the continued influence of "race" on positions in the society, several contributors argued that the problem lay with the older generations of both Asian and African parents.[37]

> "Forcing a young man like me to marry an Indian girl just because of trying to make other wanzee [old men] feel that there is equality in Tanzania, is really to give me a burden. Old beliefs on the part of the Indians are disappearing very quickly and the young generation is patient and steady about the whole thing. If only the wanzee can leave us alone to pursue our studies and to build our nation into a prosperous socialist Tanzania, inter-marriage will come, it is no problem at the moment."[38]

While the author explicitly attributed stereotypes to the older generation of Asians, he regarded the entire problem as that of the older generation, which would end with the younger generation. The real problem, in his view, were old men forcing the younger generation of Asians and Africans to live according to their direction. While this letter only cryptically criticized political

---

35 See e.g.:Baraka Majaljwa, "Big Laws for Big Heads," *The Nationalist*, May 6, 1970, No. 1876; Mary Kimisha, "Racial Harmony," *The Nationalist*, May 7, 1970, No. 1877.
36 Juma Shauri, "A dangerous experiment," *The Nationalist*, May 7, 1970, No. 1877.
37 See e.g.: Mrs. Munduli, "I'm an Asian but married to an African - Mrs. Munduli," *The Nationalist*, May 16, 1970, No. 1885.
38 T. J. Ndee, "Inter-marriage come through love," *The Nationalist*, May 26, 1970, No. 1893.

leadership, by September 1970, the correspondence had become openly critical of Zanzibar's revolutionary council:

> "I have been shocked to read that four girls in Zanzibar have been married off to members of the Revolutionary Council against their consent and the consent of their parents. This is a very backward step indeed, which will spoil the name of Tanzania abroad. According to the speeches at the mass rally in Zanzibar, there is a Marriage Decree [...]. [...] Tanzania has earned for herself a name of being progressive and wanting to build a socialist society. How will her many socialist friends reconcile these feudalist socialist intentions?"[39]

The letter suggests that Zanzibar's policy-making was relatively obscure, as the only points of reference were speeches made at a mass rally. The author, who was from the university, would have likely had good means to be informed, and yet appears to have had only very limited information on the proceedings in Zanzibar. Despite Zanzibar's seeming detachment, international media had seized upon forced marriages as well,[40] which concerned an author in *the Nationalist*. Against the international background, he pointed not only to the risks for Tanzania, but also to the contradictions of the marriage laws for the socialist aspirations of Tanzania.

A few weeks later, Karume was said to have announced the end of the policy.[41] While the article did not elaborate on political decision-making or everyday life in Zanzibar, it is likely that international and national pressure in the public sphere resulted in the elimination of the policy. The period between the report on Karume's May Day speech and the claim of abandonment of the law in early October 1970 demonstrates that the readers were able to utilize the paper as a platform of exchange of thoughts and information, and to express political critique. In fact, one reader actively sought dialogue with Asians on the subject:

---

39 H. B. Abdulla, "Inter-Racial Marriages," *The Nationalist*, September 26, 1970, No. 1999.
40 *The Times*, "Girls forced from homes in Zanzibar." September 19, 1970, No. 57975, accessed January 7, 2019, https://gdc.galegroup.com/gdc/artemis/NewspapersDetailsPage/NewspapersDetailsWindow?disableHighlighting=false&displayGroupName=DVI-Newspapers&docIndex=5&source=fullList&prodId=TTDA&mode=view&limiter=DA+11 9700101+-+119701231&display-query=OQE+karume&contentModules=&action=e&sortBy=&windowstate=normal&currPage=1&dviSelectedPage=&scanId=&query=OQE+karume&search_within_results=&p=TTDA&catId=&u=ubtib&displayGroups=&documentId=GALE%7CCS68645683&activityType=BasicSearch&failOverType=&commentary=.
41 *The Nationalist*, "End to forced marriages," October 3, 1970, No 2005.

"My dear Asian comrades, come out in the open on this subject. The call from the First Vice President was made in the open quite a few days ago. Speak the truth without fear according to our country's Constitution which allows everyone to do so. [...]"[42]

Apparently, such calls were heard by the newspaper, which soon thereafter published an interview with an Asian woman who was married to an African. While the interview confirmed some obstacles, such as parents' initial reluctance to the relationship, it emphasized that the cultural gap between African and Asian Tanzanians was small.[43] The "interracial" relationship described in the interview certainly did not reflect the experience of most Tanzanians in the social world, but it was an example of the relaxation of "racial" relations in the public sphere since the Arusha Declaration.

"It Was a Pan-African Moment" – the Decline of an African American Presence in the Discourse

The Arusha Declaration expressed the great significance of African unity, and therefore strategically strove for collaboration with all African parties.[44] The months after the declaration saw a surge of pan-African solidarity. However, while the declaration's emphasis on "non-racialism" defused "racial" tensions between Africans and Asians in Tanzania's public sphere, it also curtailed the passionate support of African Americans that had emerged in the newspaper in the mid-1960s, which now minimized the significance of "race" as a category.

Yet, in the social world, interactions and sometimes collaboration with African Americans became more frequent. At the United Nations, Tanzania's ambassador Malecela backed the Student Nonviolent Coordinating Committee (SNCC) as it transformed to meet the challenges of continued discrimination and the Vietnam War. As a result, SNCC's James Forman visited Tanzania as a guest of TANU, and was impressed by the optimistic spirit of the society.[45] Furthermore, SNCC gained a presence in the public sphere, as they explained the developments around Black Power and the escalating violence in African

---

42 John Bundala, "Let's intermarry but...," *The Nationalist*, May 6, 1970, No. 1876.
43 See: Mrs. Munduli, "I'm an Asian."
44 See: Markle, *A Motorcycle*, 50-51.
45 See: Ibid. 51-53.

American neighborhoods in the United States.[46] However, the interview and Moore's article did not elicit any response in the newspaper.

Conversely, a visit by Stokely Carmichael[47] in late 1967 strongly resonated with Tanzania's press. While his openly critical remarks were perceived with alert by TANU's leadership, the press' reaction was divided, with the *Tanganyika Standard* voicing stern criticism and *the Nationalist* showing strong support for Carmichael's critique of the luxurious style of some African liberation leaders.[48] Carmichael's remarks undermined the diplomatic efforts Tanzania's government pursued after the Arusha Declaration, namely collaboration with all African parties for the purpose of African unity. But, his critique of the accumulation of wealth not only resonated with the Arusha Declaration's goal of a classless society, but also with readers who resented members of the Liberation movements. Such concerns had not been voiced since the introduction of the immigration laws in 1965, but resurged a few months after the publication of the declaration:

> "I would like to point out to this woman and the rest of the guests that they are already being well looked after, they are living much better than an average Tanzanian who has to pay taxes. [...] Further I would like to suggest to the Government that in pursuance of the policy of socialism and self-reliance, freedom fighters who have nothing to do in Dar es Salaam should be offered some work to stop them tracing good and bad Tanzanians around the bars of Dar es Salaam.[49]

The Chief Representative of the South West Africa People's Organisation (SWAPO), Peter Nanyemba, refuted the claim, arguing that there are "certain political charlatans, masquerading as "freedom fighters" and highly capable of such idiotic indiscretion."[50] Ms. Sichaly's reference to keywords of the Arusha Declaration – "socialism" and "self-reliance" – suggests that the Declaration encouraged her to criticize freedom fighters. However, since there

---

46 See: Ferdinand Ruhinda, "Focus: On Black Power," *The Nationalist*, August 13, 1967, No. 1034; Richard B. Moore, "Reaction to riots against racism," *The Nationalist*, August 18, 1967, No. 1038.
47 Carmichael changed his name to Kwame Ture a few years later. As he was then still known as Stokely Carmichael, and also the interviewees mention him by his former name, I did not adapt his changed name in this work.
48 See: Ibid. 62-68.
49 (Miss) R. L. Sichaly *The Nationalist*, May 8, 1967, No. 950.
50 Peter Nanyemba, "Freedom Fighters," *The Nationalist*, May 12, 1967, No. 954.

was no drastic incident, which would have aroused public anger, it is likely that freedom fighters had been viewed with suspicion in the social world for a long time. Accordingly, it is unsurprising that Carmichael's remarks did not fall on deaf ears and were picked up in letters during his visit:

> "I entirely agree with Mr. Carmichael, the Black Power leader on his views concerning "Freedom Fighters." These people should not be allowed to make any noise here without taking any practical measures on the battle spot. It's time the Government exposed these traitors of African Cause of Freedom [SIC]. Joshua Nkomo is on the spot, so is Sithole."[51]

It is noteworthy that the reader interpreted Carmichael's critique as directed towards certain organizations and not individuals from all Liberation movements. The specific addressees of the reader's disdain were leaders of the African National Congress (ANC) and the Zimbabwe African People's Union (ZAPU), both of which were aligned with the Soviet Union. This contrasts with a much tamer reader opinion that was published a few months earlier. In this letter, Chenge wa Chenge, who would soon publish articles as a journalist for *the Nationalist*, raised the issue of unfocused freedom fighters. In response to an escalated crisis within the Pan Africanist Congress of South Africa (PAC), he urged freedom fighters to quit ideological debates that he considered beyond their horizon, such as the Sino-Soviet split, and close ranks for liberation.[52] This suggests that some readers viewed the liberation struggle partially in the context of the Sino-Soviet split.

While several letters targeted freedom fighters in 1967, they were quite distinct in their specific criticism. While Chenge's letter used the PAC leadership crisis as an example of misguided priorities of Liberation movements in general, the other letters questioned freedom fighters' moral integrity. After Carmichael's comments, these comments focused on the ANC and the ZAPU. The antipathy towards the ANC in comments in the public sphere may be understood through a closer look at developments in the social world.

While the PAC faced a leadership crisis that even led to a shutdown of its offices in July 1967, it had long been a prominent organizer of rallies and talks

---

51   A. S. Mponda, "Carmichael is right," *The Nationalist*, November 7, 1967, No. 1107; see also: Revolutionary, "Freedom fighters," *The Nationalist*, November 17, 1967, No. 1116.
52   See: Chenge, wa, Chenge, "Freedom Fighters," *The Nationalist*, July 31, 1967, No. 1022.

in Dar es Salaam.[53] Furthermore, Stokely Carmichael and Miriam Makeba, who was very popular in Tanzania,[54] both met with the PAC.[55] This presence of the PAC in the city as well as its affiliation with prominent African and African American figures may have increased the PAC's reputation among readers of *the Nationalist*.

While African Liberation movements maintained a strong presence in the newspaper, they vanished from comments in the readers' page. Even dramatic local events such as the assassination of Walter Mondlane of the Frente de Libertação de Moçambique (Frelimo) on February 3rd, 1969 only sparked reaction from the staff and editor, not from readers.[56] African American issues, in contrast, evoked a range of responses by readers after the Arusha Declaration. This was possibly aided by a greater presence of African Americans in the social world. Marjorie Mbilinyi, who went with her boyfriend Simon Mbilinyi to Tanzania in late 1966, observed:

> "I came at a time when a lot of young people were coming to Tanzania, drawn by the whole Arusha Declaration, socialism, self-reliance. And then I met a lot of African American folks, who chose to remain here, chose to request asylum… in some cases they were on the FBI list or whatever in the States and Mwalimu would say: 'let them remain, let them have residency.' He had a very progressive position vis-à-vis the diaspora – well African Americans as well as the… you know it was a Pan African moment."[57]

Her reminiscence confirms the general attraction of Tanzania's non-aligned socialist path, a promising alternative in the Cold War which had turned hot in many proxy wars. More specifically, it shows how discernible pan-African

---

53 See: Azaria Mbughuni, "Tanzania and the Pan African Quest for Unity, Freedom, and Independence in East, Central, and Southern Africa: The Case of the Pan African Freedom Movement for East and the Central Africa/Pan African Freedom Movement for East Central and South Africa," *The Journal of Pan African Studies* 7, no. 4 (2014): 221-222; *The Nationalist*, "Intensify Struggle for African Liberation," May 8, 1967, No. 944.

54 See e.g.: S. A. Sawa, "Action Line," *The Nationalist*, January 23, 1967, No. 861; *The Nationalist*, "Makeba to visit Dar for two performances," January 10, 1967, No. 851.

55 See: Kwame Ture, *Ready for Revolution: The Life and Times of Stokely Carmichael*, with the assistance of Ekwueme Michael Thelwell (New York, NY: Charles Scribner's Sons, 2003), 633, 636-639.

56 See e.g.: Editor, "Dr. Mondlane," *The Nationalist*, February 7, 1969, No. 1494; *The Nationalist*, "Dr. Mondlane Killed," February 4, 1969, No. 1491.

57 Marjorie Mbilinyi, interview by Harald Barre.

solidarity – continental and trans-Atlantic – was. These developments were mirrored in *the Nationalist*. Three months after Carmichael's visit, an editorial explicitly emphasized the need to support African Americans in their struggle diplomatically, and in practice:

> "But there is a second way in which African countries must prepare to help the African Americans. As the latter struggle to assert their rights they will meet intense white resistance. In the course of this struggle there will be some African Americans who will elect at some point to seek refuge among their black brothers on the continent. The likelihood is that the number of such refugees will increase as the summers in the United States get hotter. African countries are obligated to offer refuge to these brothers who elect to find peace and humanity among their black brethren."[58]

The editorial may have been the result of African American activists' lobbying efforts. However, it also likely responded to the growing appearance of African American refugees. While most cases were brief episodes that occasionally shed a dubious light on the individual African American,[59] the case of Calvin Cobb captured the newspaper's attention over an extended period of time. Only a month before Stokely Carmichael's visit, the case tested Tanzania's position towards African Americans. Having fled the U.S. because of fraud allegations, which he claimed were fabricated, Cobb sought refuge in Tanzania. However, due to the lack of an extradition agreement with the United States and Cobb's pledge to become a devoted Tanzanian citizen, he was granted the right to stay.[60] Compared to the mid-1960s, contacts with African Americans in the social world, as well as appearances of African Americans in the public sphere, had skyrocketed – not only in quantity, but also in quality: African Americans were now described as "black brethren" in an editorial of the party newspaper. Furthermore, as the episode of Cobb showed, Tanzania was even

---

58   Editor, "African Americans," *The Nationalist*, March 1, 1968, No. 1203.
59   *The Nationalist*, "Another American disappears," August 28, 1967, No. 1046; *The Nationalist*, "Expelled from Tanzania," October 17, 1966, No. 778.
60   Cobbs reappeared in the Daily News as the coach for Tanzania's Olympic boxing team. See e.g.: Temmy Sithole, "A test for our boxers," *The Daily News*, July 6, 1972, No. 62. However, in 1974, he returned to the United States. claiming that he wanted to face the charges, but left for Tanzania shortly thereafter. *The Long Island Traveler*, "At Press Time," December 19, 1974, No. 10; *The Long Island Traveler*, "Cobb Back In Tanzania," May 15, 1975. There he was arrested as a prohibited immigrant and ultimately handed over to the U.S. government.

willing to take diplomatically strong stances against U.S. interests in support of African Americans.

Yet, this development would soon be overturned. Despite the significant change in attitude in the newspaper coverage, African American issues were still overshadowed by reports on the Vietnam War, or on regional issues such as liberation struggles or the conflicts revolving around Asians living in African countries. Almost in synchrony with the increasing rejection of anti-Asian resentment, "race" as a category of solidarity declined a year after the Arusha Declaration. After the assassination of Martin Luther King Jr., African American news reports in *the Nationalist* declined and more focus was placed on local events. Sporadic reports about ongoing riots in the United States continued to appear.[61] This development steadily continued from 1967 to 1970.

The discontinuity of "race" as a category of solidarity may be explained with attempts of TANU to downplay its significance. After all, it was not part of the concept of "non-racial" socialism. However, the rapid decline of an African American presence in the newspaper may also reflect substantial gaps between African American and East African social concerns. George Hajivayanis and Salha Hamdani, who began to establish ties with the university in those years, related no personal significance to the African American struggle:

"G: [...] you had others coming in and one of them was [Stokely] Carmichael. He came and gave a talk. But I wasn't there by then. He gave it all and electrified the university campus. Completely electrified it [*laughing*].
H.: And you...
G.: I was not there.
H.: Was it somehow otherwise perceived in the media or like did you...?
G.: It was [...] in the media.
H.: And how did you [...] perceive it at the time, you personally?
G.: No we didn't really feel about it as such because we were not in Dar es Salaam.
H.: Yes, ok, so it was more like in....
S.: Yeah, well [...] African Americans, I mean they were powerful in the US and in other areas, like in maybe West Africa. [...]

---

61 See e.g.: *The Nationalist*, "Afro-American revolutionary visits Tanzania," May 25, 1968, No. 1275.

> G.: I mean the Black Panthers, [...] a lot of them came to Tanzania after they were killed in America. [...]
> S.: African American politics we're not so... [...] They did not impact so much on us. We already had [...] other issues [...]
> G.: I think Vietnam was the Turning Point. [...] Not black Americans."[62]

The quote suggests that the socialization in independent Tanzania, the exposure to socialist literature, and the connection to China and Julius Nyerere's "non-racial" politics had shifted students' foci away from an explanation of social inequality along "racial" lines. While the presence of vibrant personalities such as Carmichael inspired local debates, they did not overshadow the solidarity with class-based movements such as Vietnam's National Liberation Front. Even though opposition against the war certainly constituted a common denominator with African American activists, the Vietnam War dwarfed the experience of African Americans in Tanzania's public sphere. Furthermore, East Asia had a particular significance in Tanzania's strategy of non-alignment and, as noted in the previous chapter, China – North Vietnam's supporter – not only built the TanZam railway, but also brought Maoist literature to Tanzania. Lastly, the Arusha Declaration's strong emphasis on socialism that sought to defuse "racial" tensions amongst citizens of Tanzania inevitably put the significance of "race" into perspective altogether.

In fact, despite an evidently growing presence of African Americans in Tanzania, in 1969, African American culture increasingly became the target of an escalating debate surrounding African culture and fashion. While the country experienced its first indecent clothing campaign, Operation Vijana,[63] an African American music teacher in Dar es Salaam tried to reach out to Radio Tanzania:

> "I heard the announcer say that he would be playing 'soul Music.' This made me very happy because I am an African-American and after hearing so much European and white American music on Radio Tanzania, I was very excited to get a chance to hear some of our music. So you can imagine my disappointment when the following recording was by Tim Jones, a British Performer [...]. [...] I would like to clear up the confusion about the term 'soul Music.' This term is part of the whole 'soul Language' which has evolved from the

---

62 Salha Hamdani and George G. Hajivayanis, interview by Harald Barre.
63 See chapter 4.3.

Black Revolution in the USA. [...] It is a direct descendent of African music [...]."[64]

Unlike the request of Mr. Sampant to restore the Hindustani program in Radio Tanzania in 1966,[65] Ms. Shabaz's letter did not create any immediate reaction. Only half a year later, an editorial first mentioned "this growing habit of pupils indulging in 'digging soul' at Saturday and Sunday afternoons [...]."[66] The brief paragraph in the editorial, as well as the flurry of responses triggered by it, suggests that soul music had captured Dar es Salaam's social world. While the editor and other readers criticized soul music as a tool of "foreign elements," with one letter even calling for a ban of soul, other readers defended soul as revolutionary and genuinely African.[67] The exchanges made up a good portion of articles dealing with African Americans in general and demonstrate how visible – and audible – African American culture had become in Tanzania's social world. However, the critics of soul music implied a strong fear of commercial co-option of young Tanzanians, which was evidently not shared by its supporters, including African American residents of Tanzania.

Two months into the debate in *the Nationalist*, Coast Regional Commissioner Songambele – who had spearheaded the term 'paper citizen' in 1967 – announced a ban on soul music. While *the Standard* was first to report the ban, it did not back it.[68] This, however, may be due to the fact that *the Standard* was not yet nationalized.[69] Therefore, it was unlikely to support a restrictive government measure. *The Nationalist*, conversely, praised the decision, and emphasized its critique of soul music in an editorial and the column "Fighting Talk."[70] On this harsh note, the formerly vibrant relations to African Americans almost faded from the public sphere. *The Nationalist*'s support of Songambele's initiative is remarkable. Even though the editor had implicitly rejected Songambele's alienation of Indians, it now whole-heartedly supported his ban

---

64 Maisha Shabaz, "Soul Music," *The Nationalist*, January 16, 1969, No. 1474.
65 See chapter 3.1.
66 Editor, "Good Example," *The Nationalist*, July 30, 1969, No. 1641.
67 See e.g.: Onlooker, "Those soul diggers," *The Nationalist*, September 24, 1969, No. 1689; Monday Wamunza *The Nationalist*, September 24, 1969, No. 1689; Green Guard, "Those 'Soul' Diggers," *The Nationalist*, August 29, 1969, No. 1667.
68 See: Ivaska, *Cultured States*, 69.
69 See: Sturmer, *The Media History*, 122.
70 See: Editor, "Soul Digging," *The Nationalist*, November 15, 1969, No. 1734; Age, "Fighting Talk: The soulless souls," *The Nationalist*, November 22, 1969, No. 1740.

of African American culture. The newspaper's position may be explained by Nyerere's philosophy of "non-racialism": "race" was neither to be construed as a category of solidarity nor of differentiation.

In the social world, however, soul music and African American culture remained popular in the following years. While African American activists openly opposed the rigid measure, they felt free to debate it and play soul music in their homes.[71] Furthermore, soul did not stop being significant as a cultural reference point in Dar es Salaam's nightlife.[72] Despite TANUs intervention to quell African American political conceptualizations in Tanzania's public sphere, African American culture in Tanzania's continued to impact urban everyday life.

Tanzania's relationship with African Americans was characterized by a climax in 1967. Increasing social contacts had highlighted similarities of the struggle faced by Tanzanians and African Americans, which were accordingly projected in the media. However, while the Arusha Declaration's emphasis on a "non-racial" class struggle slowly defused tensions with "Asians" in the public sphere, it also crippled the "racial" solidarity with African Americans. African Liberation movements, however, remained almost omnipresent in the newspaper, with the curious exception of the letters to the editor. While complaints against Liberation movements in 1967 suggest some friction within the social world of Dar es Salaam, the readers' section remained overwhelmingly silent. This may have been due to decisions of the editors not to stir public opinion against the supported movements, and to only exert pressure through editorials. However, it could also reflect the acceptance of African Liberation movements in Dar es Salaam. In any case, the pan-African solidarity practiced by TANU in the late 1960s no longer included "race" in its concept. This constituted a steep departure from the ideological origins of African group cohesion in the colonial era.

4.2 Reforms on the Hill – the Pretext

As noted in chapter 3.2, the 1966 student demonstration was attributed with having influenced the Arusha Declaration, which consequently impacted student life. However, the vague and often ambivalent direction expressed in the

---

71 See: Markle, *A Motorcycle*, 126-127.
72 See: Callaci, *Street Archives*, 114.

declaration led to a rocky road, which was characterized by innovative teaching and research work, but also by sharp government intervention. Education, particularly at the university, evolved in its significance for Tanzania's nation building project. The university became a hub of interaction on a trans- and international scale. As the previous section has shown, it was often university students who would contribute their opinions, shaped by social interactions on campus, to the debates in the newspaper.

Days after announcing the Arusha Declaration, President Nyerere sought to mobilize Tanzania's youth, referring to them as 'Green Guards.'[73] This was quickly followed by a three-piece article *Education for Socialism and Self-reliance*, which called for a change in school curricula to emphasize an appreciation of physical work. In it, journalist Che Ng'ombo blamed colonialism for conditioning students of higher education towards elitism. Similarly, school books needed to be Africanized, as most were written by expatriates. Furthermore, the author emphasized that Peace Corps teachers were to be removed from primary schools.[74] While the latter aspect affirms the fear of being infiltrated by agents of Cold War super powers, the former points to the urgent role of the university to develop these text books. Furthermore, the continued impact of colonial values in the education system per se became an explicit point of criticism.

A few weeks later, *the Nationalist* published President Nyerere's thoughts on Education for Self-Reliance. In the four-page long article, he discussed some aspects already raised by Ng'ombo, such as the impact of colonial education on the country. However, in contrast to Ng'ombo, Nyerere's article contained no reference to pan-Africanism, and focused on Tanzanian society exclusively. He emphasized that colonial educational politics had not only been inadequate as they had left the country with insufficient skilled local personnel, but also inappropriate as they had been based on "race." However,

---

73 See: *The Nationalist*, "Be Vigilant Call to Green Guards," February 8, 1967, No. 875. The term appears to be inspired by China's Red Guards, which would affirm the significance of China to Tanzania's socio-political vision.

74 See: Che Ng'ombo, "Education for Socialism and Self-Reliance," *The Nationalist*, February 10, 1967, No. 877; Che Ng'ombo, "Education for Socialism and Self-Reliance: Part II," *The Nationalist*, February 16, 1967, No. 882. A third article situated the Arusha Declaration in the pan-African struggle and emphasized the aesthetics of "racial" pride. This can be seen as a precursor to a debate surrounding fashion and "racial" pride a year later – see: Che Ng'ombo, "Education for Socialism and Self-Reliance," *The Nationalist*, February 24, 1967, No. 889 and discussion in chapter 5.3.

he took pride in the achievements of his government such as vastly expanding education, tackling racism, and advancing African self-consciousness. Regarding the latter, he lauded the University College of Dar es Salaam (UCD), which had provided materials on African history and pointed to the significance of national dances and songs, as well as civic classes.[75] It is remarkable that Nyerere explicitly pointed to the colonial state's destitute educational system, the concurring dependency of the Tanzanian nation on expatriates, as well as the destructive force of racism. The Arusha Declaration and Education for Self-Reliance were attempts to obtain independence from contemporary world powers.[76] However, perpetuated dependency due to people's socialization in the colonial state's value system was a central point of criticism. Therefore, Nyerere viewed education in general, and the university in particular, as key to achieving true independence.

While the government's decision to remove students in late 1966 had shocked young people, the reforms that accompanied the Arusha Declaration were welcomed by them.[77] In fact, George Hajivayanis remembered that students of higher education from certain backgrounds were particularly enthusiastic about the goals the Arusha Declaration outlined:

> "I had read Marx and I had read Mao and [...] so on. Especially at the A level, I became quite radical. And I was a student [...] when the Arusha Declaration was declared [...]. So we also carried these [posters] that will say "away with capitalism" and so on. So we participated, students in Arusha. Ilboru Secondary School in Arusha, my school, [...] we all supported Ujamaa. Because we came from [...] not well-to-do families [...]. So by the time I came to university, I was half baked already. And [...] when I came to the university I became communist. I radicalized. I remember my uncle – my uncle was a priest – he had given me a big cross. I wanted to throw it away but I felt, well, it was my uncle who gave it to me. He was a priest, father Otto Frech, I took it and I gave it to my cousin."[78]

His recollection affirms the significance students' discussion of both political theories as well as their support of the Arusha Declaration. Furthermore,

---

75 See: Nyerere, Julius K. "Education for Self-reliance." *The Nationalist*, March 10, 1967. No. 901.
76 See: Melchiorre, "Building Nations," 147-149.
77 See: Melchiorre, "Building Nations," 198-199.
78 Salha Hamdani and George G. Hajivayanis, interview by Harald Barre.

the changes in socialization in the school system and policy reforms not only influenced their paths in the university. It also put social norms brought by European missionaries in perspective, as the giving away of the cross symbolized. In contrast to radicalizing youth in Western Europe and the United States, Tanzanian students came overwhelmingly from poorer backgrounds, and they considered their government to be an ally in revolutionizing the nation. However, as this section will show, the seemingly smooth convergence of the independent society and the government's vision turned out to be a tense and occasionally conflicted process.

The reform process turned out to be complicated. A fundamental problem was that the university was dependent on foreign personnel. A year after the events, the head of the UDC's History Department, Terrence Ranger, published *the Emerging Themes of African History*, which was based on lectures at a conference hosted at the university in 1965. His introduction, which was certainly written under the impression of the changes debated after the Arusha Declaration, admitted that in 1965, the question of African history as being "sufficiently *African*" [in italics in publication] was not discussed far enough.[79] Despite Ranger's critical reflection, the university had, as Nyerere's article shows, built African history research from the ground up, and thereby contributed to building a nation on an African foundation.

Yet, the challenge of making African history "sufficiently African" – or rather making Tanzanian higher education "Tanzanian" – was at the heart of the rhetoric of Nyerere's critique after the Arusha Declaration. Being convinced that the British educational system alienated students from the surrounding society early on, Nyerere urged reforms in education by including elements of practical work into society – ideally in agriculture and maintaining their facilities. This was meant for not only students in primary and secondary education, but also university students who needed to establish projects practicing self-reliance.[80] A university commission to examine changes was established a day after Nyerere's statement. While not naming any individuals, *the Nationalist* highlighted that a group of lecturers,

---

79 See: Terrance Ranger, ed., *Emerging Themes of African History: Proceedings of the International Congress of African Historians held at University College, Dar es Salaam, October 1965* (London: Heinemann, 1968), ix-xi.
80 See: Nyerere, "Education for Self-Reliance," 6-7.

soon to be known as the Committee of Nine,[81] had proposed major structural changes to the university. The suggested reforms included hiring practices to be focused on East Africa and the utilization of vacation for extra-curricular student activities. While the article named several high ranking members of TANU that would speak at the conference, it displayed university staff as the driving force.[82] *The Nationalist* went on to report about Minister Babu's call to use the university to overcome the socio-cultural amnesia which colonialism had brought upon the society in Tanzania, and build a classless society.[83] Compared to reactions after the demonstration six months earlier, the newspaper's tone on education was sympathetic to students, and seemed to leave the authority to shape decisions in the hands of the lecturers.

However, the newspaper's portrayal of the proceedings of the reforms did not entirely reflect the conditions during the conference: By ensuring that it was overrepresented at the conference, TANU was able to lay down its vision of reform, namely, an augmented role of TANU and its sub-organizations, the TANU Youth League (TYL) and Umoja wa Wanawake (UWT).[84] Thus, although the Arusha Declaration promised academic freedom, the reforms of the university threatened tighter control by the party. Former lecturers remembered that controversial debates were encouraged, but within parameters that were predetermined by the party. These limitations were ensured by TANU's overwhelming presence at the conference.[85] This direction of the post-Arusha reforms was in line with Nyerere's vision of a one-party state. However, in light

---

81 Although the reforms in academia after the Arusha Declaration were advanced by foreign intellectuals of the Committee of Nine, other foreigners viewed the reforms and the international leftist imprint as highly problematic. In his article *Tanzaphilia*, Kenyan political scientist Ali Mazrui, then teaching at Makerere College, expressed his concern that academic freedom was being given up. The University College of Dar es Salaam, he argued, had evolved from an institution to analyzing socialism into one that promoted socialism. See: Mazrui, "Tanzaphilia," 25-26.

82 See: *The Nationalist*, "Reform 'Varsity urge Lecturers," March 11, 1967, No. 902.

83 *The Nationalist*, "Turn College into Socialist Institution: Dar two-day education meeting ends," March 13, 1967, No. 903.

84 See: Bertram B.B. Mapunda, "University of Dar es Salaam's immediate response to Arusha Declaration," in Kimambo; Mapunda; Lawi, *In Search of Relevance*, 179-182.

85 See: McCracken, "Terry Ranger," 178. Mapunda's argument and McCracken's recollection suggest that the line of conflict between the Committee of Nine lecturers and remaining staff was less clear than suggested by Melchiorre, who mostly identified the reform phase as a struggle between liberals, a majority of moderate socialists and Marxists in the committee.

of the concern the 1966 expulsion of students had caused, many lecturers were likely uneasy about TANU's stronger involvement on campus.

Yet, the Arusha Declaration was also utilized by staff to articulate opposition to the government. *The Nationalist* reported that Vice-Principle Honeybone urged the government to reinstate the students dismissed from the university after the 1966 student demonstration. They, he argued, "were not being allowed to play [a] full and proper role in the current national mobilisation and without them the UCD could not play its full and proper role in the service of the nation." The topic was not permitted for discussion during the conference to reform the university,[86] which hinted at TANU's attempt to control processes at the university more rigidly. However, it is remarkable that the party newspaper published such positions that were sceptical of party decisions, even though the critique clearly had to be articulated in the confines of the Arusha Declaration.

Education for Self-Reliance: Debates and Activism

The immediate months after the reform were shaped by contradictory developments. While the reforms gave academics rhetorical structure to argue for changes, the reform process itself was shaped by tight party control. Beyond the public expression of opinions, the progressive staff utilized the declaration to overhaul existing institutional structures and implemented reforms that emboldened academic debates. The goal of obtaining independence from colonial values and world views boosted this development. *The Nationalist* announced that the conference had "recommended a course of political education to be compulsory for Tanzanian students, and emphasis should be laid 'on the teaching of Tanzanian socialism against the African and international background.'"[87] This common course initially faced logistical shortcomings and was unpopular with lecturers and students. However, students and lec-

---

86   *The Nationalist*, "Professor Clarfies Remarks on Students," March 13, 1967, No. 903. Mr. Honeybone's argument does not seem to have been that outrageous as Nyerere agreed to permit the students back to the subsequent term. See: John Carthew, "Life Imitates Art: The Student Expulsion in Dar es Salaam, October 1966, as a Dramatic Ritual," *The Journal of Modern African Studies* 18, no. 3 (1980): 541, accessed February 6, 2019, https://www.jstor.org/stable/160370

87   *The Nationalist*, "Stress on Socialism at the University," March 15, 1967, No. 905.

turers worked on turning the program into a high-level course.[88] The development of a common course likely benefited from a pioneering spirit among the staff, which was already exploring inter-disciplinary work before the declaration.[89] Thus, while the university was urged to reform itself institutionally, its social composition was not a product of the Arusha Declaration, but of the motivation of the international staff.

Walter Rodney, who would soon be known as one of the crucial protagonists in the post-Arusha reform process, recalled that he was drawn to Tanzania as Ghana no longer provided a pan-African harbour after the coup against Kwame Nkrumah in 1966.[90] His reminiscence highlights the mobilizing effect of pan-Africanism on the pre-Arusha era in Tanzania. Hired by Terence Ranger in 1966, his colleagues remembered Rodney's skill in discussing African diaspora and Marxism.[91] While Rodney was not a local scholar, he had evolved out of a pan-African Marxist intellectual network that included luminaries such as C.L.R. James.[92] With this background, he did not only contribute to the leftist intellectual fervour that characterized the department of history, but also brought a pan-African perspective to the university. The university had a vital role in a nation that sought to remain independent and unified, as the Cold War and colonial wars tore into Africa and other regions of the global South.

Rodney hit the nerve of many students when he came to Dar es Salaam. The president was not alone in his concern over students being motivated by individual profit over the common good of the nation. After his graduation in 1970, Yoweri Museveni recalled the contrast between Tanzania's pan-Africanist image and the indifference towards pan-Africanism he experienced among students upon arrival in Dar es Salaam. He recalled frustration with

---

88 See: Issa G. Shivji, "Lionel Cliffe, 1936–2013: A comradely scholar in Nyerere's nationalist Tanzania," *Review of African Political Economy* 41, no. 140 (2014): 285, accessed January 25, 2019, https://doi.org/10.1080/03056244.2014.873162.

89 See: Hamilton, Marybeth. "Terence Ranger: Life as Historiography." Accessed January 28, 2019, http://www.historyworkshop.org.uk/terence-ranger-life-as-historiography/;McCracken, "Terry Ranger," 178.

90 See: Walter Rodney, "The Black Scholar Interviews: Walter Rodney," *The Black Scholar* 6, no. 3 (1974): 38, accessed September 19, 2014, http://www.jstor.org/stable/41066348.

91 See: Hamilton, "Terence Ranger" McCracken, "Terry Ranger," 178.

92 See: Clairmont Chung, ed., *Walter A. Rodney: A Promise of Revolution* (New York: Monthly Review Press, 2012), accessed May 2, 2018, http://site.ebrary.com/lib/alltitles/docDetail.action?docID=10659285, 9, 20.

this situation and the lack of alternative to the TYL. It was the reason why students formed the University Students African Revolutionary Front (USARF) shortly before Stokely Carmichael's visit.[93] Marjorie Mbilinyi recollected the beginning of her career at the university in the same vein:

> "The university, it wasn't just about gender, it was about race, it was about concepts. Because there was a real growing tension between any leftist movement to promote some form of socialism and mainstream elements in the university. The department of education was a good example ... it had some very conservative people. And these were not the Brits only; but also young Tanzanians coming back from USA with their PhDs. They were hostile to any form of [...] Marxist rhetoric."[94]

Her quote reiterates the significance of expatriate staff that remained in the university administration as well as that of African students returning from the U.S., whose views of society were distinctly influenced by capitalism. While British administrators may have been influenced by a colonial outlook, African graduates coming home from abroad brought Cold War mentality into the country. Their concepts seemed to conflict with the rhetoric of the Arusha Declaration, but, as Aminzade argues, resonated with the higher levels of the country's administration. Whereas the party was more supportive of rapid Africanization according revolutionary concepts, the officials in the administration were more strongly socialized by British higher education, and more accepting of Western social concepts.[95] USARF was one group that permitted pan-Africanist and leftist students at the UCD to organize and discuss despite the pre-dominance of an unsympathetic administration. However, as George Hajivayanis called to mind, lecturers were also seen within the framework of the Cold War and colonialism:

> "[...] the most interesting guy of them all was this Guayanese [...] called Walter Rodney. He was part of the student movement, he, in fact, matured in Tanzania. So [...] there was very often at the University of Dar es Salaam there was this racial thinking coming up very often, you know. You know you had [...] these lecturers who had a different language than the Ujamaa language and they were from the West, it brought in some tension. And Rodney from

---

93 See: Yoweri Museveni, "Activism at the Hill," in Hirji, *Cheche*, 12-14.
94 Marjorie Mbilinyi, interview by Harald Barre.
95 See: Aminzade, *Race, Nation, and Citizenship*, 119, 156.

the Caribbean was closer to students and there were conflicts even sometimes between lecturers themselves. [...] because [...] there was this tension because of their colonial history I mean which you could not discard. [...] There was a Department of English and Foreign Languages. So when we all met, we said no we are going to have the department of foreign languages. English as a foreign language. Before it was a language now it's a foreign language. They just couldn't believe it: 'What do you mean! How can English be foreign?' 'Because English is foreign. Here we speak Swahili.'"[96]

His recollection suggests that Rodney's Guyanese background made him more appealing to students in and around USARF, and that conversely, lecturers from "the West" were seen as perpetuators of colonial structures. The example of the "Department of English and Foreign Languages" demonstrates a collision of different perceptions, with local students understanding the significance of colonially introduced languages as a means of power, and the lecturers showing no consciousness or concern for the problem.

USARF was born in a context of heightened pan-African consciousness, with founding members coming from Tanzania and beyond. As explored in chapter 4.1, ideas of Black Power and its proponents galvanized the campus, including USARF. In the immediate aftermath of Stokely Carmichael's visit, USARF organized a teach-in on African Liberation. Two letters to the editor in *the Nationalist* demonstrate that pan-African solidarity and liberation were of primary concern to the movement. However, they also show that the student organization had to navigate the conflicts between different Liberation movements. While one reader praised the participation of South Africa's PAC and the Zimbabwe African National Union (ZANU), he criticized the ANC and other unnamed Liberation movements. However, in the other letter, USARF's secretary Tshabangu apologized for appearing partial regarding the Liberation movements.[97] The apology may merely reflect an attempt to maintain open channels with all Liberation movements, but it could also have been triggered by the fear of governmental backlash. Nyerere's position of collaborating with all African parties was a cornerstone of Tanzania's foreign policies; and only weeks earlier, Stokely Carmichael had caused harsh reactions by attacking other African governments.

---

96 Salha Hamdani and George G. Hajivayanis, interview by Harald Barre.
97 See: Baitu Waitu *The Nationalist*, November 27, 1967, No. 1124; O. M. Tshabangu *The Nationalist*, November 27, 1967, No. 1124.

It is likely that President Nyerere gave greater significance to preserving the reason of state, over protecting civil liberties in Tanzania, particularly with regard to diplomatic relations. This was in line with Tanzania's original policies, as detailed in chapter 2.5, but was again confirmed in the public sphere two years later. In anticipation of a youth seminar to be held at UDC, an editorial in *the Nationalist* urged:

> "For, the purpose [...] is [...] to make Africa truly independent and truly emancipated, and truly one. However, in order that this work can be correctly undertaken, it has to be completely divorced from confusion and doubts. [...] The youth of Africa have no alternative but to participate fully in the struggle for the liberation of Africa. The youth of Africa have no alternative but to fight colonialism, neo-liberalism and Imperialism. The youth of Africa have to "die a little" for the liberation of Africa."[98]

This reassuring call with militant undertones apparently resonated with the tone of the seminar, namely with the contribution of Walter Rodney, who was – in line with his pan-Africanist and Marxist background – devoted to working with African youth. His presentation evidently made such an impression, that it was printed in *the Nationalist* a few days later. In the paper, he argued that the African revolution was a long-term process. Adhering to the language of the Arusha Declaration and Nyerere's subsequent paper on Education for Self-Reliance, Rodney highlighted the ambivalent role of the educated Africans, who had gained a privileged position in the course of independence, but were socialized by Western education. His paper took a turn as he began describing the educated African elite as petty bourgeoisie who, with a few exceptions, supported capitalism. While praising the diplomatic strategy of non-alignment, Rodney alleged that a few socialist states spent more resources on "watching the so-called communists than they do watching the petty-bourgeois counter-revolutionaries." In the last columns, Rodney lauded Zanzibar as the only African country "where a neo-colonial elite has been removed from power since it hijacked the African revolution."[99] It is remarkable that the newspaper printed the lecture without any commentary, as it contained certain criticism that may very well be applied to Tanzania's administration. The newspaper's initial granting of space and lack of criticism

---

98 Editor, "Youth Seminar," *The Nationalist*, December 6, 1969, No. 1753.
99 See: Walter Rodney, "Ideology of African Revolution," *The Nationalist*, December 11, 1969, No. 1756.

may be seen as an indication of the approval Rodney's views held in the public sphere.

However, merely two days later, an editorial, supposedly written by president Nyerere himself, harshly attacked Rodney's views.[100] The editorial intimidatingly questioned whether Rodney was suggesting that the Tanzanian government should be overthrown by force. While acknowledging that Rodney had the freedom to think, he was not free to use a seminar hosted in Tanzania as a platform to promote the overthrow of any independent African government. Such rhetoric, the text went on, would cause turmoil in other nations or hatred towards Tanzania. The editorial ended with a very unsubtle reminder that Rodney was merely a guest and that revolutionary rhetoric could not veil the damaging potential of his paper.[101] The very drastic and public rebuttal of Rodney's text may have come as a surprise, because George Hajivayanis recalled the presidential support students received on some diplomatically sensitive issues:

> "And [...] even the embassies were not happy about us. For example, during the hijacking of planes, [...] I remember the Palestinians had hijacked this plane. Her name was Leila Khaled, she had hijacked a plane, you know, to announce to the world that the Palestinians were being oppressed. And we supported it. The Ambassador in Tanzania, I mean the British ambassador in Tanzania, was so upset he literally on his own wrote a letter to Nyerere to press not to allow this again. But it helped us a lot because then Nyerere was quite upset. He asked him whether he knew that Tanzania was an independent state. It was no longer a colony of Britain."[102]

His recollection suggests that students felt emboldened by the president's support against Great Britain and his tolerance of their support for Palestinian tactics. However, Nyerere himself had severed ties with Great Britain after Rhodesia's Unilateral Declaration of Independence, and the relationship between the countries had been strained ever since. Furthermore, Israel's official image had been severely damaged after the Six Day War, boosting public

---

100   See: Issa G. Shivji, "Remembering Walter Rodney," accessed February 19, 2019, monthlyreview.org/2012/12/01/remembering-walter-rodney/.
101   See: Editor, "Revolutionary Hot Air," *The Nationalist*, December 13, 1969, No. 1758.
102   Salha Hamdani and George G. Hajivayanis, interview by Harald Barre.

solidarity with the Palestinians.[103] Therefore, Nyerere's defense of USARF political positions may have been rather useful to his own diplomatic agenda.

The case of Rodney's critique of African governments was different. Beyond seeing the need to contain a diplomatic threat in pivotal pan-African relations, the aspect of fear of internal turmoil may have been prominently on the President's mind. In October, just a couple of months earlier, *the Nationalist* had announced the arrest of several high-ranking TANU members who were alleged to be involved in a coup attempt by Oscar Kambona, who had left for self-exile in 1967.[104] The events probably increased a feeling of insecurity that had been fed by regional unrest, colonial threats and internal crises such as the 1964 mutiny and the 1966 student demonstration.

Yet, also among the students who worked closely with Walter Rodney, the presidential editorial caused fear, and the students in USARF and in the TYL agreed not to publish the proceedings of the seminar in the recently created magazine *Cheche*. While this decision illustrates the fragility of academic freedom, it is noteworthy that the main reason was securing future influence through *Cheche*.[105] However, looking back, another USARF member, Issa Shivji, wrote that a 'comrade' destroyed papers in fear after the publication of the letter.[106] Compared to other countries, which students fled from, the sense of personal safety was apparently relatively high in Tanganyika, at least on the mainland. Yet, concerns for personal consequences and retributions inhibited the academic freedom promised by the Arusha Declaration. The episode had no immediate consequences beyond a letter in which Walter Rodney clarified that his remarks were personal, not targeting the Tanzanian government, and that he would never call for revolution in a country in which he did not live.[107] Nonetheless, the exchange illustrates the confusing atmosphere progressive students faced, as they were urged to explore and engage in revolutionary ways, and yet, they were confronted with unexpected and forceful rejection from the highest level of government.

USARF particularly thrived in the immediate years after the Arusha Declaration and often appeared in articles in *the Nationalist*. After establishing itself

---

103   See e.g.: *The Nationalist*, "Israel is aggressor - Mgonja," June 23, 1967, No. 990.
104   See: *The Nationalist*, "Kamaliza, titi face plot trial," October 27, 1969, No. 1717; Aminzade, *Race, Nation, and Citizenship*, 168-169.
105   See: Karim F. Hirji, "Tribulations of An Independent Magazine," in Hirji, *Cheche*, 39.
106   See: Shivji, "Remembering Walter Rodney."
107   See: *The Nationalist*, "Dr. Rodney," November 25, 1967, No. 1123

as a local pan-African institution, USARF went on to challenge events such as "Rag Day" and the "Rag Day Beauty" competition, which it considered to be conservative university traditions.[108] In contrast to the private owned newspaper *the Standard*,[109] the TANU newspaper was remarkably supportive of the joint action of USARF and the campus TYL writing "when the "rag" students realized they had been out-manouvred [SIC], they initiated a heated verbal exchanged [...]"[110] After the organizer of "Rag Day" accused USARF of manipulating TYL, *the Nationalist* gave USARF space to respond. Under the headline "College TYL, Revolutionary Front are one," it was quoted: "No imperialist master-minded manouvre [SIC] will succeed to drive a wedge between us."[111] USARF also took a prominent position in challenging scholars, such as the visiting scholar Seth Singleton, to a public discussion on Frantz Fanon.[112] After Singleton refused to participate in a public debate USARF and the campus TYL appealed unsuccessfully to Prime Minister Kawawa to expel Singleton.[113] Just as in the context of "Rag Day," USARF was criticized in its connection to TYL, and was accused of being steered by foreign elements. The two organizations reaffirmed their unity and rebuffed the critique arguing: "how can an African be called a foreigner in an African country?"[114] USARF's success, as well as its unchallenged support in the TANU newspaper, is indicative of the dominance of pan-Africanist views, as well as the tolerance for independent organizations under Education for Self-Reliance in the late 1960s.

USARF may have benefited from its close association with the campus TYL or from its tactics that were explicitly aligned with Education for Self-Reliance. Furthermore, while USARF's sabotage of "Rag Day" had been con-

---

108   During "Rag Day," students would dress in rags as a display of solidarity to poor people. Progressive students opposed it as a meaningless spectacle. See: Zakia Hamdani Meghji, "Sisterly Activism," in Hirji, *Cheche*, 78. Beauty pageants were decried as capitalist and degrading to women. See: Chapter 4.3
109   See: Zakia Hamdani Meghji, "Sisterly Activism," in Hirji, *Cheche*, 78.
110   *The Nationalist*, "'Rag Day' at the Hill flops," November 11, 1968, No. 1421.
111   *The Nationalist*, "College TYL, Revolutionary Front are one," November 13, 1968, No. 1423.
112   See: *The Nationalist*, "Students challenge lecturer," July 31, 1969, No. 1642. Psychologist Frantz Fanon had been important to anti-colonial movements world-wide, as his work put the question of the psychological impact of colonialism on societies and the prerequisites for successful liberation on the table.
113   See: *The Nationalist*, "Sack Lecturer - Students demand," August 8, 1969, No. 1649; Karim F. Hirji, "The Spark is Kindled," in Hirji, *Cheche*, 22-24.
114   *The Nationalist*, "Varsity T.Y.L. unveils plot," August 16, 1969, No. 1656.

tained to campus, other student protests became violent, spurring harsh critique by Nyerere. Shortly after the Arusha Declaration, students rioted in the former Dutch bank and were swiftly scolded by the President.[115] A few years later, amongst increased fears of foreign influence, students accused two lecturers, Mr. and Mrs. Freyhold, of espionage and besieged their home. While the initial reaction was cautiously sympathetic with the students,[116] later government statements suggest discomfort with such crowd dynamics. Interestingly, the article differentiated the students' action. It praised UDC students and urged them to remain vigilant, but warned: "Green Guards and other revolutionaries should avoid falling into 'traps of the enemy' by behaving recklessly."[117] This public differentiation may reflect the questionable image the TYL had gained off campus. Whereas the youth organization had enjoyed a constructive public image up to independence, after the union with Zanzibar, the youth organization's policing of public space was seen as increasingly intrusive.[118] While *the Nationalist* certainly would not have attacked the TYL in general, it probably had closer ties to the campus TYL and USARF since students were in regular correspondence with the newspaper.[119] Such relations may have prompted TANU and its newspaper to portray the organized students in a more favorable light.

Not only was USARF's protest against suspicious lecturers and customs like "Rag Day" more nuanced and thereby less dangerous for TANU's diplomatic strategy, but USARF also spearheaded projects in practical work. The university administration established a limited scope of self-reliance projects – students had to clean their own rooms – and the larger projects died quickly. USARF, on the other hand, began pioneering large variety of projects. A rec-

---

115   See: *The Nationalist*, "Nyerere rebuffs Green Guards 'hooliganism'," March 17, 1967, No. 907.
116   See: *The Nationalist*, "Students besiege Lecturer's house," March 15, 1969, No. 1525; *The Nationalist*, "Saboteurs Warned: University College not a hiding place - Kawawa," March 21, 1969, No. 1530.
117   *The Nationalist*, "Mgonja urges Dar College students to be vigilant," July 10, 1969, No. 1624.
118   See: James R. Brennan, "Youth, The TANU Youth League and Managed Vigilantism in Dar es Salaam, Tanzania, 1925-73," *Africa: Journal of the International African Institute* 76, no. 2 (2006): 236-238, accessed July 14, 2015, http://www.jstor.org/stable/40027110.
119   See: Salha Hamdani and George G. Hajivayanis, interview by Harald Barre.

ollection of George Hajivayanis helps understand the effects and running of USARF's implementation of Education for Self-Reliance.

"[O]ne trip was to go to Dodoma with Rodney and all other comrades [...], and we spent a lot of time in the villages trying to [...] help to the peasants. I mean the dire conditions in the villages and [...] and what was there in the urban areas was a big contrast. In the villages they hadn't even water. Let alone other luxuries. And that gave us a lot of impetus and [...] we [...] tried to do our best, but then we didn't have any resources as such, but we tried anyway somehow. [...] [F]or instance, if you wanted to go somewhere, you have to hire a bus. Sometimes we got the money from the TANU Youth League, [...] and sometimes we had to just [...] contribute ourselves. Because we didn't have any resources, so that gave us a lot of life. [L]ife became interesting. Development studies became interesting because what we were studying now was more relevant than before. We were learning how to transform ourselves."[120]

As suggested above, USARF benefited from its close relationship to the TYL, which helped USARF logistically. Other projects were shouldered by USARF independently. George Hajivayanis' eager reminiscence of facing logistical challenges, organizing abounding projects, while gaining new perspectives on society suggests the great creative and intellectual impact the Education for Self-Reliance had on students. It appeared to have the impact that Nyerere desired after the 1966 student demonstration – now students dramatically altered their view of society, as they related to the impoverished countryside and attempted to serve the population.

Furthermore, George Hajivayanis recalled being highly critical of official Education for Self-Reliance projects in schools:

"It is that [...] Education for Self-Reliance [...] it was implemented in secondary schools. Students had to cultivate, they had to farm like chicken farms, and so on. And what was happening [...] in the schools [...] the head-teachers they were now taking all these eggs [...] consuming them and the students were being exploited. So there was a contradiction between the students and the teachers. They were producing [...] in the gardens they had chickens and so on [...]. They never benefited from this [...]. So there was a contradic-

---

120   Ibid.

tion there. So the students, they became our supporters as well because we were speaking on their behalf."[121]

While not specifying whether this extended to both private and governmental schools, the quote illustrates how the problems between parts of the administration and students continued into the post-Arusha era. Meanwhile, it was students, along with motivated and accepted teachers such as Rodney, who were encouraged to engage in community work and in the schools because of the Arusha Declaration. Such interaction, the quote suggests, permitted ideas from the academic sphere to reach students in primary and secondary schools. It also gave university students a critical view into the society, which helped them to reflect on their own position, but also developed a belief on political and administrative development within the society.

However, progressive students' initiative to identify existing dependencies did not exclude the university itself. After the new common course had turned out to be unpopular, USARF decided in 1969 to start open ideological Sunday classes. The events were initiated clandestinely and independent of administrative or TANU help.[122]

> "Everyone had a part to play. One day somebody talked about class struggle, the next time somebody talked about, I don't know, whatever they call it in a capitalist economy, [...] someone talked about Engels and Marx, the end of German classical philosophy, and so on. It was essentially debating... So students who are going to church passed where we used to meet. But it was the most important thing [...] that helped students because then it was not just [...] talking about Marx and Marxism and Lenin and Leninism, but now reading it understanding it and explaining it."[123]

Beyond providing insight into the lively academic discussions that tried to explore the applicability of theories in various contexts, the quote inconspicuously reaffirms the presence of tensions between leftist students and students who were devoted to religious service. Yet, ultimately it was not conflict with

---

121 Ibid.
122 Karim F. Hirji, "The African University: A critical comment," accessed February 19, 2019, https://www.pambazuka.org/education/african-university-critical-comment.
123 Salha Hamdani and George G. Hajivayanis, interview by Harald Barre.

other students nor, as far as it can be traced back, influence from foreign secret services[124] that ended USARF's independent academic activism.

As Melchiorre concludes, USARF's demise was a planned and concerted effort of TANU in order to bring independent student politics under control.[125] However, despite the confrontation between Rodney and TANU's leadership in *the Nationalist*, the newspaper coverage did not immediately reflect the confrontation. In July 1970, *the Nationalist* published a highly favorable review of *Cheche*. It distinguished the magazine from other students' publications:

> "[...] especially of 'sensational' publicity of campus 'scandal' of inane kind or another usually involving such subjects as sex or petty-bourgeois student politics [...]. All in all, it can be said without any fear of contradiction that when the University of Dar es Salaam can be wholly devoted to the production of youths of the quality and seriousness of TYL and USARF students responsible for this publication instead of the reactionary technocrats and bureaucrats at present mass produced, then and only then will it make good its claim to being a people's university."[126]

The "contradiction" came within a week. A letter to the editor criticized USARF and the Campus TYL for focusing on foreign theories in its first two issues of *Cheche*. So far, the author argued, the magazine had failed to relate such theories to the Tanzanian situation. He concluded by forcefully rejecting the claim that the university "mass produced "reactionary bureaucrats and technocrats.""[127] Hirji retrospectively suspected Editor Benjamin Mkapa behind this letter.[128] It appears probable that a leading member of TANU used the readers' section to issue such a warning to the students under the guise of a pseudonym. However, the fact that both positions were printed suggests that

---

124 Hirji mentions that he found out decades later that one of his lecturers was in fact working for the Central Intelligence Agency and transition, in which Mazrui published his critique, was funded by the CIA. See: Karim F. Hirji, "The Spark is Kindled," in Hirji, *Cheche*, 24; Colin Leys, "Letter," *London Review of Books*, August 2, 2018, 15, accessed February 19, 2019, https://www.lrb.co.uk/v40/n14/mahmood-mamdani/the-african-university.

125 See: Melchiorre, "Building Nations," 162-163.

126 G.K., "'Cheche' - Organ of the Moment: Book Review," *The Nationalist*, July 25, 1970, No. 1945.

127 Mwana Wa Matonya, "'Cheche' can do more," *The Nationalist*, July 31, 1970, No. 1950.

128 See: Karim F. Hirji, "Not So Silent a Spark," in Hirji, *Cheche*, 55.

Mkapa had initially no objections against the sympathetic portrayal of US-ARF and its magazine and that the critical rejection of *Cheche* was rather the product of intervention by other members of the TANU leadership.

Regardless of who was behind the alarming letter to the editor, the magazine as well as USARF was banned in November 1970, and the newspaper did not question the step. On the front page, *the Nationalist* relayed that the reasons given to the students were the redundancy of USARF and the foreign origin of the name Cheche – a translation of Lenin's *Iskara*. The newspaper continued with a short response from USARF.[129] The public explanation was weak, as the students were accused in earlier disputes of not being sufficiently 'internationalist.'[130] It may have occurred to the editor that this was a questionable justification, for a day later, an editorial stated that all work in Tanzania was supposed to be organized under TANU and therefore there was no need for USARF. The editor expanded by saying that outside opinions would have less weight in TANU debates, and most members of USARF were also members of the campus TYL.[131] The entire statement of the dissolved USARF highlighted conflicts with the government and the administration as the reason for its demise:

> "Perhaps it would be correct to say that it was the tourism debate that started the systematic strangling of the revolution at the Hill of which the banning of USARF and *Cheche* are but a culmination. It started with an exchange of views between us and the Minister responsible for the 'industry.' The exchange was a fiasco as the Minister seemed incapable of understanding either the economics of the 'industry,' or the ideological implications. We therefore put our views in the press, triggering a useful debate that however earned us a multitude of enemies. Threats against us were to be heard even in the parliament."[132]

In the tourism debate months earlier, the now nationalized competitor of *the Nationalist*, *the Standard*, had published an article which contended that the Western developed tourism concept would not benefit Tanzanian society. Subsequent critics argued that colonial relationships would be reinforced

---

129   See: *The Nationalist*, "Hill Students' Front asked to cease," November 13, 1970, No. 2040
130   See: Aminzade, *Race, Nation, and Citizenship*, 187.
131   See: Editor, "Students' Front," *The Nationalist*, November 14, 1970, No. 2041.
132   Karim F. Hirji and Naijuka Kasihwaki, "Appendix E: Our Last Stand," in Hirji, *Cheche*, 210.

and potential spies would have another avenue into the country.[133] The quote from USARF's final statement confirms that in their view, the government was largely made up of conservative, Western-leaning politicians. It was only after the critique of the administration became public that the group's image in *the Nationalist* began deteriorating. The fact that their ban became a front-page matter indicates the great significance of the organization for changes in academic life in Dar es Salaam.

Although, according to the editorial, most USARF members were also part of the campus TYL, the ban had devastating effects on the pan-African dimension of organized student activism:

"So really the unity of foreign students [...] collapsed [...]. Because this was the thing that brought us together. Now it collapsed."[134]

Somewhat surprisingly, in supporting the ban, Nyerere sacrificed one of his political cornerstones – "non-racial" pan-Africanism. Student organizations had been one of the few areas where a version of pan-Africanism had been practiced that focused in its activism class, not "race." The fact that Nyerere was swayed by the conservative block and sacrificed this prospect of African unity for the unity of the party may be seen against the background of the foundation of the University of Dar es Salaam (UDSM) in 1970. As the University of East Africa was dissolved and the UCD turned into a national institution, considerations for pan-African students may have lessened. Probably more crucially was the fear of independently organized students.[135] The lingering party leadership's fear was likely exacerbated by an alleged attempted coup d'état that year. The so-called Treason Trial against the suspects dominated the headlines.[136] The concern of another coup attempt only six years after the short but violent events in Tanganyika in 1964 may have reaffirmed in President Nyerere the need to contain opposition, including academic critique, within the confines of TANU.

---

133 See: Aminzade, *Race, Nation, and Citizenship*, 188-189.
134 Salha Hamdani and George G. Hajivayanis, interview by Harald Barre.
135 See: Melchiorre, "Building Nations," 200.
136 Since May 1970, *the Nationalist* was filled with articles and reports about the 'treason trial.' Aminzade argues that it was the climax of a conflict with TANU members who viewed presidential power as overreaching. See: Aminzade, *Race, Nation, and Citizenship*, 168-170.

By 1970, a lot of the initial enthusiasm progressives had for the Arusha Declaration gave way to the realities of a power struggle against a conservative leaning administration and the party's determination to control the political debate. Despite this development, progressive students had made visible and lasting contributions to the debate around independence.[137] Furthermore, no other group of students contributed as actively to the TANU newspaper as progressive, leftist students. This illustrates that *the Nationalist* provided a space for controversial debate, regardless of a climate of fear surrounding Cold War aggressions and the possibility of coup d'états.

4.3 Gender – the Articulation of Women's Critique in the Public Sphere

The Arusha Declaration had not only called for "racial," but also gender equality. The years after the declaration were to show massive changes in the portrayal of roles and opportunities for women. Social values would be debated against the background of colonialism and the Cold War. The emphasis on working women as part of the nation building project resulted from an increasing number of low-paying jobs in the formal economy.[138] The party's interest in advocating new roles had been visible in *the Nationalist* since its inception. In contrast to the years before the declaration, women began shaping the newspaper discourse critically both as journalists and readers. And while, as shown in chapter 4.1 "race" devolved into a more subtle topic in the public debates in the newspaper, concerns around gender issues skyrocketed.

Although women, driven by TANU's pledge for equality, were crucial agents in the independence campaign during the 1950s, they only had begun to voice themselves in *the Nationalist* a few months before the Arusha Declaration. Reforms in gender roles that had been advocated for in editorials in the mid-1960s were mere visions for Tanzanian society. Accordingly, it is not surprising that Marjorie Mbilinyi, remembered friction and struggle as she immigrated to Tanzania:

"I have come to a new place. I'm adjusting to marriage with my old boyfriend, [...]. And then all the politics of marriage when you have a baby and things

---

137 See chapter 5.2 for a discussion on the impact of ideological classes on campus life after USARF's ban.
138 See: Callaci, *Street Archives*, 64-65.

like that and negotiating that and finding out how other people negotiate. And then dealing with real outright, outrageous forms of blatant sexism at the university, statutory sexism. You know, when they write down:' You can't get a house without a letter from your husband's employer that he does not have a house.' This is... that is blatant, it is not just hear-say. I mean it was there, it was, procedure at the university, you can't receive the funding staff normally receive to go on leave. That a letter from the employer of your husband was required saying that my husband has not received annual leave money ... from his employer. Ridiculous and of course he wasn't asked to do the same thing. So this was not just me, just normal... normal stuff. [...] the terms under which I was employed, they were outrageous."[139]

Remarkably, her statement reflects a particular sense of bewilderedness in light of the formal discriminatory regulations at the university, where she was hired well after the publication of the declaration in early 1968. The extent of sexism not just in social practice, but also in prevailing regulations from colonial times, also surprised other contemporaries, as an exchange in the Nationalist's 'Action Line' shows. In one comment, a reader mentioned that female teachers who had become pregnant used to be dismissed in colonial times. This practice, the reader alleged, had been changed for the good of the nation, and requested to apply the same changes to school girls. The Ministry of Education, however, responded that the rules had not changed and that pregnant teachers or school girls had displayed immoral behavior and constituted a bad influence.[140] The exchange demonstrates that sexist regulation from the colonial era was still practiced and defended by the administration. However, the reader's assumption that the regulation had been abolished suggests that the public image of the government was more progressive.

In fact, the government handled gender relations ambivalently. On one side, the Ministry's response suggests that the administration took a stubborn stance regarding the regulations it had inherited. On the other side, when she embarked on a PhD project, Marjorie Mbilinyi recollected that there was actually strong concern and eagerness to find solutions regarding the discrimination against school girls:

---

139 Marjorie Mbilinyi, interview by Harald Barre.
140 *The Nationalist*, "Action Line," June 10, 1967, No. 979. Similar regulations applied to factory workers, where women were not allowed to work night shifts based on a 1957 code. See: A. A. Riyami, "Night Work for Women," *The Nationalist*, October 9, 1968, No. 1393.

"[A]s a research assistant [...] it was suggested: go to the ministry and find out what they see as priorities to do research. So I think they saw a woman and said: 'Ok, we have [an] issue of pregnant school girls, what do we do about it' [...] And the other one was: 'why are parents deciding not to educate their daughters - we want them to do so.' So that's also interesting, right. They were concerned and that was 1968, yah. And this was not an external donor, this was people within the ministry [...].[141]

As shown in chapter 2.4, the British colonial administration had not considered the education of women a priority, and rather a luxury. Conversely, newspaper editorials in the mid-1960s had described empowered women as an ideal. After the Arusha Declaration, the ministry sought to deal with the basic problems that stood between such visions. One problem that both the administration and TANU faced in this regard was that the party's women's section did not have strong connections to school girls.[142] Accordingly, solutions could not be implemented through the party. Similar to a few years earlier, in terms of the issues with racism,[143] the university was seen as an institution that could provide answers. The systematic request of academic research can be seen as a direct implementation of the Arusha Declaration in that it strove to do research that was immediately relevant to the society.

Destitutes, Prostitutes and Working Mothers

Despite TANU intent to alter and approximate gender roles, the rules and values of education left over from the colonial era had a strong normative imprint on peoples' minds. A common topic was the question of how to deal with unemployed urban populations. As noted in chapter 2.3, it had been common practice of the colonial state to deport unemployed urban dwellers to the countryside. In 1967, a reader praised the administration for this practice, but wondered why it was not also applied to prostitutes.[144] Just two days later, the newspaper reported that Coast Regional Commissioner Songambele had stressed that anybody without work in the city, including women,

---

141 Marjorie Mbilinyi, interview by Harald Barre.
142 See: Editor, "U.W.T." *The Nationalist*, September 20, 1968, No. 1377.
143 See chapter 1.1.
144 See: S. B. Buberwa, "Why not also for those women?," *The Nationalist*, April 17, 1967, No. 932.

was to be sent to do work in the countryside.[145] More than a year later, the question was picked up by Hannah Kassambala, who frequently wrote articles on the women's page, then called 'Mainly for Women.' She argued that most women regarded the constant harassment of prostitutes by police with apprehension, and wondered why customers and pimps were not equally targeted. In a subsequent interview, an officer from the Ministry of Local Government and Rural Development argued that most women were not rounded up because of prostitution, which was hard to prove, but because of the status of being unemployed.[146] Her article suggests that Ms. Kasambala had evolved in her journalistic vigour as she shone new light on the topic of prostitution. She appears to have been encouraged by a general scepticism of women regarding the treatment of prostitutes. While the officer dismissed her criticism on legal grounds, her article constituted a new interpretation of gender roles in the public sphere.

The topic remained low-profile until an editorial deplored the practice of the administration. It condemned readers' comments against prostitutes and destitutes as "bourgeois," and argued that the Arusha Declaration had made clear that they should be cared for wherever they live. As they were Tanzanian citizens, they were not to be seen as a problem, but an obligation.[147] One letter that the editor likely responded to, came from a Mrs. Aggy Chacha. The reader, whose background is unknown, wrote:

"Equalizing single women to married women will invite and encourage the following: Many single women and girls will not again care to get married [...] which will now result in an increase of a great number of prostitutes and lowering the name and image of our nation. [...] It is my contention that our government will not think of reversing the hailed policy and allow a group of parasites to participate and enjoy any privileges which they are not entitled to principally."[148]

The author's world view fit within Christian middle-class values that tried to influence the expanding urban population, namely the growing number

---

145 See: *The Nationalist*, "Sent-back women till land for rice," April 19, 1967, No. 934
146 See: H. R. Kassambala, "Repatriation of prostitutes: Is it the answer?," *The Nationalist*, August 21, 1968, No. 1351.
147 See: Editor, "Destitutes," *The Nationalist*, July 22, 1969, No. 1634.
148 Mrs. A. Chacha, "Maternity leave," *The Nationalist*, July 8, 1969, No. 1622.

of young working women.¹⁴⁹ It is notable that the editor of *the Nationalist* sharply attacked her position as well as that of the city administration that organized the deportations. The diverging position can be well explained with the split Aminzade observed between TANU and administration.¹⁵⁰ While the Western educated administration held conservative views such as deportation for example, the party and its newspaper actively questioned these official positions.

Mrs. Chacha's concern for equalizing single and married women revolved around a hotly contested topic: paid maternity leave. In the *Nationalist*, the topic was discussed in 1968 on the page 'Mainly for Women,' where edited views of two working mothers were published. An introductory comment contended that women were increasingly aware of the need to "come out of the shell of their femininity and speak about their rights." The first contributor, Mrs. Mulokozi, argued:

> "Whenever maternity leave with pay is in discussion, some men insist that maternity leave is not sick leave. This is a rash answer without much thought attached to it."¹⁵¹

Paid maternity leave, she continued, would offer women the opportunity to properly take care of their newborns, and return to work after recovery. The other interviewee, Mrs. Marealle, pointed to the fact that maternity leave not only prepared a strong future generation, but was also in line with the Arusha Declaration, as it helped fight "discrimination based on sex."¹⁵² The fact that the women had formed highly differentiated opinions on the topic indicates that maternity had been part of public, but unpublished debates, before.

The newspaper provided women a space to articulate and publicly express their perspectives on the matter. It furthermore shows how women and journalists utilized the Arusha Declaration to bolster their case and describe the existing gender roles as unjust. However, as the case of Mrs. Chacha shows, Christian morals were quickly utilized to justify the exclusion of unmarried women from such claims. When Second Vice-President Kawawa announced the actual introduction of paid maternity leave in state and parastatal orga-

---

149   See: Callaci, *Street Archives*, 69–71.
150   See chapter 4.2.
151   *The Nationalist*, "Opinions on Maternity Leave with Pay," September 4, 1968, No. 1363.
152   Ibid.

nizations, the law at the time only applied to married women.[153] It is hard to establish if the decision reflected the conservative view of the administration, or if it was an attempt to symbolically pave the way to more equality, while not alienating conservative groups.

The outrage against discrimination against unmarried women came swiftly. A week after the announcement, a dismayed reader contended:

> "I am not at all convinced that children born by married women are the only ones who contribute to the building of the nation [...]. We, unmarried women, are singularly responsible for proper up-bringing of our children so that they may grow to prove worthy mothers and fathers; to pave the way for the nation on a realistic basis. If it is a matter of gratitude, we should thank all conceiving women and grant them equal human rights and privileges, otherwise it is not justifiable to state that Tanzania has resolved to follow the road leading to socialism."[154]

The quote illustrates that the government was critically reviewed, and that *the Nationalist* readily granted readers space to voice such criticism. Once more, the argument of unmarried working women relied heavily on the Arusha Declaration's promise of equality and socialism. Subsequent letters supported debating the issue, but accusations that equated single mothers with prostitutes were dismissed carefully.[155] The exchange shows that encompassing moral condemnation of single women by readers such as Mrs. Chacha did not resonate with all readers. However, the abovementioned editor's call for solidarity with prostitutes and destitutes remained an outstanding position at the time.

The input from *the Nationalist* to advance women's equality and independence continued in further works, as journalist Hannah Kassambala pointed to the lack of infrastructure for working mothers in another article. In a report about nursery schools, she argued that they were too few and too expensive, even though they would be very helpful for working mothers.[156] The

---

153 See: *The Nationalist*, "New deal for maternity women from July 1," June 6, 1969, No. 1595.
154 Veneranda Joe, "Maternity Leave," *The Nationalist*, June 13, 1969, No. 1601.
155 See: A. K. Mwalwisi, "Maternity leave," *The Nationalist*, July 29, 1969, No. 1640; A. K. Mwalwisi, "Maternity leave," *The Nationalist*, July 2, 1969, No. 1617; Chacha, "Maternity leave."
156 H. R. Kassambala, "Nursery schools - a new development." *The Nationalist*, June 28, 1969, No. 1614.

debates around paid maternity leave showed how the party newspaper gave female journalists and readers space to question existing norms and regulations. While the legislation addressed only part of the demands, resistance against continued discrimination remained and significantly shifted the discourse from purely Christian moralist opinions.

Debating Opportunities and Obstacles

Christian morals mixed in a discourse of black self-appreciation accompanied much of the early post-Arusha years. The issue of 'decent' clothing had already been voiced in *the Nationalist* after the 1966 student riots, but it was only after the Arusha Declaration that the debate around indecent fashion gained traction in the newspaper. Readers protested after UWT had announced a meeting to debate the issue. While miniskirts were deemed shameful, readers considered them a marginal issue in Tanzania. Instead of discussing 'imperialist' dresses, they argued that the implementation of the Arusha Declaration should be discussed.[157] This appeal, however, was futile, as the TYL discovered the issue of fashion and launched 'Operation Vijana' with official support in January 1969.[158] While Ivaska found many letters focusing on the female body and the display of nudity, a good number of opinions uttered in *the Nationalist* focused on the issue of Africanization and black pride, as their critique lay on bleaching one's skin and the wearing of wigs. "African women (and men) are naturally beautiful and handsome though not artificially so,"[159] one reader commented. And an editorial explained the recent ban on beauty contests in the same vein. The editor contended that miniskirts and make-up were based on colonial mentality, and were about cultural domination.[160] After the ban on miniskirts in early 1969, the topic quickly faded from the pages. One female reader praised the ban, but wondered why the government allowed the import of magazines which advertised the very products that Tanzania tried to ban from society.[161] Such contradictions between rhetoric and practice could be regularly found in *the Nationalist* itself, where cinema advertisements set the example of the very gender roles the TYL and TANU sought to ban.

---

157 See: Hussein Mtabuzi, "Mini-skirts," *The Nationalist*, September 7, 1967, No. 1055.
158 See: Ivaska, "'Anti-Mini Militants Meet," 591-594.
159 L. N. Njoki, "Cultural Revolution is timely," *The Nationalist*, October 14, 1968, No. 1307.
160 See: Editor, "Colonial Mentality," *The Nationalist*, August 30, 1968, No. 1359.
161 See: Mrs. A. Sanga, "Dress Fashions," *The Nationalist*, February 8, 1969, No. 1495.

The debates and, in certain times and places, hostile atmosphere,[162] must have impeded women's attempts to struggle for equality. Najma Sachak recollected:

> "I have to say that the rest of us did not appreciate the cultural directive at all, which, thank goodness, ended after a while. We, women, solved the problem by wearing kaftans or long evening dresses to work on the campus at the time."[163]

As women developed strategies to avoid being targeted by TYL vigilantes, they used the public space in the newspaper to advocate for ways to gain equality. In late 1967, the 'Mainly for women' page launched the recurring topic 'Women and Employment.' Clearly annoyed with the ongoing debate about fashion, one unnamed author wrote:

> "This is an appeal to both men and women. In Tanzania men have taken so much interest in women's affairs like cosmetics, mini-skirts and hair straightening that on occasions these have been the cause of uproars during many National Assembly sessions. I hope now that we have embarked on a more serious subject – namely employment opportunities for women – our men will not desert us."[164]

The journalist's appeal did not help to tone down the anti-miniskirt debate, which climaxed in 'Operation Vijana,' but it constituted the beginning of a debate on how to develop opportunities for women. These debates were meant to encourage breaching male domains and were occasionally supported with images, which likely made the career path more imaginable. Over the course of the next years, the women's page presented career options for girls in various fields such as banking, teaching, or the prison service.[165]

While these examples of advice were still outnumbered by tips for the household and child rearing, the quality of articles that advocated for women's equality rose. Such articles were often based by interviews with women and men that illustrated the complexity of gender roles in a more personal and

---

162 See: *The Nationalist*, "Police call," 127-128.
163 Email Correspondence with Najma Sachak, 18.01.2019.
164 *The Nationalist*, "Women and Employment," August 26, 1968, No. 1045.
165 See: *The Nationalist*, "Careers for girls - Banking," March 1, 1969, No. 1513; *The Nationalist*, "Careers for girls in Prison Services," March 29, 1969, No. 1537; *The Nationalist*, "Career for Girls: Teaching," July 24, 1968, No. 1326.

narrative style. A turning point where such perspectives entered the debate was the controversy that accompanied the introduction of a new marriage code. The new law was supposed to reconcile the plethora of regulations and customs that Tanzania had inherited from British indirect rule, and sought to strengthen women's rights. However, the proposal was hotly contested, as it permitted polygamy, dependent on the first wife's consent, but not polyandry. Critics viewed the law as a consolidation of existing discrimination, whereas proponents either argued it the secured more rights for the first wife, or that it was in line with "traditional" or "natural" gender orders.[166] As the country started a debate on the reformation of the marriage law, journalist Hannah Kassambala's articles put into question whether marriage was even an ambition of young women in the city:

> "A married man with five children had this to say. [...] Nowadays girls are shattering the old picture of desparate [SIC] young women always on the look out [SIC] for a husband to catch. [...] A married woman commenting on the subject said that girls have become more independent nowadays and have changed their attitude towards marriage. Work and earning their living has given them independence from men, they have also given them independence from their parents. In towns where they must live in order to work, they depend on themselves instead of depending on their parents."[167]

Her article shows that men and women from the older generation were well aware of the dependency that gender roles inflicted on women, and that they saw the advantages that working life in the post-colonial city offered to young women. In particular, the women interviewed noted the traditional double dependency of women on both their parents and future husband. Their perspectives suggest that young women were regarded as more independent than previous generations. In a comment a couple of months later, Hannah Kassambala pointed out how regulations impeded young women's abilities to achieve the independence:

> "Recently a Palestine Arab girl took part in hijacking a plane. [...] We had already seen women make war, fighting bravely, militating in revolutionary groups. [...] A few years ago I visited the Women Section of the Police Force

---

166 See: Ivaska, *Cultured States*, 170-188.
167 H. R. Kassambala, "Girls in bid for marriage reform," *The Nationalist*, July 19, 1969, No. 1632.

in Dar es Salaam. I wanted particularly to know why women were not riding motor cycles. The answer was that, they were not allowed to do so because they were women. What a disappointing answer. As we all know Women Police in Guinea ride motor-cycles. The only difference between them is that the Guineans do not face a bureaucracy which thinks that women are too delicate to ride motor-cycles."[168]

While her article explicitly urged women to take the initiative in the struggle for equality, she lamented the formal hurdles women faced, similar to Marjorie Mbilinyi's observation regarding the university. Hannah Kassambala bolstered her case by comparing the situation in Tanzania to the progress in gender equality in other societies. She contrasted gender equality in Guinea, which was usually portrayed as a politically close ally,[169] and the prominent role of female Palestinian activists, whose activities gained increasing popularity in Tanzania.[170] Based on these comparisons, she suggested that Tanzania was lagging behind. As described in chapter 1.4, the attempt to build the argument for greater gender equality had already been present in the letters to the editor in newspapers in the Kilimanjaro region in the 1950s. However, in the current climate, positions such as Hannah Kassambala's, collided with moralist and traditionalist opinions. While the former seized on the importance of gender equality in Tanzania's socialist nation building project, the latter sought to gain momentum by placing emphasis on the image of African tradition. In this sense Nyerere's concept of African socialism included a spectrum of antagonistic imagery into the national narrative.

Despite the backlash from conservatives, female voices increasingly targeted structural forms of gender discrimination, at least in the public sphere. Under the headline 'Yes we've got a grouse,' an unnamed correspondent featured the portraits and experiences of four young women. The layout of the article, which covered the whole page, brought the reader literally face-to-face with the women.[171] Their perspectives were introduced in a resolute tone:

"OUR WOMEN today are very much disturbed and angry and many are seemingly disillusioned. Why? Because they want to be given equal opportunity

---

168 H. R. Kassambala, "Call to Tanzania women," *The Nationalist*, October 4, 1969, No. 1693.
169 This published affinity increased even more after the coup against Ghana's President Nkrumah. See e.g.: *The Nationalist*, "Walk-Out at Addis," March 4, 1966, No. 586.
170 See chapter 4.2.
171 See Image 6.

as men enjoy in the service of the nation. They are angry with what they generally described as discriminatory practices and prejudices directed against them in the Civil Service, parastatal organisations and even in commercial houses."[172]

The introduction contrasted strongly with the debates that focused on the morality of polygamous marriages and the idealization of rural women over allegedly immoral urban women.[173] While the party, and particularly the Youth League, concerned itself with African authenticity, the English TANU newspaper provided women space to criticize the social order and the administration that maintained it. Even TANU's Swahili newspaper *Uhuru* criticized the mistreatment of women in its pages,[174] although the focus appears to have been on men's behaviour rather than the political administration of the country.

Discriminatory practices and regulations continued to be denounced. Another article in the Nationalist's women's page denounced the victimization of unmarried mothers in the taxation system. While men could easily claim child allowance, unmarried mothers would have to prove that there could be no claim by a father. Fathers, however, would automatically have the legal right of parenthood and could claim benefits accordingly. Even divorced or widowed mothers could only claim a meagre 'supplementary allowance.'[175] It is remarkable that *the Nationalist* published such critical assessments of the administration of the country from its staff in regards to gender relations, while it eventually supported the dissolution of the critical student organization USARF. It is possible that TANU feared autonomously organized critics as political threats, while it felt in control over journalists and independent scholars whose critical assessment it welcomed and actively supported.

---

172 *The Nationalist*, "Yes, We've got a grouse: Why discriminate against us?," January 31, 1970, No. 1797.
173 See: Lal, *African Socialism*, 22.
174 See: Emily Callaci, "Dancehall Politics: Mobility, Sexuality, and Spectacles of Racial Respectability in Late Colonial Tanganyika, 1930s–1961," *The Journal of African History* 52, no. 03 (2011): 75-76, https://doi.org/10.1017/S0021853711000478
175 See: *The Nationalist*, "Working girls and P.A.Y.E." April 11, 1970, N. 1855.

Academia, Politics and Gender Discrimination

Half a decade after *the Nationalist* had urged women to assert their place in male-dominated job sectors, the women's pages pointed to basic obstacles faced by women, namely inadequate education:

> "Exponents of women emancipation dream of the day when all women would stop all dependence on men. They believe that one of the factors which will herald the day is education. Education for girls in fact, has become the expected panacea to so many womens' [SIC] problems. When we talk of polygamy, we hope that it will disappear as more and more girls become educated. So will girls' early marriages and ignorance with their disastrous consequences on child bearing and child upbringing. In fact any talk on girls' education which does not point out that its late arrival to women is responsible for putting womens' [SIC] progress behind that of men, is rare."[176]

In the interview, Principal Secretary to the Ministry of National Education Mwingira, acknowledged that girls receiving less education had caused so much concern, that they had requested Marjorie Mbilinyi from the UCD to research the reason behind the high rates of girls dropping out of school. The main problem was that school girls were married forcibly by their parents and there was no law to prevent this. This parental attitude barred many girls from obtaining secondary education.[177] Mbilinyi's book became background of an article a few months later. The author, H.K. – presumably Hannah Kassambala – quoted Mbilinyi, highlighting the discrepancy between the "progressive role" women were expected to take while being excluded from educational institutions. H.K. combined her own experiences as a school girl with Mbilinyi's research outcomes and concluded that: "The situation does not seem to have changed much!"[178] The article did not only demonstrate how the post-Arusha administration sought to utilize academia to provide answers to social problems they faced, but also showed how journalists eagerly integrated research from the university in their own work.

---

176   *The Nationalist*, "Problems of women education," April 18, 1970, No. 1861.
177   See: Ibid.
178   See: H. K., "Girls' education in Tanzania: Book Review," *The Nationalist*, October 24, 1970, No. 2023.

Although Marjorie Mbilinyi had rejected the topic of school girl pregnancies as being too sensitive,[179] she identified it as one factor for the high dropout rate of girls in secondary schools. H.K. wrote with apparent disquiet:

> "It was also found out that some parents feared the 'misconduct of some female school leavers.' I should think that complaint has just been given an official stamp by Mrs. Mbilinyi, for no problem of girls education has been so much talked about recently than this one."[180]

H.K.'s comment indicates that she viewed other factors as more important, but the topic became part of an increasingly heated debate. In the course of the debate around paid maternity leave, Hannah Kassambala interviewed the Commissioner for Social and Welfare Services on the Affiliation Bill. The new law was to secure a support payment for the children of unmarried mothers by the father. The commissioner acknowledged that the amounts were too low for the subsistence of children of unmarried mothers, but emphasized that this bill was merely the beginning of improving the chances of such children.[181] Once more, the bill suggests that not only journalists, but also the administration regarded the unequal treatment of children born in or out of wedlock as problematic. However, the interview indirectly pointed to a significant problem in overcoming the abuse of school girls. When asked about the background of school girl pregnancies, the commissioner said that the men were often

> "quite old and sometimes with families of six or more children. Among them you will find 'seemingly respectable men, some holding very high position in their jobs. [...] Men who are brought here sometimes stoop to very low tricks to get young girls they want, but girls should also learn to guard themselves against these tricks.'"[182]

The quote indicates that in Tanzania's increasingly nationalized economy, men affiliated with the administration played an essential role in the abuse of young women and school girls. In explicitly pointing to the responsibility of the country's administration for what was seen as an urgent social problem,

---

179   See: Marjorie Mbilinyi, interview by Harald Barre.
180   H. K., "Girls' education."
181   See: H. R. Kassambala, "Help for unmarried mothers," *The Nationalist*, April 12, 1969, No. 1548.
182   Ibid.

the women's page of *the Nationalist* led a debate in the public sphere which would put the country's leadership under scrutiny in the upcoming years. The women's page did not hesitate to push on with its critical analysis:

> "Whenever a girl kills herself in the process of trying to take her unborn illigitimate [SIC] baby out, everybody is angry and asks why she had to turn to such desparate [SIC] ends. [...] In my opinion the answer is clear, society is out to punish mothers of illigitimate [SIC] children in a big way. [...] But I think worse still, certain regulations and laws passed by the State take part in discriminating against them and adding to the stigma. [...] In a socialist country like this one, all the children are equal and should be given equal chances of growing up. [...] The State should encourage [the mothers] [...] instead of discouraging them with regulations which make conditions against the proper care of their children."[183]

The quote demonstrated to the reading public quite dramatically, the gap between the nation's aspiration of socialist equality and the lethal consequences of discriminatory regulations. Despite the articulation of such critical perspectives, Principal Secretary in the Ministry of National Education, Mwingira affirmed the general position that pregnant school girls should be expelled.[184] Another article also took on the ongoing debate on 'soul music,' which the administration blamed for moral decay.[185] Dancing to any music, however, should be considered a normal social activity, the author argued. Parents should engage themselves in their children's social life so that they can "enjoy their young world innocently."[186] However, the official perspectives that blamed 'soul music' or girls "habits"[187] were challenged by an article that gave "a chance to a few women to air their views."[188] One of them, Christina Nsekela, was a well-known figure in Dar es Salaam. As head of the family planning association Chama cha Uzazi na Malezi Bora Tanzania (UMATI), she had been publicly present and advocated family planning for married and divorced women. Coming from a Christian school background, she assured the public that UMATI would turn away unmarried

---

183 *The Nationalist*, "Why some girls abort," August 2, 1969, No. 1644.
184 *The Nationalist*, "Problems of women."
185 See chapter 4.2 for an analysis of the debate around banning 'soul music.'
186 See: *The Nationalist*, "Why girls go wrong," November 28, 1970, No. 2053.
187 *The Nationalist*, "Problems of women."
188 *The Nationalist*, "Sex Education in Schools," June 6, 1970, No. 1903.

women seeking advice on birth control.[189] School girls, she argued, were best protected against men's irresponsible abuse if they had sex education in school. She deemed that this would enable school girls to consciously resist men who were protected by generous laws even though they should be treated like criminals. A teacher, Mrs. Mulokozi, agreed that sex education would empower girls, and described how "these irresponsible, so-called leaders" exploited the bad infrastructure, offered school girls a lift and sexually assaulted them.[190] The article showed how the topic of gender discrimination became a vehicle for a critique of transgressions of the administration.

As mentioned above, the topic of school girl pregnancies was a particularly sensitive topic, as Mbilinyi's research identified it as a factor for parents to not send their daughters to secondary schools. However, in another article, *the Nationalist* vividly described the extent of sexual harassment women faced, even if they were able to obtain education and qualifications:

> "Tamali is an ex-standard seven girl but is also a qualified typist. [...] But it is months now since she qualified and she is still without a job. [...] "I have been to many interviews, but they tell me the same thing: 'Give us something you have got, then we will give you a job; When I ask them what is that something I have, they tell me, you are not a baby, you know what we mean. You have got something in your body, if you can't give us that something then you can't get a job." By "they" Tamali meant the people responsible for employing new staff in government ministries, parastatal organizations and companies."[191]

The quote not only illustrates the challenges even qualified and educated women faced, but also the abuse and discrimination that was actively committed by the administration. Women were forced to choose between unemployment and risking becoming unmarried mothers. The author went on and denounced the active cover-up of the problem by a "prominent minister" when a UWT member tried to discuss the issue in parliament.[192] Although the article went not as far as to name any implicated officials, its scathing critique was a remarkable trend. The continuous publication of increasingly outspoken assessments suggests that the editorial board of *the Nationalist* supported the trend.

---

189 See: Callaci, *Street Archives*, 92-94.
190 See: *The Nationalist*, "Sex Education in."
191 *The Nationalist*, "Why girls go."
192 See: Ibid.

4.4 Conclusion: Debating New Concepts and Struggling with Old Structures

The Arusha Declaration emerged out of a realization of the need for greater independence from colonial structures and foreign domination. Even though the social world continued to be shaped by regulations and practices from the colonial era, the newspaper debates turned out to reflect a minimized significance of "race" as a socio-political category. This may also be attributed to a greater participation of young people in the debates, as the letters to the editor suggest, which considered racism to be a problem caused by the older generation. As "race" lost its significance, the meaning of gender roles was transformed, and the significance of women to the nation building project was reiterated.

One of the fields most immediately affected by the reforms was education, and particularly higher education. Here, the developments were ambivalent. On the one side, colonial regulations and a conservative administration faced challenges from reformers. On the other side, the aim to utilize academic research for the development of the nation more directly clashed with concerns over academic freedom. In this regard, the university administration became increasingly intolerant over independently organized students, as was most dramatically evident in the ban of USARF. Yet, one of the most direct results of the reforms was the official encouragement of innovative research and study methods. Former students' recollections as well as articles in *the Nationalist* evoke the image of the university being a political battleground, as independently organized students' and lecturers' activism challenged other lecturers, the university administration, foreign heads of state, and the Tanzanian administration.

As shown in chapter 4.3 female academics spearheaded research that aimed to address the gender inequalities which were an increasing concern in the public and political spheres. A growing concern for gender equality also manifested itself in *the Nationalist's* women's page 'Mainly for women,' which departed from being a fashion and housekeeping advice column and morphed into introducing critical perspectives into the ongoing debates. While the aspect of advice-giving for cooking and child rearing was not abandoned, the quantity and quality of articles that sought to put reader's opinions into perspective surged. In this phase, the coverage of gender roles strongly departed from colonial imagery. Even though the social world was evidently strongly shaped by regulations and values that emanated from the colonial era, the public sphere was transforming rapidly. Despite the continued presence of letters to the editor that argued for gender inequality, journalists and readers began to vehemently oppose these conservative views.

Even with these obstacles to a transformed understanding of gender roles, the TANU newspaper evidently supported the promotion of the women's page as a vehicle for a critique of the government and the administration. Its staunch support for protest against gender roles that had been shaped in the colonial era was likely boosted by the Arusha Declaration. The administration, however, was composed of Western educated personnel who supported strongly divided gender roles supported by Christian missionaries and colonial administrators.[193] The division between party and administration that Aminzade had observed can be identified as a main explanation for the *Nationalist*'s support of increasing government criticism. Regardless of these tensions, the immediate years after the Arusha Declaration witnessed the rise of gender as a vital category around which newspaper debates revolved.

Conversely, in *the Nationalist* and the university, the significance of "race" for the debates hit a watershed moment during this period. While interest in the African diaspora skyrocketed in 1967, it continually declined in the subsequent years. Ironically, the African American presence in Dar es Salaam's social world increased as students, activists and refugees entered the country. Thus, after the discovery of the relationship between the African American struggle and the independence struggle in Africa, this may have merely reflected hype that abated when African American perspectives became less of a curiosity. As the recollections of Salha Hamdani and George Hajivayanis have shown, other conflicts, such as the Vietnam War, were more significant and relatable to leftist students. However, it is possible that other sections of Dar es Salaam's society related to the African diaspora on a cultural level much more closely, as the debate on the significance of soul music among teenagers suggests. This social group, however, would have contributed less to the newspaper debates.

While "race" continued to differentiate individuals' positions in Tanzania's social world, *the Nationalist* almost completely reversed its portrayal of Tanza-

---

[193] Even though the research for this book has not identified the driving force behind the conservative gender ideals up to the mid-1960s in *the Nationalist*, it seems likely that not only adherence to the colonial middle class ideal, but also a certain Christian family ideal, drove this reporting.

nia's citizens from Asian backgrounds. The editor not only toned down his own attacks on Indians, but actively criticized readers for using "racial" stereotypes instead of seeking solutions to inequality on a class basis. Whether the decline in hostile comments based on "race" was the result of such interventions, or the exodus of Asians from Kenya caused sympathy for the "racial" minority, or that *the Nationalist* simply chose to censor such letters to the editor, cannot be verified on the basis of this material. In either scenario, the phase from 1967-1970 was an explicit turning point, and the affirmation of replacing the debate on "race" with a debate on class marked a conscious departure from the colonial concept of "race."

The determined push back against using "race" in the newspaper debates demonstrates that the category had decisively been rejected in the aftermath of the Arusha Declaration. TANU not only ensured its authority over the discourse on "race" but also over critical academics. The official reprimands and eventual ban of USARF led to varying degrees of fear and disillusionment as former students' recollections have shown. While TANU's assertion of authority certainly hampered the possibility to organize the students of international African backgrounds, the post-Arusha phase helped develop approaches and ways of teaching that changed Tanzania's educational system from the British system it inherited. Yet, it sacrificed the unofficial pan-African structures at the university in order to implement a national one-party system.

It is striking that the newspaper covered critics of gender relations and independently organized students so differently even though both had identified significant weaknesses in the administration. While Nyerere could not accuse the students of elitism as in 1966, he still argued that they were introducing a foreign ideology. Yet, the government relied heavily on foreign advisers, as the example of the tourism-debate had shown. Therefore, and against the background of fear of political turmoil, USARF's outspoken criticism was probably seen as a greater threat by the administration than accusations of its complicity in sexual harassment. Regardless of the continuing struggles in the social world, the colonially shaped categories of "race" and gender in the public sphere were fundamentally re-imagined by the turn of the decade.

5 1971-1974: Achieving Liberation from Colonial World Views?

While Tanzania's social world was shaped by internal struggles, January 1971 marked a watershed moment that impacted the entire region of East Africa for the entire decade. In Uganda, in a long-orchestrated military coup, Idi Amin ousted Prime Minister Milton Obote.[1] He quickly displayed an authoritarian willingness to commit excessive violence.[2] The shock and dismay that the coup had caused for President Nyerere and the Tanganyika African National Union (TANU) became evident when new party guidelines (*Mwongozo wa TANU*) were published in 1971. The Arusha Declaration had touched upon the dedication to pan-Africanism,[3] but the new guidelines made pan-African liberation a central framework.

On the new guideline's front page, the Amin coup was described out as a threat to the African revolution, and described as a catalyst for TANU to:

> "Spell out the aims of the Tanzanian and the African revolution, and to identify the enemies of this revolution [...]. [T]he present situation in Africa shows that there is no people in any African state which has achieved the stage of total liberation. [...] That is why revolutionary parties in in-

---

1 See: Garth Glentworth and Ian Hancock, "Obote and Amin: Change and Continuity in Modern Uganda Politics," *African Affairs* 72, no. 28 (1973): 248-250, accessed February 28, 2019, https://www.jstor.org/stable/719846.
2 See: Alicia Decker, "Idi Amin's Dirty War: Subversion, Sabotage, and the Battle to Keep Uganda Clean, 1971-1979," *The International Journal of African Historical Studies* 43, no. 3 (2010): 489-490, 501-503, accessed February 28, 2019, https://www.jstor.org/stable/23046822
3 See: *Arusha Declaration*, 2.

dependent African countries, such as TANU, are still in fact Liberation movements."[4]

By placing Tanzania in the context of a continental liberation struggle that had seen violent transgressions in several independent states including the "treachery and counter-revolution" in Uganda,[5] TANU emphasized the urgency of the struggle on the one side, and the potential of solidarity and unity, on the other side.

The document's subsequent analysis of the Tanzanian view reflects the party's perspective on developments of the preceding years. In fact, *Mwongozo wa TANU* seemed to acknowledge some of the criticism that both academics associated with the University Students African Revolutionary Front (USARF) and female journalists had expressed regarding exploitative leadership. The guidelines stated that the country had not only been unable to change the colonial government structure, but also adopted colonial working and leadership habits. Furthermore, some leaders were actively avoiding the leadership code. To redress these problems, the party needed to take over guidance of all activities, including control of the parastatal institutions, and guarantee that the people would be involved: "The duty of our Party is to ensure that the leaders and experts implement the plans that have been agreed upon by the people themselves."[6] While the criticism was aimed at developments that had been denounced in *the Nationalist* and by USARF – namely a conservative administration and overreaching leaders in the parastatals – the solution contained a potential structural contradiction. Despite the goal of democratizing processes in the society and economy, guidance and authority was to be in the hands of leaders. Very much in line with the ban of USARF a few months prior, this approach did not consider independently organized domestic entities as part of a solution to the problems it described.

As such, the new party guidelines reinforced potentially contradictory developments: They encouraged criticism, and thereby placed particular significance on the public articulation of opinions. However, as the party and administration retained all control, accountability was a burden which could be rejected depending on an individual leaders' political strategy. Therefore, the

---

4   "T.A.N.U. Guidelines on Guarding Consolidating and Advancing the Revolution of Tanzania, and of Africa," *The African Review* 1, no. 4 (1972): 1-2, accessed February 28, 2019, https://hdl.handle.net/10520/AJA00020117_2.
5   Ibid. 2.
6   See: Ibid. 3-7.

tensions that surfaced in the years after the Arusha Declaration would not be solved.

5.1 The Comeback of "Race"?

The *Mwongozo wa TANU* did not mention the aspect of "race" explicitly. As the new guidelines were based on the Arusha Declaration, its "non-racial" ideals were indirectly reiterated. Yet, the document explicitly targeted structures emanating from colonialism which could have easily been seen as aiming to address the continuing dominance of Asians in the economy. Furthermore, Zanzibar's Sheikh Karume advocated for Tanzanian citizenship based on the premise of being a "black African, which appears to have been met with enthusiasm at a mass rally for the new guidelines.[7] Thus, although racism had declined in publicly expressed opinions in the party newspaper, it clearly remained a popular motive. Furthermore, in Uganda, Amin's government viciously targeted Asians in particular, leading to another mass-exodus of Asians from that East African country and increasing fear in Asian communities throughout the region.[8] However, while the developments reflected the persistence of "racially" based antagonism, the dramatic events in Uganda also gave rise to voices that condemned racism. Furthermore, they helped develop "non-racial" pan-Africanism as progressive scholars who fled from authoritarian regimes and Liberation movements converged in Dar es Salaam.

"Race" as a Category of Difference

The first year after the publication of the new guidelines had little effect on the discourse on "race" in *the Nationalist*. Despite reports about an exposed ring of Asian smugglers, some of whom had no Tanzanian citizenship, the newspaper did not publish any letters debating the topic. However, in April 1972, the topic of favoritism and exploitation in Asian-owned shops became predominant in the readers section, and the accusation of 'paper citizens'

---

7   See: Aminzade, *Race, Nation, and Citizenship*, 202.
8   See: May Joseph, *Nomadic Identities: The Performance of Citizenship*, Public worlds v. 5 (Minneapolis: University of Minnesota Press, 1999). https://doi.org/10.5749/j.ctttvc1p, http://www.jstor.org/stable/10.5749/j.ctttvc1p, 44.

resurfaced.⁹ This development seemed to reinsert "race" as a category in the newspaper discourse.

One could say that the merger of *the Standard* and *the Nationalist* in April 1972 brought new readers who were more inclined use "race" as a category to explain inequities in the social world. Or perhaps the re-composed staff of the newly created *Daily News* was less restrictive towards the publication of these views. However, these explanations seem implausible. For, as discussed in chapter 1.2, the readers from both newspapers were almost identical, and the staffs from both newspapers were not antagonistic towards each other. Thus, vastly different approaches towards freedom of expression seem unlikely. It appears more probable that the resurgence of hostility towards Asian traders in the readers' section was triggered by increased reports about restrictions against the Asian population in Uganda.¹⁰ Such reports may have corresponded with readers experiences in the social world, and prompted them to voice their views in the public sphere. Yet, in contrast to the peak of racism in the newspaper discourse in 1967, such opinions did not go unchallenged:

> "[L]et me state that he [Mr. R.J. Rukombe, a reader who accused Asians of being 'paper citizens'] is an outright racist. [...] He also appears to be anti-Tanu, he is at least disgracefully ignorant of the main principles and objectives of Tanu as enshrined in the constitution of Tanu."¹¹

The quote suggests that the discourse in the newspaper following the Arusha Declaration had either shaped readers' opinions on "race," or that they were more so encouraged to speak in favor of explanations that were based on economics instead of "race." In the following months, a heated debate ensued in which some readers and journalists discussed the controversial topic and others condemned exploitation without framing it in "racial" terms.¹² Resentment against Asians became even more widespread when the emigration of

---

9 See e.g.: R. J. Rukombe, "Paper citizens should reapply," *Daily News*, May 5, 1972, No. 9; Nancy Angy, "Farvouritism in shops," *Daily News*, April 6, 1972, No. 1.
10 See e.g.: *The Nationalist*, "Asians to get new rules for Ugandan citizenship - Amin," December 10, 1971, No. 2372.
11 Anti-Racist, "Blame individuals," *Daily News*, May 11, 1972, No. 14.
12 See e.g.: Mongeri Mayowa, "Shopkeepers in Mwanza exploit us," *Daily News*, May 25, 1972, No. 26; Proper, "We aren't serious about Asians," *Daily News*, July 15, 1972, No. 69; *Sunday News*, "Suggestions to beat the Dukawalla Exploitation," June 18, 1972, No. 1017.

highly educated Asians became a topic in the newspaper.[13] However, other readers, who were also dismayed by the exodus, pointed to "racial" discrimination in South Africa, and thereby underlined the danger of a general condemnation on a "racial" basis.[14] The publication of such opinions reflects conscious attempts to frame social problems outside the parameters of "race."

Even though Amin's restrictive policies in Uganda were initially met with some sympathy, and possibly triggered corresponding sentiments among some readers, the narrative shifted as Amin's politics unfolded. With regard to the exodus of Asians in Kenya in the late 1960s, the increasingly vicious treatment Asians suffered at the hands of Uganda's Idi Amin ultimately spurred sympathy for Asians. In one article, journalist Jenerali Ulimwengu pointed out that Amin was using divisive politics to secure his power. While he was now targeting Asians, soon he would single out another group, Ulimwengu argued.[15] Other readers still viewed Asians as being exploitative, but were nonetheless sympathetic to their plight:

> "Amin's decision to stop these smugglers, as I call them, is good, but the act to expel them from the country is not only bad but also brutal. Imagine a person being thrown out of the country where he had settled for years, [...]. Is this humanity? Think of the poor innocent family of the affected person who have never participated in the economy smuggling [...]."[16]

While printing a spectrum of letters to the editor from presumably African readers, the newspaper ran articles with an 'Asian' perspective. In its column 'Face the people,' the *Sunday News* published an interview with a "Dar 'Asian,'" Mr. Amir Bhimji. He denounced the press for not having published letters to the editor that were written by his friends, thereby contributing to the unfair stereotypes Asians faced. He acknowledged that Asian business people were oriented towards gain, but doubted that African business people would

---

13 See: Said A. Saidi, "Why educate these ungrateful citizens?," *Daily News*, June 12, 1972, No. 41. Throughout the entire period of publication, South Africa was defined as the main foe of Tanzania and African liberation (along with the other white supremacist regimes in Southern Africa). Thus, comparing opinions and conditions in Tanzania with apartheid in South Africa amounted to a strong critique.

14 See: K. O. Liwelallo, "Students who run away," *Daily News*, June 8, 1972, No. 38.

15 See: Jenerali Ulimwengu, "Need to re-examine mentality on race," *Daily News*, August 25, 1972, No. 105.

16 O. N. Kabanga, "Amin is right and wrong," *Daily News*, September 8, 1972, No. 116.

act differently. The interview also gave readers insight into government measures that Bhimji considered damaging, such as the Building Acquisition Act. The law severely impacted poorer Asians who had invested their life savings in housing and who were no faced with significant economic loss.[17] Such interviews and the exchanges in the 'People's forum' had the potential to bridge gaps based on stereotypes which were not addressed in daily exchanges in the social world.

While the Building Acquisition Act apparently did not hurt rich people as much,[18] it was a turning point that noticeably spurred large-scale emigration of Tanzania's Asian population. The nationalization may be seen as a continuation of the Arusha Declaration, but Hirji remembered it as a watershed moment in which increasingly successful social integration began to fall apart. Until the passing of the law, he had considered the common experiences of young people in the National Service to be particularly transformative and unifying.[19] Others concurred and found that parental fears for their safety were unfounded. While the reminiscences of Asian National Service[20] recruits do not mention "race"-based intimidation in the camps, they do reiterate that many relatives looked for ways to get around the National Service requirement. Furthermore it does not appear to have been uncommon that Asian, as well as African girls, tried to get a doctor's certificate for "light duty services."[21] Whereas a multitude of young Asians were seen as draft dodgers, Asian recruits who did not seek preferential treatment were still met with particular scrutiny as Najma Sachak remembered:

> "When I arrived, they asked me for a Light Duty certificate because I was an Indian. And every Indian girl and many African girls, let's face it, arrived in the camp with a 'LD-Cheti', it was called - Light Duty Certificate. And I didn't have one. So I got tested by a big commander to carry my suitcase on top my

---

17 See: Khassim Mpenda, "We are victims of historical conditions, says Dar 'Asian'," *Sunday News*, July 23, 1972, No. 1022

18 Kassum remembered that his father, owner of several real estates, reacted indifferently to the change. However, as a long-term politician in Tanzania, Kassum may have been inclined to portray the family's relation to the country rather favorably in his memoirs. See: Kassum, *Africa's Winds*, 69.

19 See: Hirji, *Growing up*, 111, 144-145.

20 See chapter 3.2 about the origins of National Service.

21 See: Najma Sachak, interview by Harald Barre; Rama Bhikhabhai, "Life at National Service camp," accessed March 5, 2019, https://michuzi-matukio.blogspot.com/2014/12/life-at-national-service-camp-by-rama.html#links.

head to and from the gate – it was rather far – and the offices. I had to do that – go, come, go, come – six times. On the sixth, I put it down and at that point I suppose the fellow decided (he had had his fun). So he said: 'Alright, let's see how you do the HD,' you know Heavy Duty, 'afterwards.'"[22]

Even though the discriminating experience can be interpreted as a test to prevent conflict with the harsh conditions in the National Service camp, it is indicative of the stereotypes Asians faced. In any case, in the camp, the element of "race" kept being a factor:

"And then of course, the whole notion of being an Askari [soldier] [...]. Which got me into trouble because every time I questioned something, or even did something well, my Indianness was brought up to the forefront. Like when I ironed my uniform with starch, applied it, 'wanga' it was called - proper starch applied, then brushed on your uniform. And when I did it to perfection it was remarked that – I was brought forward to be shown, they said: 'look this is a *mhindi* [member of Tanzania's Indian community] Askari who can do this, when at home she has houseboys to do that.' And I got into trouble because I objected to that statement, I said: 'I am not here as a *mhindi*. I am here just as an Askari, you should not refer to my Indian origin, okay, I'm not that.' And I got punished in prison for just opposing what the company commander had said. Because that was punishable, you do not to talk back to your superior in the army."[23]

The strict punishment reflects the authoritarian and militaristic circumstances that were inherent to the National Service camps, but such punishments were not perceived as "racial" discrimination. Yet, as in the recruiting office, "racial" stereotypes influenced the perception of individual actions or merits. This illustrates the persistence of "race" as a category in the public sphere. However, the prejudicial view of Asians having a safer and in some cases even comfortable background often corresponded with conditions in the social world, even if the individual from that group tried to distance themselves from such privilege:

"I got a research job at the University of Dar es Salaam. I remember one of the first things I decided was that I would never have a servant, that I would do all my work. And so I did all my washing and all my clothes and ironing

---

22 Sieder, "Erzählungen analysieren - Analysen."
23 Ibid.

and so on, okay? Until my neighbor, [who] was an Indian, brought his servant back home from his village in Handeni, [...] he came from a modest Indian background. [...] [A]nd he said 'You have to give him some work as we don't have full-time employment for our houseboy.' [...] 'You've got to employ him some of the time. So you give him two afternoons a week and you pay him, um, he'll wash your clothes and so on.' But I said, 'but I wash my own clothes, I've resisted this for a long time.' [...] 'so the why did you bring him from this village?' He said, 'he wanted to come to the city. [...].' [...] I finally employed him twice a week."[24]

The episode illustrates the complexity of social relations. Najma Sachak, who was possibly influenced by the philosophy of Education for Self-Reliance, consciously decided to live without a servant. Yet, her socio-economic status put her in a position where she felt obliged to employ an African "houseboy," which perpetuated stereotypical "racial" hierarchies. However, it also constituted an employment opportunity for the servant who intentionally pursued it. Yet, National Service provided a chance to live somewhat removed from the economic conditions which cemented such prejudice, as the confrontation with the officer showed. Like Karim Hirji, Najma Sacha examined National Service retrospectively and found it to be a transformative phase:

"And so National Service was a socializing experience - I would never have had it, if I had not done it. I learned to live with young girls, who were supposed to be above 18, 16 - above 16, the voluntary intake was supposed to be that. Um but, I noticed that they were really 12/13 because they became adolescents in the camp. Right in front of my eyes, you know. And I mean, people like me, the older girls had to explain to them the notion of what was happening to them. So that was, you know, here was an Indian girl trying to explain to young – something I was not required to do at home. [...]Yah I look back over it, sometimes at it and I say 'I wasted all that time.' Sometimes I laugh and say 'well it was a different way of getting socialized, a socializing experience, where you are learning to live with people who had not at all the background that I came from.'"[25]

Najma Sachak's recollection of young women collectively working to guide girls through puberty demonstrates how "race" became an insignificant as-

---

24   Ibid.
25   Ibid.

pect. This demonstrates that National Service was an important space that enabled Tanzanians from different backgrounds to interact outside the boundaries of the neighborhoods and economic relations that caused separation and tension. As such, National Service transformed and diminished the meaning of "race" as a category of perception. Yet, National Service had little impact on the "racial" tensions in the nation's social world, as National Service only targeted the younger generation and was avoided by many recruits.

The limits of transforming the society to a "non-racial" one was cemented by the Building Acquisition Act, which resulted in an increasing number of Asians leaving the country altogether. However, from the perspective of those who had embraced the ideal of "non-racialism," Tanzanian youth could have been key to a society free(er) of "racial" stereotypes, as Najma Sachak's following reflection on the relevance of her time in the camp suggests:

> "[B]ut when I think back over it, sometimes I think, you know, 'were those 10 months really worth it, wasn't there a different way of being that person' Yes! If we had been brought up differently."[26]

Her quote points to the generational gap that was also observed by Hirji. While she acknowledges the impact of National Service, her quote highlights the formative experiences in families and local communities. National Service provided a chance to live outside of these structures and less influenced by "racially" determined factors. Yet, it only reached a small section of Tanzania's population for a limited period of time.

"Race" as a Category of Solidarity

Pan-Africanism had been fundamental to Nyerere's politics since he formed the first TANU government. However, due to his emphasis on "non-racialism," he sought to define it in political terms. The early 1970s would see this seemingly ambivalent stance presented to the international pan-African community. As this section will show, the Tanzanian government tried to navigate between pan-African ideals, diplomatic pragmatism, and sympathies in Tanzania's public sphere. Whereas the Arusha Declaration had given little consideration to pan-Africanism, in 1971, the new guidelines of TANU put a strong emphasis on pan-African solidarity with Liberation movements and

26   Ibid.

"revolutionary African countries." Additionally, even African Americans were indirectly considered:

"Similarly it is our duty to establish fraternal and revolutionary relations with those American citizens fighting for justice and human equality."[27]

However, the new guidelines implied certain limitations in terms of the interpretation of pan-Africanism, as it did not even mention the "racial" component of "revolutionary Americans." Given the intensive lobbying of African Americans for their cause of "racial" equality and pan-African collaboration, as well as the increasing presence of African Americans in Dar es Salaam's social world, this suggests that TANU viewed this relationship with some unease.

Meanwhile, the coverage of African Americans resurged in *the Nationalist*, and continued to increase after the *Nationalist* and *the Standard* were merged into the *Daily News*. Beyond a growing number of visiting African American activists and politicians,[28] two main catalysts contributed to this dynamic. First, the trial of Angela Davis, a figurehead to socialism, pan-Africanism and gender equality, rose to international prominence as well as in Tanzania. Secondly, the idea of a Sixth Pan African Congress (6PAC)[29] began to materialize, and ultimately Tanzania agreed to host the event.[30] The planning of the event, which would be held at the University of Dar es Salaam (UDSM), became part of public debates, and the Congress would be a unique congregation of Liberation movements, political parties and organizations from various backgrounds.

Initially, *the Nationalist* merely reported about the trial of Angela Davis,[31] but her acquittal became a front-page story in the *Daily News*. Enthusiastic

---

27 "T.A.N.U. Guidelines," 4.
28 See e.g.: *The Nationalist*, "Afro-American leader moved by our spirit," December 12, 1971, No. 2374, Gora Ebrahim, "Africa must unite: Dr. Shirley G. DuBois talks to Gora Ibrahim," *Sunday News*, July 22, 1973, No. 1973.
29 The first Pan African Congress was initiated in 1919 by W.E.B. Du Bois, who was considered by many as one of the fathers of pan-Africanism. While the first four congresses were organized and dominated by African Americans, the fifth Pan African Congress in Manchester was dominated by Africans, many of whom were future leaders of the independence movements. See: Hakim Adi, "The African Diaspora, 'Development' & Modern African Political Theory," *Review of African Political Economy* 29, no. 92 (2002), accessed September 9, 2019, https://www.jstor.org/stable/4006813.
30 See: Markle, *A Motorcycle*, 152-156.
31 See e.g.: *The Nationalist*, "Trial of Angela Davis moves to another city," November 4, 1971, No. 2341; *The Nationalist*, "Angela Davis pleads not guilty," July 29, 1971, No. 2257.

letters in the *Daily News* after her acquittal suggest that Angela Davis had an impact on Dar es Salaam's public sphere.[32] In a poem, a reader provided insight on the symbolism of Davis' persona:

> "Angela,
> The gun is your best companion
> Because it speaks the language
> Of that sick society,
> Your hair is always awake
> Because you are proud of
> Your own-being
> You sobbed after your acquittal
> Because you saw the images
> Of your comrades kissing
> The chains and dust
> In the amerikkkan prisons!"[33]

The fact that such a poem was printed, suggests that Angela Davis was an important figure in public debates, and not only in the coverage of the *Daily News*. Even though the details mentioned in the poem could have been learned from the *Daily News*' coverage, it seems likely that the emotional embrace of her in the public sphere was supported by her presence in other arenas. Furthermore, the poem reflects a high consciousness of African American activists' criticism of the U.S. judicial system, as the reference to the Ku Klux Klan in the phrase "amerikkkan prisons" shows. One arena where views and ideas of pan-Africanism were discussed was the university. Here, lecturers such as Walter Rodney connected the African American struggle with debates about independence in Africa, as Fatma Alloo, who was on campus as a young woman, remembered:

> "I was there when Angela Davis came. [...] She came in the 70s [...] I have never forgotten the image...with her huge Afro, tiny woman with a huge Afro descending in a helicopter!. [...] Huge impression. At the campus, ayayay, the students went crazy. [...] [W]e were also discovering their history of slavery. And Walter Rodney talks a lot about this in his book. So to see her and

---

32   See e.g.: Teophilius M. Bidi, "Letter to Angela Davis," *Daily News*, June 12, 1972, No. 41.
33   Paul Y. Mlaguzi, "To Angela Davis," *Daily News*, June 20, 1972, No. 48.

she had just [...] taken part in [the] Black Panther Movement, that kind of thing."[34]

As in the poem, this reminiscence emphasizes the significance of style and fashion, such as her 'Afro.' Even though the ban on soul music was still in place, aspects of African American culture remained strong and were interpreted as political messages and stirred up emotion on campus. The degree of sensation that surrounded Davis can be gauged by the repercussions of her visit in 1973. In one comment, infuriated journalist Jenerali Ulimwengu lambasted the director of Information and Broadcasting for not arranging a face-to-face interview with "this heroine of ours."[35] The commentary not only speaks to the gravity of Davis' visit, but displays a strikingly open criticism of Tanzania's government. Riyami responded by pointing out that Davis had been a guest of TANU, not the government, and went on to quote TANU Press Officer Msungu. According to him, Davis had asked only to be interviewed at scheduled meetings and rejected to do private interviews. Jenerali Ulimwengu's comment points to the continued level of skepticism towards the administration. In fact, the exchange constituted a novelty, as a sub-editor of the *Daily News* openly criticized the government on the basic matter of transparency. This new level of objection was probably rooted in Ulimwengu's background as a student activist at the UDSM,[36] but may have further been spurred by TANU's new guidelines. However, the ultimate trigger for Ulimwengu's outspoken article appears to have been the impact of Davis as a pan-African symbol of resistance, which underlined the significance of "race" on a cultural level.

While Angela Davis' visit reinserted an intercontinental dimension of pan-Africanism to Tanzania's national debate, the agenda of the upcoming 6PAC was debated in the *Daily News*. Even though TANU hosted the event and strongly supported its organization, it also ensured that the events would unfold according to the state's political strategy, namely that it would not allow participation of non-governmental organizations.[37] TANU publicly questioned the African American organizing committee's emphasis on "race" early on. Furthermore, the government assured the U.S. ambassador that

---

34 Fatma Alloo, interview by Harald Barre
35 See: Jenerali Ulimwengu, "Why did you keep her from us?," *Daily News*, August 31, 1973, No. 423.
36 See: Melchiorre, "Building Nations," 201.
37 See: Markle, *A Motorcycle*, 142, 147.

the congress would not become a platform for Black Power.[38] Such public criticism and confidential pledges could have been interpreted as an indication that Tanzania would sacrifice freedom of speech during the congress for diplomatic accommodation of the United States and other governments.

However, as the 6PAC was about to commence, an encounter between Foreign Minister Malecela and the U.S. Ambassador suggests that Tanzania was not willing to humor foreign governments at all costs, and that it was quite open to pointing out the persistence of racism in the United States. While "non-African" states were not invited to the congress, the U.S. ambassador sought to be granted observer status on the grounds that he was an African American, and that the United States was home to the second-largest black population in the world.

When the congress opened, the seemingly enraged ambassador cabled to the Department of State:

"MALECELA COUNTERED WITH OBSERVER STATUS NOT BEING GRANTED AND THAT, IF I INVITED, ALL OTHER AMBASSADORS ACCREDITED DAR WOULD EXPECT SAME PRIVILEGE. HE ADDED, LAUGHINGLY (AND I INTERPRETED AS MOST SERIOUS), COMMENT THAT, 'WHILE U.S. MAY HAVE SECOND LARGEST BLACK POPULATION, YOU STILL REPRESENT WHITE POWER.'"[39]

The ambassador's suspicion that the decision was made to placate those who were disappointed that opposition groups from Caribbean states had been barred[40] was probably justified. Yet, as Malecela mockingly castigated U.S. structural racism, he had evidently absorbed and utilized the rhetoric and concepts of African American activists. In fact, "white power" had been juxtaposed to "Black Power", after the slogan had been popularized by Stokely Carmichael.[41] A year later, Carmichael conceptualized "the white power structure" in his book *Black Power*.[42] Although he had been vilified after his 1967

---

38 See: Ibid. 154-157.
39 Embassy Dar es Salaam, *Sixth Pan African Congress*, 3 vols. (1974); Electronic Telegram, DAR ES SALAAM 1958; STATE 129503, 2.
40 See: Ibid.
41 See: Simon Hall, "The NAACP, Black Power, and the African American Freedom Struggle, 1966? 1969," *The Historian* 69, no. 1 (2007): 58, https://doi.org/10.1111/j.1540-6563.2007.00174.x.
42 See: Kwame Ture, (formerly known as Stokely Carmichael) and Charles V. Hamilton, *Black Power: The Politics of Liberation* (New York: Vintage Books, 1992), 2-32.

visit, Carmichael's concept and terminology had been adopted by a ranking member of the Tanzanian government.

Even during the 6PAC, the impact of African American thought remained tangible, it was softened by an official affirmation of racism being a mere symptom of economic structures of exploitation.[43] For instance, Frelimo, Mozambique's Liberation movement, which was most prominently supported by TANU, quoted its president Samora Machel stating that a "white power" structure could not be altered through Africanization.[44] These somewhat ambivalent dynamics suggest that while African American activism was particularly attractive on a cultural level, its assertions regarding power structures resonated with many of Nyerere's observations on Tanzania's continued dependency even after national independence. Black Nationalist political strategies that focused on (temporarily) exclusively "race"-based collaboration[45] found no official backing. In fact, even former USARF students and Walter Rodney would disagree on the matter with the students arguing that the significance of "race" in the North American context was not equally applicable in Tanzania.[46] In the case of TANU, the rejection of Black Nationalism was consistent with its Arusha Declaration as well as the new party guidelines. The exclusion of non-governmental representatives, however, was disappointing to many activists, but it was in line with the Nyerere's pragmatic diplomatic stance.[47]

The TANU government had disappointed the African American organizers less because of its determined push back against the significance of "race" in the liberation struggles, than because of its insistence that the 6PAC was organized as a congress of governmental organizations. However, outside the official program, non-governmental views of Caribbean opposition groups, as well as a critical position paper of Walter Rodney, were circulated.[48] The party newspaper did not present such dissenting opinions to its readers,

---

[43] See: Seth M. Markle, ""Book Publishers for a Pan-African World": Drum and Spear Press and Tanzania's "Ujamaa" Ideology," *The Black Scholar* 37, no. 4 (2008): 161-165.

[44] See: *Resolutions and Selected Speeches from the Sixth Pan African Congress* (Dar es Salaam: Tanzania Publishing House, 1976), 102-103.

[45] See e.g. Ture, (formerly known as Stokely Carmichael) and Hamilton, *Black Power*.

[46] See: Shivji, "Remembering Walter Rodney."

[47] See: LaTasha Levy, "Remembering Sixth-PAC: Interviews with Sylvia Hill and Judy Claude, Organizers of the Sixth Pan-African Congress," *The Black Scholar* 37, no. 4 (2008): 44-45, accessed September 19, 2014, http://www.jstor.org/stable/41069282

[48] See: *The Nationalist*, "Professor Clarfies Remarks," 165-166.

which illustrates that governmental stability and "non-racialism" remained lines which TANU would not cross for the sake of freedom of speech or academic freedom.

However, two years later, the Tanzania Publishing House (TPH) covered not only the official program of the congress, but also prominently published Rodney's paper.[49] Walter Bgoya, who was then managing the TPH, remembered having greater freedom to engage with activists and Liberation movements after leaving government services in 1972.[50] Regarding opposition groups and critics of independent African governments, TANU enforced a restrictive official program and newspaper coverage. However, beyond the official agenda, the congress permitted the participants to congregate and exchange ideas about the political development of African nations after colonialism. In this unofficial dimension, the congress enabled expressions of alternative perspectives and, with some delay, even the publication of prominent critical views, such as Rodney's.

Regarding the (in)significance of "race" as a cornerstone of the struggle, most of the Liberation movements concurred with TANU. The *Daily News* covered the official section of the congress, as it printed speeches which reiterated the "non-racial" stance. One page gave voice to the Liberation movements, which expressed in brief statements their support of Nyerere's position.[51] The officially, strictly governmental framework of the 6PAC was disappointing to the organizing committee and its prominent sponsor C.L.R. James.[52] However, it could be considered as a climax of Tanzania's "non-racial" version of pan-African solidarity, particularly towards the African Liberation movements, who were not all eagerly supportive of the congress:

49　See: Rodney, Walter. "Towards the Sixth Pan African Congress: Aspects of the International Class Struggle in Africa, the Caribbean and America." In *Resolutions and Selected Speeches from the Sixth Pan African Congress*, 21–34. Dar es Salaam: Tanzania Publishing House, 1976. Rodney's paper was clearly influenced by debates with colleagues and students in Dar es Salaam, demonstrating the creative and critical role of the university. See chapter 5.2 for a discussion of unfolding debates at the UDSM.

50　See: Bgoya, "From Tanzania to Kansas," 105-106.

51　See: *Daily News*, "Sixth PAC: The voices of Freedom Fighters," June 24, 1974, No. 675.

52　See: Judy Claude, "Some Personal Reflections on the Sixth Pan-African Congress," *The Black Scholar* 37, no. 4 (2008): 49, accessed September 19, 2014, http://www.jstor.org/stable/41069283 James had been a prominent sponsor of the Congress, but as TANU excluded non-governmental and opposition groups from the Congress, he withdrew from the position.

"Within [...] the congress there was quite a rift [...]. African progressives did not want the Congress to be dominated by the Black Nationalist line being pushed by black delegates from countries in the West. Delegates from the Portuguese colonies, as well as the African National Congress, were united on this, while PAC's position was closer to that of the Black Nationalists. [...] I know Frelimo for instance, Marcelino dos Santos in particular was very skeptical of the very idea of [the] Congress."[53]

The quote suggests that the confrontation between TANU and the organizing committee extended to the Liberation movements. It appears that the divide Walter Bgoya observed went beyond the Sino-Soviet split that had impacted USARF's relations to the Liberation movements years earlier. However, in regard to the looming breakdown of Portuguese colonialism,[54] Frelimo's "non-racial" position gained additional weight over positions that sought to tackle the "race" question first. A front-page commentary in the *Daily News* stated:

"The struggle of Black people for true freedom, dignity and emancipation has become inseparable with the world-wide struggle against all forms of injustices. [...] The recent example in Portugal is a great lesson for all of us. For it is a fact that the victories recorded by Africans fighting in Mozambique, Guinea Bissau and Angola has given rise to the crumbling of a fascist regime in Portugal and therefore brought nearer the hope of the Portuguese people for a more just society."[55]

The quote illustrates the significance of developments in the social world to positions in the debates within the public sphere. The Portuguese revolution constituted a welcome affirmation of TANU's position on the liberation struggle, as well as its vision on Tanzania's road to complete independence: Not "race," but class consciousness was crucial for a nation's political development. Tanzania's support of the Liberation movements which had aroused indignation in the 1960s must have appeared as a vindication to many. After a decade of continuously covering the struggle, as well as the occasional infighting among the movements, a decisive victory was in sight.

---

53   Walter Bgoya, interview by Harald Barre.
54   See for instance: David Birmingham, *A Concise History of Portugal*, Cambridge Concise Histories (Cambridge: Univ. Press, 1993), 169–78.
55   *Daily News*, "Comment," June 20, 1974, No. 671.

While readers had remained largely silent on the liberation issue, Salha Hamdani and George Hajivayanis called to mind how progressive students devoted time to collaborate with the Liberation movements on a practical level:

> S.: "You [...] cannot imagine the people who are in the [...] field, living during war, they would need something small like a needle. [...] Yes, when clothes get torn, they needed to sow them. [...] And we used to collect for them. [...] The University of Dar es Salaam was really conscious. [...] [Y]ou know these people needed needles and immediately they sent the idea. We said, 'Ok we have to collect that.' So a thread was also sent and things like that, [...] small, but it was basic [...]."
> G.: "Cause students went to town everywhere to beg for second hand clothes. [...] For anything whatever you heard you would give it to us."
> S.: "Yeah, and then they would take it away."
> G.: "To the Liberation movements. [...] But that's the thing that engaged us in these movements, they engaged us, they gave us impetus."[56]

Their recollections demonstrate that the silence of readers in the newspaper was not indicative of any irrelevance the Liberation movements had to Tanzanians in general, and university students, in particular. Students worked with the movements, and citizens donated to their cause. And while the readers' section did not reflect a lively discourse on the movement, the campus turned out to be a hub which keenly absorbed and discussed their impetus. Looking back, Walter Bgoya considers the movements' impact as crucial for Tanzania, as they contributed to a national narrative:

> "[W]e debated the ideological issues; Socialism vs Capitalism, Imperialism. So those debates which were taking place around the Liberation movements were filtering into the newspapers people were reading; there were radio broadcasts. People were awakening also – it was not just [...] the party [...]. Liberation movements through their own work were raising consciousness among the people here. And in my view, when they left in 1975, there was a kind of a lacuna left because those debates no longer were taking place in the way they were taking place publically and consistently during the years before 1975. So, yes, the Liberation movements contributed quite a lot to

---

56   Salha Hamdani and George G. Hajivayanis, interview by Harald Barre.

our mobilization and the consciousness of the Tanzanian people. [...] I think many people would probably agree with that."⁵⁷

With his background of studying abroad and working in the Ministry of Foreign Affairs, Walter Bgoya was probably more exposed and interested in the views of the Liberation movements than most Tanzanians, as he notes himself. Yet, a certain section of society was highly receptive to the experiences and opinions that were brought into the country. His recognition of the impact of the collapse of the Portuguese colonial regime, which prompted the departure of the respective Liberation movements, supports the notion of the importance of the movements to Tanzania's public sphere in arenas apart from the readers' page in the *Daily News*.

Moreover, the Liberation movements did not only impact debates in Tanzania, but also augmented Tanzania's attraction to other intellectuals. Ugandan Professor Yash Tandon described the presence of the movements as a factor to move Tanzania in 1973 after living in exile in London due to the Amin coup. According to him, their presence as well as that of pan-Africanists and leftist intellectuals from various backgrounds turned Dar es Salaam into a place where extraordinary networks and debates developed.⁵⁸ His recollection confirms that a "non-racial," socialist interpretation of pan-Africanism was consolidated among intellectuals in Dar es Salaam and this new interpretation of pan-Africanism was particularly alive at the university campus.

The era after the Idi Amin coup was shaped by highly ambivalent developments regarding the significance of "race" for Tanzanian society. His despotic regime spurred an alliance of pan-African groups, as intellectuals and activists fled to Dar es Salaam. Meanwhile, his uncompromising stance on "racially" inscribed socio-economic relations spurred both anti-Asian sentiment and sympathy for Asians, and the debate on how to resolve socio-economic gaps between "racial" groups in Tanzania grew. While the relations between young Africans and Asians improved, as noted by Karim Hirji, it was ultimately insignificant as Tanzania's nationalization of property deterred many Asians from seeing a future in the country.

"Race" was effectively downgraded not only as a category of difference, but also as a category of solidarity. The 6PAC sanctioned TANU's "non-

---

57 Walter Bgoya, interview by Harald Barre.
58 See: Yash Tandon, interview by Harald Barre, February 13, 2018, Oxford. The other factors that Tandon remembered as an attraction for going to Tanzania were the presence of exiled Prime Minister Milton Obote and Nyerere's Ujamaa politics.

racial" approach to liberation and ending exploitation. The anticipated end of Portuguese colonialism bolstered TANU's political stance on "non-racialism," even though the cultural agency of "race" remained a factor in this period. However, "race" remained culturally significant, as the shockwaves that surrounded Angela Davis visit suggest. Just like Stokely Carmichael's visit six years earlier, it was an African American symbol of resistance that spurred a declaration of solidarity and as well as a critique of the government, even if only for a brief period.

5.2 The University – A Contested Space

The networks between students and Liberation movements point to the significance of the university as an arena in the public sphere. However, since the ban of USARF, the threat of tighter control of student activism loomed over the campus. Despite the ban of the pan-African student organization USARF in 1970, the UDSM remained a vital site for international research and activism. Therefore, it is not surprising that its campus became the physical space in which not only the official, but also the informal part of the 6PAC converged. After the nationalization of the University in 1970 and the ban of the student organization USARF, activist students and lecturers struggled to organize and publish critical analyses of the society. Despite the repression, students found creative ways to integrate foreign students clandestinely, as George Hajivayanis recalled:

> "So what [...] needed to be done for USARF was done through TANU Youth League for legitimacy. [...] Nobody mentioned [...] USARF. Because that was [...] an organization that also had foreign students. So we never talked about it. But they would come in as well. Nobody would know about it. We would walk into TANU Youth League, invite all those who are interested and maybe mention who they are. That's how we got through it."[59]

His recollection reflects students' determination to express their views on the progress of African socialism despite the occasionally intimidating confrontations. Furthermore, the TANU Youth League (TYL) on campus was not completely in line with the party, as it possibly tolerated the participation of

---

59 Salha Hamdani and George G. Hajivayanis, interview by Harald Barre.

foreign students. Moreover, the banned magazine *Cheche* was in a way "reborn" when students founded its successor – *Maji Maji*.[60] Salha Hamdani, who joined the magazine's board, underlined the continuity between *Cheche* and the new publication:

> "And we used to have [...] quite [...] interesting articles, progressive articles. We never really ran into a problem, except I remember once, but I have forgotten the incident. I think once there was an article [...] that created a lot of problems. I think it talked on the [...] government or something like it. We were warned [...] 'if you make another mistake, we're going to....' But otherwise it was not as vocal as [*Cheche*]. [...] But this was - it was a continuation [...] of *Cheche*."[61]

The quote reflects a degree of uncertainty. *Maji Maji*'s resemblance to *Cheche* was demonstrated in the progressive quality of articles, but the fear of repression suggests that *Maji Maji* had to soften its tone compared to its predecessor.

In 1971, a major crisis between student leadership and the university administration was to foster hesitance, if not fear in the academic community. The danger of open confrontation was imminent. Possibly due to an increasing tension between the independent Dar es Salaam University Students Organisation (DUSO) and the party affiliated campus TYL, the university administration took action against DUSO, and eventually expelled and deported its president, Kenyan national Symonds Akivaga.[62] However, *the Nationalist* and the campus TYL's reaction to the crisis suggest that it was not due to a competition between the two student organizations. Rather, it was part of TANU's continued endeavor to control the university.[63] However, not all party organs, namely the campus TYL and *the Nationalist*, turned out to be supportive of the party's handling of the crisis.

The heterogeneity of TANU was also reflected by the confidence Akivaga displayed in the party newspaper as the crisis unfolded: At the moment of his arrest, he passed on a note from Vice-Chancellor Pius Msekwa, which

---

60 *Maji Maji* was a reference to the so-called Maji Maji war against the German colonial government. See: Karim F. Hirji, "From Cheche to MajiMaji," in Hirji, *Cheche*, 113.
61 Ibid.
62 See: Ibrahim Oanda, "The Evolving Nature of Student Participation in University Governance in Africa: An Overview of Policies, Trends and Emerging Issues," in *Student Politics in Africa: Representation and Activism*, ed. Thierry M. Luescher (s.l.: African Minds, 2016), 68-69.
63 See: Melchiorre, "Building Nations," 202.

detailed the punishment of "rustication with immediate effect" to journalists of the newspaper.[64] Had he mistrusted the entire party, it appears likely that Mr. Akivaga would have passed the note to fellow students who could have published the content clandestinely. His confidence was supported by the fact that the incident and part of the note were prominently covered in a front-page story. As well, an editorial argued that there was an over-reaction from both sides, but calling the riot-police to remove Mr. Akivaga went too far. The editorial went on to question why the TYL did not help de-escalate the unfolding crisis, while at the same time publishing part of a statement from the TYL:

> "In fact it has been well near impossible to communicate in any form and at any level with the administration. Students, teachers and workers have been unwilling victims of the reluctance to communicate."[65]

The episode points to the heterogeneity of TANU and institutions affiliated with the party. The Nationalist's skepticism towards the action against DUSO's president is particularly striking, as the newspaper had been instrumental in communicating and defending the end of USARF. Meanwhile, the TYL's statement underscored that it did not view DUSO, as the cause for fundamental problems at the university, but rather the university administration itself. In the following months, the campus TYL maintained its critical stance towards the university administration, as it questioned the legitimacy of an investigating committee. Furthermore, it called for Mr. Akivaga's return and readmission to Tanzania and the university. Moreover, the TYL criticized the general underrepresentation of students in the decision-making processes of the university, and called for amending the University [of Dar es Salaam] Act of 1970.[66] In light of these public statements, as well as George Hajivayanis recollection of progressive and critical students using the campus TYL as a base, it seems unlikely that the TYL sought the confrontation with DUSO, nor did the university administration hope to enhance the power of such an outspokenly critical TYL.

---

64   The Nationalist, "Dar University Student Leader Deported," July 10, 1971, No. 2241.
65   Editor, "Campus Confrontation," The Nationalist, July 12, 1971, No. 2242.
66   See: The Nationalist, "Varsity TYL says 'no' to Mungai Report," November 25, 1971, No. 2395; The Nationalist, "Varsity Tanu brach wants Akivaga back," September 9, 1971, No. 2293.

Despite the defiant stance of the TYL and DUSO, the expulsion must have been intimidating to students, particularly to non-Tanzanian citizens, as the administration could use open criticism as an excuse to potentially destroy an individual's career. Looking back, Marjorie Mbilinyi noted the rough atmosphere created by politics: "[P]eople could also be nasty in what they were doing when they wanted, when there are issues like this of power and control."[67] Even though a politically active life on campus was not comfortable and fraught with many risks, students and campus activists such as Issa Shivji and Karim Hirji, as well as academic staff such as Walter Rodney and Marjorie Mbilinyi, protested against the restrictive stance of the university's administration.[68] The continued pressure in the form of protests and boycotts appear to have been successful, as the *Daily News* reported in 1972 about Mr. Akivaga's return to the University and student politics where he would form a new DUSO government.[69]

However, less than two months after the election of this provisionary government by all students, the newspaper reported that the government had been overthrown after accusations of Akvivaga exhibiting dictatorial behavior. In this instance, the *Daily News* ran two conflicting stories, with the first claiming the "regime" was toppled with the support of Tanzanian and international students. The article went on to allege that Akivaga had attempted to sideline the TYL. The second, subsequent article reported that Ugandan and Kenyan students condemned the coup and decried Vice-Chancellor Msekwa's acceptance of violence.[70] Given the strong support students, lecturers and the TYL had rendered to Mr. Akivaga, it seems unlikely that he attempted to torpedo those groups. Considering the sympathy former students and lecturers

---

67 Marjorie Mbilinyi, interview by Harald Barre.
68 See: Janet Bujra, "Gender and Politics in Africa: an Interview with Marjorie Mbilinyi - ROAPE," Review of African Political Economy, accessed March 1, 2019, http://roape.net/2017/08/24/gender-politics-change-africa-interview-marjorie-mbilinyi/;Lewis, R. *Walter Rodney's Intellectual and Political Thought*. (Kingston: Press University of the West Indies, 1998), Accessed May 20, 2019, https://books.google.de/books?id=1XkCzBiP7N0C; Yahya-Othman, Saida, ed. *Yes, In My Lifetime: Selected works of Haroub Othman*. (Dakar: Mkuki Na Nyoka, 2013), accessed June 15, 2019, https://books.google.de/books?id=SdwWAgAAQBAJ.
69 See: *Daily News*, "Duso head," July 6, 1972, No. 62; *Daily News*, "Akivaga forms new DUSO government," July 11, 1972, No. 65.
70 See: *Daily News*, "Akivaga's regime overthrown," September 1, 1972, No. 111; *Daily News*, "Kenyans, Ugandans denounce Hill 'Coup'," September 4, 1972, No. 113.

expressed for Akivaga even in hindsight,[71] it appears to be probable that the university administration, namely Vice-Chancellor Msekwa, were involved in the coup, as well as the initially positive responses to it.

Curiously, the coup either did not provoke any letters to the editor, or the *Daily News* chose not to publish them. Readers may have overlooked these developments in 1972, as they were only published on page five and no longer featured on the front page. It is also plausible that TANU's leadership had intervened with the newspaper on the Vice-Chancellor's behalf in order to stem any further public damage. However, at the beginning of the confrontation in 1971, the assertion of students' rights were not limited to campus, but also postulated in *the Nationalist*. A "Perplexed Observer" pointed to the abyss between the administration's actions and the new party guidelines:

> "In effect, it appears that the students were merely seeking a dialogue on the points of difference with the University Authorities. 'Mwongozo' encourages that positions and affairs of our country be run by DISCUSSION [capitalized in primary source.] at every level. [...] In the circumstances, can we afford to give the impression that a Vice-Chancellor is above dialogue with his students? Other contradictions and curiosities relating to this incident are puzzling. Why doesn't the press publish the students['] letter or a more detailed substance of its contents? Furthermore, how is it that while the press is making some reporting of the crisis, Radio Tanzania is by-passing this occurrence? Strange!"[72]

The reader's comment is remarkable in that it not only expressed indignation at the university administration's disregard for the new party guidelines, but also comprised an explicit critique of the press' handling of the matter. As such, it constituted a direct challenge, as the new party guidelines called for transparency of the party media and supported the students' argument.

The crisis demonstrated the heterogeneity of TANU, as well as the institutions and executives that were affiliated with it. A general tension between students and TANU had developed over students' claims for representing post-colonial, revolutionary perspectives for the country independent of the party.[73] However, the party did not respond homogenously to this poten-

---

71 See: Salha Hamdani and George G. Hajivayanis, interview by Harald Barre; Yahya-Othman, *Yes, In My Lifetime*, 302.
72 Perplexed Observer, "University puzzle," *The Nationalist*, July 26, 1971, No. 2254.
73 See: Oanda, "The Evolving Nature," 65-66.

tial conflict. In fact, in the early 1970s, the campus TYL appears to have been an advocate for students critical of the administration. Also the party newspapers, *the Nationalist* and starting 1972 the *Daily News*, published a spectrum of perspectives on the conflicts including those of critical students. Nonetheless, even the newspapers were criticized for not being transparent, illustrating the potential of the new party guidelines on public debates despite the increasingly adverse conditions on campus.

"So Almost All Students Became Aware" – Localizing and Democratizing Research & Education

The escalating tensions and confrontations between students and the administration did not occur unnoticed. In 1972, Ali Mazrui and William Tordoff concluded that:

> "[t]he revolutionary wing of the student body of the University of Dar es Salaam has had its political claws blunted. Militantly zealous expatriates in Dar es Salaam have declined in influence. And those who used Uganda's problems following the January 1971 coup as an additional excuse for radical slogans have now been forced to cool down following the official rapprochement between the Governments of Tanzania and Uganda." [74]

Even though this assessment rightly identified a political backlash against "revolutionary" students, it was too positive in its evaluation of relations between Tanzania and Uganda. Just before the publication, Amin would launch air raids against northern Tanzanian cities and affirm lasting hostile tensions between the two governments.[75] As noted in chapter 5.1, developments in Uganda would be seen with mounting scepticism.

Mazrui and Tordoff went on to argue that the 1966 suggestions to reform the university had been diminished:

> "The so-called 'Committee of Nine' advocated a more doctrinal form of socialism than Nyerere himself intended; they were expatriate members of

---

74 William Tordoff and Ali A. Mazrui, "The Left and the Super-Left in Tanzania," *The Journal of Modern African Studies* 10, no. 3 (1972): 427, accessed March 18, 2018, http://www.jstor.org/stable/160129.
75 See: George Roberts, "The Uganda–Tanzania War, the Fall of Idi Amin, and the Failure of African Diplomacy, 1978–1979," *Journal of Eastern African Studies* 8, no. 4 (2014): 693, accessed March 4, 2019, https://doi.org/10.1080/17531055.2014.946236.

staff and, perhaps significantly, did not attract any Tanzanians to their ranks. The views of this group would appear to have become of diminishing influence [...]. A Revolutionary Front still exists among the student body de facto, but has concerned itself with mini skirts as well as more weighty political matters."[76]

The article agreed with Mazrui's assertion of foreign leftist dominance within the university as expressed in his 1967 Tanzaphilia article. However, as the previous section has shown, leftist scholars were not only keen to empower local voices, but also adapted their own academic conclusions based upon their input. And while the campaign about decent clothing had also reached the campus, scholars emphasizing gender equality faced resistance from other leftist scholars.[77] Hence, it was not an exclusive characteristic of leftist students but rather of the conservative leaning administration.

Furthermore, students and lecturers were joined academically by local politicians like Abdulrahman Babu. While he had been demoted and eventually removed from the cabinet, as Mazrui and Tordoff noted,[78] he was and remained part of pivotal political acts.[79] Furthermore, Babu was in regular exchange with academics and went so far as to entrust his works to their critique, even when he wrote from prison after the assassination of Zanzibar's Cheikh Karume.[80] Hence, the narrative, which claimed that leftist academics were foreign and therefore marginalized, was misleading.

Despite intimidating developments, such as Babu's arrest, and continuing tension between parts of the administration and a range of lecturers and students, academic life continued to be characterized by innovative and critical research and teaching. Deborah Bryceson, who had emigrated from the United States and commenced her studies at UDSM in 1972, remembered that

---

76 See: Tordoff and Mazrui, "The Left," 438.
77 See chapter 5.3.
78 See: Tordoff and Mazrui, "The Left," 427.
79 Lionel Cliffe wrote that allegedly not President Nyerere, but Abdulrahman Babu and Ngombali Mweru had drafted the critical new party guidelines. See: Jan Burgess et al., "A Tribute to A. M. Babu," *Review of African Political Economy* 23, no. 69 (1996): 323, accessed March 18, 2018, http://www.jstor.org/stable/4006376.
80 See: Issa G. Shivji, "The Life & Times of Babu: The Age of Liberation and Revolution," *Review of African Political Economy* 95, no. 95 (2003): 109, accessed March 20, 2019, https://www.jstor.org/stable/4006743.

debates were undeterred, creative, and critical. Particularly, ideological sessions on Sunday mornings drew a pan-African crowd of students and lecturers. This diverse group of academics concerned itself with the lasting impact of colonialism on Tanzania and its attempt to develop a socialist society.[81]

Her recollection is indicative of the resilience of students' and lecturers' dedication to critical research and teaching. Despite the ban of USARF and the Akivaga crisis, academic life on campus had inspired a student who had just arrived from the United States. Furthermore, even an institution started by USARF, the ideological Sunday classes, had survived repression at the hand of the university administration. So did the interdisciplinary courses which had been developed after the Arusha Declaration. This new curriculum was shaped significantly by left-leaning academics.[82] Retrospectively, local students, such as Salha Hamdani, evaluated these interdisciplinary classes as pivotal for their socio-political consciousness:

> "Development studies were extremely crucial [...], [b]ecause like some of us [...] who were taking science subjects such as biology like myself, others were taking engineering, chemistry. [...] So, normally science students were not so conscious [...] even medical students. But what they did at the University of Dar es Salaam, they said: 'no, we cannot leave the students, they will just become bureaucrats; we have to introduce these development studies.' It was a compulsory subject. If you failed in development studies, you repeat a year!! [...] This was more about current affairs, politics [...]. [...]. So almost all students became aware. They knew what was [...] happening in the world. We knew all that. We had to know, we had to read all these books like Rodney's [*How Europe Underdeveloped Africa*]."[83]

The quote illustrates that the academic dimension of Education for Self-Reliance, which built a level of consciousness for local conditions against the backdrop of independence from colonialism, had become institutionalized. Making the interdisciplinary classes mandatory ensured that a multitude of students became conscious of the social world around them. Furthermore, the reminiscence demonstrates that local scholars' works, such as Rodney's *How Europe Underdeveloped Africa*, were directly included in the syllabus. This illustrated the significance of international perspectives.

---

81 See: Deborah Bryceson, interview by Harald Barre
82 See: Hirji, "The African University," 4.
83 Salha Hamdani and George G. Hajivayanis, interview by Harald Barre.

However, Rodney's work was a product of local research and, on top of that, discussion with local students. Issa Shivji remembered that Rodney did not exert his profound reputation to force his academic opinions on the students, and also gave way in discussions. Even his publications were influenced by the perspectives of local students who disagreed with him, for instance, the evaluation of Ujamaa socialism or, as mentioned above, the significance of "race" for the Tanzanian context.[84] The experience shows how, on the one hand, lecturers strove to localize and democratize research and education. On the other hand, transnational experiences and practices inspired further methods in Tanzania. Marjorie Mbilinyi considered her work in African American communities in the U.S. South as pivotal to her outlook:

> "I joined the Fayette County Voter Registration Project based at Cornell University and went the summer after the hot summer to Fayette County, [Tennessee] [...], [...] we did things like taxi driving, and we were there to bear witness, and I suppose we gave some suggestions and all this, but these people were highly organized. Which taught me a lot when I came here, because here I rapidly became a part of people involved with much more what you'd call 'participatory activist research,' whether it is participatory activism or research as a teacher."[85]

Being aware of the significance of communities' knowledge, perspectives, and structures, Marjorie Mbilinyi and her colleagues strove to connect these approaches with Education for Self-Reliance at the Department of Education at the Institute of Adult Education.[86] Beyond this personal experience, Brazilian educator and philosopher Paulo Freie's work inspired Marjorie Mbilinyi and her colleague Budd Hall:

> "I still remember seeing my first copy of the penguin edition of Pedagogy of the Oppressed in the living room of the home of Marjorie Mbilinyi [...]. Marjorie and I were so excited that a scholar had written such a powerful book about the political and transformative potential of education and using examples from literacy and adult education. He gave voice to the work of linking learning and political action which Marjorie, myself and so many

---

84 See: Shivji, "Remembering Walter Rodney."
85 Marjorie Mbilinyi, interview by Harald Barre.
86 See: Ibid.

others in Tanzania and around the world were engaged in. He gave us a theoretical platform and a discursive structure with which we could go forth in our meetings and our papers to strengthen the role of education and learning in the transformative movements of our times."[87]

Freire's impact on the Institute for Adult Education was significant, but at the same time, TANU reforms such as the new party guidelines, were important for initiatives at the Institute of Adult Education and Department of Education as well. While their work was founded in the Arusha Declaration's call for self-reliance, the guidelines supported the academics' attempts to raise community consciousness for their own empowerment, and to challenge a culture that reinforced unquestioned hierarchies. In 1974, Budd Hall described the institute's implementation of their programs:

> "A study group leader is not a teacher! This may be the most difficult aspect of the campaign to convey to new participants. [...] A teacher in most countries especially in rural areas is a person who 'knows.' The learner or pupil is someone who does not know. [...] In order to break away from this kind of education which cripples the minds of children and is equally inappropriate for adults study group leaders are chosen and trained."[88]

While the scholars were supported by the 1971 new party guidelines in their goal to advance self-empowerment of communities, they had to go through governmental and party structures[89] which were inevitably hierarchal. This also impacted the work of the academics. Marjorie Mbilinyi recalled the transformative impact on the Institute for Adult Education and the limitations placed upon it as it moved to the university campus:

> "[W]here a lot was going on, was the Institute for Adult Education [...] they were doing some fascinating stuff [...]. Although there were a lot of the actions at the university... but if you're talking about interesting developments

---

87 Hall, Budd L. "Surf On Paulino - Poem for Paulo Freire." Accessed March 19, 2019. https://www.academia.edu/5712588/Surf_On_Paulino_-_Poem_for_Paulo_Freire. See also Marjorie Mbilinyi, interview by Harald Barre.
88 Budd L. Hall, "Revolution in Rural Education; Health Education in Tanzania," *Community Development Journal* 9, no. 2 (1974): 135, accessed March 19, 2019, https://www.jstor.org/stable/44255658.
89 See: Ibid. 133-134, 137.

in adult education [...], it wasn't the university, not then. Later they moved it to the main campus, but by then they had become much more tame."[90]

While Marjorie Mbilinyi's quote suggests that academics faced obstacles on campus, their work that challenged existing social hierarchies found support in other places, like the government newspaper. In one article, a correspondent took a reluctant stance towards the Tanganyika African Parents Association (TAPA) and questioned whether it was overreaching by calling for school girls' decent clothing and getting involved in other cultural aspects of young peoples' cultural expression. Rather, the author continued, TAPA should protect children by insuring they receive more nutritious food and eliminating the primacy enjoyed by fathers, who frequently cause damage through alcoholism.[91] Quite in the spirit of the new party guidelines as well as the philosophy of Marjorie Mbilinyi and Budd Hall, the article concluded:

> "There is need for TAPA to reappraise the orientation of its goals. TAPA must be interested in finding out why children behave the way they do, rather than insisting that the parent is always right."[92]

The article reiterated the highly ambivalent developments in Tanzania. Whether in research, higher or adult education, new and innovative avenues and methods to achieve a self-reliant, democratic and egalitarian society were explored. These initiatives were supported by the government and the party in parts, while others sought to curtail critical research. At the same time, public spaces, such as the TANU newspaper, remained open to call out authoritarian practices and structures.

Despite such encouraging aspects, the element of fear and concern that activist academics experienced since the late 1960s must have increased despite the *Mwongozo wa TANU*. Against this background, the debates in academia appear to have had an emotional toll. This is reflected in Yash Tandon's *The Debate*. Published in 1982, the book examines the debates in academic articles from the 1970s. In the introduction, Abdulrahman Babu, by then released from prison and in exile, wrote:

---

90   Marjorie Mbilinyi, interview by Harald Barre.
91   *The Nationalist*, "The changing role of TAPA," December 28, 1971, No. 2386.
92   Ibid.

"Here is a vigorous, sometimes too vigorous, discussion on what are probably the most burning questions of the day – imperialism, finance capital, monopoly capitalism, neo-colonialism, and classes in the neo-colonies."[93]

The quote demonstrates the passionate willingness to debate the country's past, present, and prospects, in light of the unabated significance of colonialism. Up to 1974, students were captivated by particular academic courses and structures at the university. At least some academics, like for instance Walter Rodney or Marjorie Mbilinyi, consciously tried to produce academic works in collaboration with students and non-academics. These seized on initiatives of TANU to democratize public discourse and to achieve independence from the social structures that emanated from the colonial period. However, while facing an increasingly authoritarian university administration, academics appear to have pushed debates to the point where an atmosphere of constructive academic exchange was in danger.

5.3 Gender – A Struggle Against Colonial Laws and Values

The abovementioned critique of Abdulrahman Babu of the manner in which the academic exchange was conducted resonated well with Marjorie Mbilinyi's reflection on the challenges she faced when she strove to include "race" and gender in the debates:

"The progressive left at the university was dominated by dogmatic Marxists who had no conception of, nor tolerance for, the notion of (class/gender/race) intersectionality. They demanded a 'purist' static class analysis that could not grapple with the grey areas of structural change and power relations/struggles in post-colonial Tanzania. My critical analyses of race and gender were labelled diversionary in studies of colonial education and agriculture policies."[94]

Academics' blindness to "race" as a category that determined social dynamics was rooted in a Marxist emphasis on class as a causal force. This was possibly aided by Nyerere's own political emphasis on "non-racialism." However, the analysis of inequality between men and women and the promise of equality

---

93 A. M. Babu, "Introduction," in *The Debate*, ed. Yash Tandon, 1. print (Dar es Salaam: Tanzania Publ. House, 1982), 1.
94 Bujra, "Gender and Politics."

had been an integral part of socialism in general, as well as TANU's position since the 1950s. Therefore, it is remarkable that a significant number of academics refused to integrate gender in their conceptual framework. Nonetheless, as the following section will show, conditions in the social world were challenged in published research and newspaper debates. Activists were able to conduct and advance their research on gender relations. In fact, against strong resistance, women successfully struggled for rights and concessions in new laws such as the new marriage act.[95] Furthermore, gender roles continued to be a prominent and hotly contested topic in the newspaper. Against constant backlash, readers and journalists questioned the social roles of men and women, as well as the political structures that upheld them, paving the way for stronger laws that would further level the playing field between men and women.

"Traditions Can Be Changed" - Debating Gender Roles

As noted in chapter 5, the new party guidelines appeared to adopt much of the women's explicit critique of the government and its administration, as they vowed to provide more government accountability. The party newspaper not only continued to publish positions that highlighted various forms of discrimination, but also encouraged academic research in this area. University student Deborah Bryceson recollected *Daily News* editor Benjamin Mkapa's support as she submitted a letter to the editor that dealt with the highly controversial topic of birth control. She considered the debates in the readers' section to be reflective of the debates on campus. Nonetheless, she was surprised that an essay of hers on birth control was published despite the prevalent social taboos against family planning and contraceptives.[96] As already seen in the support for Majorie Mbilinyi's research on the causes for gender discrimination, there was considerable support among the country's leadership for debate that tested avenues toward gender equality.

Bryceson's letter touched upon a topic that had been controversial since the late 1960s. In *the Nationalist*, the issue of birth control originally surfaced in a report about Chama cha Uzazi na Malezi Bora Tanzania (UMATI) and

---

95 See: Nakazael Tenga and Chris M. Peter, "The Right to Organise as Mother of All Rights: The Experience of Women in Tanzania," *The Journal of Modern African Studies* 34, no. 1 (1996): 151, accessed March 26, 2019, https://www.jstor.org/stable/161742.
96 See: Deborah Bryceson, interview by Harald Barre.

its head, Ms. Nsekela.[97] The association had been founded in the 1950s. At the time, its membership was composed of Asian and Europeans. As it was the only provider of contraceptives in the country, the struggle over different views on of the role of women in the nation was projected on UMATI.[98] While printing a spectrum of opinions, *the Nationalist* supported UMATI and family planning in an editorial in 1970, and referenced President Nyerere's own backing of it.[99] Even though the government supported the independent organization UMATI, there was deep suspicion over the organization's power as a gateway to imported contraceptives.[100] In this sense, critics feared that foreign domination would be exerted on Tanzanian citizens through UMATI.

Deborah Bryceson's article noted the continually heated debate and attempted to highlight the very contradiction in social acceptance and refusal of foreign product:

> "Mr. Bashome, a University student set forth his opinion [on contraceptives] in an emotionally charged poem viewing birth control as the following: "These drugs are evil, they spoil the female lot. Un-African, unsocialist, inhuman, reactionary."
>
> If he regards contraceptives as un-African because they were introduced by the colonialists, then presumably electricity is also un-African and Tanesco [Tanzania Electric Supply Company] must go along with Umati. His assertion that contraceptives are unsocialist reveals his ignorance of socialist countries' policies towards family planning. […] Chinese women plan the size of their families […]. Women's use of contraceptives facilitates the realization of socialist equality."[101]

Her reference to socialist China was a common argument in published opinions that touched upon the inequality between men and women in Tanzania.[102] This resembled illustrations in the World War II newspaper *Heshima*, in which Chinese fighters armed with modern weapons was a symbol of progress. China retained this role of a symbolic reference point

---

97 See also chapter 4.3.
98 See: Callaci, *Street Archives*, 92-93.
99 See: *The Nationalist*, "Family Planning," October 11, 1969, No. 1704; Editor, "Family Planning," *The Nationalist*, October 5, 1970, No. 2006.
100 See: Callaci, *Street Archives*, 92-95.
101 Deborah Bryceson, "Contraceptives are invaluable," *Sunday News*, April 1, 1973, No. 1057.
102 See e.g.: *The Nationalist*, "The Chinese Woman," July 24, 1971, No. 2253.

for proponents of gender equality, social progress, and independence. This dynamic reiterated the significance of international comparison to local debates about independence.

However ultimately, both critics and supporters of UMATI and family planning argued the need to assert Tanzania's independence and nation building. The main distinction in the debate was the image of women's roles in the nation. Many readers viciously attacked women who demanded self-determination, as well as for their alleged laziness and obsession with luxuries.[103] Comments about female decency or modernity, which had emerged in *the Nationalist* in late 1966 for the first time, continued to pour into the readers' section. As mentioned in chapter 4.3, these sentiments culminated in the party-enforced 'Operation Vijana,' which targeted Western-styled fashion, particularly worn by women. However, in contrast to the fashion debate in the late 1960s, these comments were vociferously contested. After several articles that addressed mini-skirts or buibui's as not fitting to the country's culture, an unnerved reader named Jane Gebahai responded:

> "I definitely do not understand what we mean when we say culture. [...] Why do men wear ties if they are after culture. [...] When we change to minis, there are complaints and operations against it. When we stick to "buibui" there are still complaints. [...] I suggest it is high time the authorities and particularly those who always suggest such unnecessary operations let freedom flourish!!!"[104]

Clearly, Deborah Bryceson's article and the letter to the editor of Jane Gebahai constitute outspoken rejections of domination over female self-determination. Furthermore, the 'Women's special page' emphasized not only the limited agency women had regarding their own bodies, but also how the entire discourse was dominated by men.[105] Yet, while the authors' input revolved around a similar goal, the assertion of women's self-determination, Gebahai seems to have less faith in the system, as she criticized TANU's support for 'Operation Vijana' a few years earlier. Despite evidently crumbling confidence in the party, the party newspaper continued to publish female voices, and

---

103 See e.g.: T. Mketasunga, "Men to serve in all bars," *Daily News*, May 4, 1972, No. 8; Kajogolo Nebma, "Birth control amounts to witchcraft," *Daily News*, March 20, 1973, No. 282; Deadat Kahanta, "Luxury leads girls to prostitution," *Daily News*, June 12, 1972, No. 41.
104 Jane Gebahai, "Contradiction in dressing styles," *Daily News*, June 24, 1972, No. 52.
105 See: *Sunday News*, "No more than a biological factory," February 11, 1973, No. 1050.

even explicitly refuted male domination over women's bodies. In doing so, the newspaper contested opinions that limited a woman's role in the nation to that of a mother. Rather, they seized upon the Arusha Declaration's promise of equality to all citizens, and pointed to the prestige of women's liberation for the socialist nation.

Meanwhile, neither of these women were representative of the opinions of poorer, often illiterate women in Tanzania. Yet, both academics and journalists made conscious efforts to include the perspectives of those women, who had less means to express and publish their opinions in the debates. In the *Nationalist's* 'women's page,' two community workers and a member of Umoja wa Wanawake (UWT) shared their experiences dealing with women's problems in towns. According to them, married women had to sustain the family, while husbands spent as much as possible on their luxuries. Furthermore, husbands often withdrew financial support, or even took their wives income.[106] At least indirectly, the English-written government newspaper's coverage gave voice to marginalized groups such as working women. These perspectives articulated a rare counter narrative of city women being lazy and concerned with luxuries.

However, while husbands were described as the root of women's problem, women also vigorously condemned the dominance of men in key sectors of the economy and the administration, which made it nearly impossible for women to find regular employment because of discrimination in education and sexual exploitation. Community worker Mrs. Loiza Kazi pointed to the gendered, inter-generational dimension of this problem:

> "In our cities and towns at the moment, mothers are undergoing a terrible period. Most mothers are terrified that their daughters may become pregnant before they are married. [...] Many mothers living in towns hadn't opportunity to go to school when they were young and they are anxious of the many educational opportunities around them. So you will find that many of them take the trouble of providing their daughters' school requirements themselves even if the fathers do not care. When their daughters do not finish their education it is a big tragedy to them. [...] I urge our government to pass more stringent laws which will deter the men from putting our school girls in the family way."[107]

---

106 See: *The Nationalist*, "Our problems in the cities," September 11, 1971, No. 2295.
107 Ibid.

Her quote rejects the blame frequently put on pregnant, unmarried women in letters to the editor, and even though she can be seen as part of what Callaci termed 'advice givers' – Christian women, who urged young women to led a religious life to avoid the perils of the city. With the opinion of UWT worker Jane Mongi, the article went even further:

> "All girls primarily move to towns because they want jobs and they think they will find them there. Yet they find that one stumbling block to their ambition are men who won't give them job unless they agree to their propositions of which the No. 1 is having pre-marital relations with them. This is a number one problem facing girls in towns."[108]

Her quote reiterated men's responsibility for the sexual exploitation of women and demonstrated how such men took advantage of being in key occupational positions. Furthermore, and in contrast to Kazi, her views provided readers insight into the motivations of the marginalized group of young women, who sought material and personal independence. Such reports highlighted the image of working women, which had been part of the nation building project since the early 1960s. However, they also markedly pointed to the challenges women faced in the social world.

Engaging in debates with the public at large in the newspaper inspired further academic research, as Deborah Bryceson recollected.[109] In 1973, she and Marja-Liisa Swantz launched a survey on women workers in Dar es Salaam, which differentiated the urban experiences of women. It showed that some parastatals, like the textile mill Urafiki, supported their workers in family planning after their first child was born, whereas other employers feared that female workers would exploit the paid maternity leave, even though none of the interviewed women had benefitted from it. Such fears even amounted to the plan to stop hiring women, which was thwarted by TANU.[110] These findings underline that the party was actively committed to implementing their ideals on gender equality even if businesses, apparently without proper cause, worked against it. The policies of Urafiki suggest that alternative employment practices were attempted. Overall, the research

---

108 Ibid.
109 See: Deborah Bryceson, interview by Harald Barre.
110 See: Marji-Liisa Swantz and Deborah F. Bryceson, "Women Workers in Dar es Salaam: 1973/74 Survey of Female Minimum Wage Earners and Self-Employed," Research Paper No. 43 (University of Dar es Salaam, Dar es Salaam, 1975), 7, 18.

outcomes suggest that TANU attributed great significance to gender equality for its nation building project, even in the face of economic concerns.

The study itself was independently launched by Swantz and Bryceson. The latter interviewed employees at a number of ministries, and she recollected that she could conduct her research without objection or interference from the authorities.[111] The study indicates that there were strong structures for independent research, and that the administration and the party remained committed to exploring the causes for the difference between their ideal of gender equality and the realities in the social world.

The study also shed some light on the realities of urban relations between men and women, arguing that many women merely sought temporary alliances with men and not marriage. This, the scholars concluded, was a strategy to find independent income in the city,[112] which was, as noted above, extremely difficult for women. This dynamic was not limited to the social world, but was increasingly articulated in the newspaper publications. While some complained about high bride prices, others debated their legitimacy.[113] And, while some readers praised bride wealth as an African tradition,[114] another merely retorted: "Traditions can be changed."[115] The views on women's struggles in the economy had hitherto been largely limited to publications of journalists and academics. However, the topic of marriage and bridewealth spurred a flurry of readers' responses which peaked in a back and forth exchange in 1972 and 1973. Interestingly, the opinions in the letters were not necessarily organized along gender lines as the names of the authors suggest.[116] Both men and women were open to critical positions on the existing conditions of gender relations in the social world, and were eager to express their opinions in newspapers.

---

111 Email correspondence, Deborah Bryceson, 31.03.2019.
112 See: Swantz and Bryceson, "Women Workers in," 4.
113 See e.g.: Leo T. Mnyanga, "Dowries in Tanzania too high," *Daily News*, May 4, 1972, No. 8; Hammie Bajab, "Parents know better on dowry value," *Daily News*, May 24, 1972, No. 25; Nicolas Kunambi, "Daughters aren't for sale," *Daily News*, June 6, 1972, No. 36
114 See e.g.: K. O. Liweliolo, "Dowries are traditional in Africa," *Daily News*, June 10, 1972, No. 40; Kina R. Moki, "Don't trouble us; you have everything," *Sunday News*, September 10, 1972, No. 1027.
115 Leonard A. Mwakilufl, "Traditions can be changed." *Daily News*, June 20, 1972, No. 48.
116 Many authors published under pseudonyms. Therefore, the gender background of authors could not be verified in the newspapers analyzed in this work.

In-depth opinion pieces on the effects of marriage on the disempowerment of women were published by journalists such as Scholastica Mushi. In an article in the "For women" page, she decries marriage as a source of cheap labor, and that wives barely receive any schooling, and are not allowed to make public appearances. As previous articles on the women's page pointed out, women rarely earned money, and those who did often had their income taken away by their husbands.[117] In this context, she describes wives in outraged terms:

> "What else are wives but mere household tools – tools to satisfy the demands of men! Underdogs. That is what women still are as far as men are concerned. [...] These socio-economic disparities have, in fact, been the real heart of the matter – the very cause that calls for the liberation of women. For, like all other class struggles, this has put women on both the offensive and defensive!"[118]

As in Bryceson's article in support of family planning, Mushi related the matter of gender relations to socialism and described it as part of a class struggle on the way to an egalitarian society. The debates in articles and between readers in the "People's Forum" not only provide insight into the gendered social hierarchies in Tanzania, but also how readers, capable of reading and writing in English, perceived them. In this context, they did not only think in terms of the respectability of the nuclear family, but questioned such social institutions fundamentally. Particularly in light of the editor's willingness to profoundly dispute readers' opinions,[119] and the fact that the party newspaper provided space for both critical readers' as well as journalists' opinions reflect TANU's willingness to fundamentally challenge the social status quo. However, the concerns which were brought to light by research and in the newspaper also show that a significant part of the administration benefited from gender hierarchies.

As chapter 5.2 demonstrated, scholarship at the university was motivated by a desire to overcome academic preconceptions. Therefore, scholars tried be guided by the subjects of the research. Swantz and Bryceson's research paper

---

117　See: Scholastica Mushi, "The Master and his marital servant," *Sunday News*, June 4, 1972, No. 1015.
118　Ibid.
119　Some examples of this were editorial interventions against academics' letters to the editor or debates on "race", discussed in chapters 4.2 and 4.1.

expressed similar impetus, as the conclusion was introduced as an attempt to "highlight the opinions of women workers towards their roles both at home and at work in the hopes of suggesting a course of action direct at coming to grips with urban women's economic and social needs."[120] In such a manner, academia, particularly the emerging women's studies, journalists and women living in the broader public were in an interactive relationship through the *Daily News*, which was providing space to a debate that both inspired research and was informed by research and activism. Both are testament to supportive agents or structures in the country's administration and party.

Yet, even though independent scholarship was encouraged, female scholars were subjected to many of the structures in the social world that reinforced male dominance, whether through laws from the colonial era or the regulation of clothing styles. And while female researchers were able to develop space to launch and work on their projects on campus, student life was strongly shaped by sexism.[121] Female students were themselves affected by misogynist and sexist cartoons that students published on a bulletin board outside the cafeteria, called "Punch." Even though Deborah Bryceson did not recall being affected directly,[122] her recollection indicates that male dominance at campus was massive, and in some ways, vicious and intimidating. Fatma Alloo, also a young woman at the time, responded to the question of how she experienced networks at the university where "there were all sort of 'isms.' [...] The other thing that I would say is it was very male."[123] The fact that she emphasized the marginal position of women on campus in the same vein as the heated political debates suggests that the experience was quite impactful. While Fatma Alloo and Deborah Bryceson's recollections were certainly shaped by years of research and activism, the contemporary engagement of students and impediments in the social world. Academia also gave women a chance to reflect, conduct research, and eventually organize,[124] as the research paper of Swantz and Bryceson illustrates. The debates in *the Nationalist* and *Daily News* can very well be seen as a foundation for broader activism, because they exposed the larger society to alternative views.

---

120   Swantz and Bryceson, "Women Workers in," 23.
121   See: Ivaska, *Cultured States*, 131-133.
122   See: Deborah Bryceson, interview by Harald Barre.
123   See: Fatma Alloo, interview by Harald Barre.
124   See chapter 6 for the evolution of women's activism after 1974.

Furthermore, events in the social world also seem to have impacted the public sphere in favour of women's liberation. After an All-Africa Women's Conference in Dar es Salaam in 1972, even male journalists such as Jenerali Ulimwengu self-critically addressed the problem:

> "[L]et us say it, a woman has been the wretchedest [SIC] of the family, the tribe, the nation, the earth – ever since the – myth about Adam and his rib. [...] Instead of coming out against the practice of subordination of women, we, the men, have conveniently hidden against such transparent slogans as 'African culture,' which seeks to keep the African in perpetual slavery."[125]

However, he concluded that women's liberation should be considered as part of the common struggle against capitalism, and women should collaborate with men: "The demand is for revolution, not a sexual revolution, but a socio-economic Revolution."[126] Thus, Ulimwengu's article seemed to be in line with the resistance Marjorie Mbilinyi faced at the university, where her focus on "race" and gender was decried as divisionary.

Other journalists drew more concrete conclusions from the conference as recommendations to women were articulated. Scholastica Mushi explicitly urged women to question and redefine the values which were determined by a male-dominated society.[127] Her article reflects the impact of such conferences on engaged women, and it also bore the potential to reach a broader public that did not attend the conference. In fact, a week later, the newspaper published an article in which Mushi reported that men were discussing her previous publications. She presented a spectrum of opinions, but reiterated that even those men who were sympathetic to women's liberation would rarely support it for fear of social sanctions. This suggested the continued significance of mechanisms of paternalism, which had shaped the society at the latest since entering the world economy in the colonial era. However, it also indicates that it was a topic that reached and stirred up debate within the society. This is affirmed by both men's and women's letters to the editor that continued to reject the assertions of "natural" hierarchies between men and

---

125 Jenerali Ulimwengu, "Capitalism vis a vis plight of women," *Daily News*, July 28, 1972, No. 81.
126 Ibid.
127 See: Scholastica Mushi, "'But I am only a woman!'," *Sunday News*, August 13, 1972, No. 1024.

women.[128] As such, the debates questioned social structures, and challenged dominant perceptions of particular gender roles and norms.

Gender Discrimination and Government Critique

Contesting the social structures in the public sphere inevitably included a critique of the administration which was responsible for reforms or a lack thereof. As the escalating tensions at the university showed, this was a delicate matter. However, in the party newspaper, contributions from the public continued to aim at the responsibility of the government and the party for gender discrimination.

In 1971, the topic of paid maternity leave for unmarried women re-emerged in *the Nationalist*, and would continue to spark debates in the newspaper and its successor until an amended law would be passed in early 1975. However, until then, the topic was hotly contested by some that considered it to be sanctioning "immoral" behaviour. However, an increasing number of readers regarded the exclusion of unmarried working women from this benefit as undue discrimination. For instance, one irritated reader asked the party's women's organization UWT to clarify its stance towards the law. She wrote that while some, such as Member of Parliament Lucy Lameck argued that unmarried mothers should benefit from the law equally, others rejected that notion as they argued this would increase prostitution. The latter position, however, she considered fatal for the relevance of the organization:

> "For the problem of unmarried mothers are some of the commonest among young girls. If UWT refuses to help them solve these problems, then I cannot see how the organisation hopes to interest their young girls in joining. [...] Married women who make a habit of selling their bodies to other men besides their husbands are also prostitutes even though they got maternity Leave with pay. [...] [W]hat about the new born baby of the unmarried mother? Is it going to suffer the loss of the attention of his mother just because he is born out of wedlock? Is this not discrimination in a State which professes socialism where all people are equal despite their background?"[129]

---

128 See: Laurence J. A. Mushi, "Tanzania Breweries," *Daily News*, April 2, 1973, No. 293; Adelbert C. Mghamba, "Relax pressure on women," *Daily News*, April 11, 1973, 301.

129 Elizabeth Kimaro, "Is UWT for married women only?," *The Nationalist*, July 15, 1971, No. 2244.

Such comments indicate that UWT's image in the population was ambivalent, which is further supported by the finding of Swantz and Bryceson's above-mentioned research paper.[130] The comment as well as the findings of the study underline that TANU and its sub-organizations had to make themselves relevant to the needs of the population. In contrast to articles and letters from the early and mid-1960s, published opinions had shifted significantly, as they identified the power structures that were continued by the moral values of the nuclear family model. The author of the letter above seemed to embrace the nuclear family, as she considered premarital pregnancies a mistake, but nonetheless made the case to support unmarried mothers. In doing so, she emboldened the group's significance by arguing that TANU's women's section will lose its relevance if they would not embrace these women. Thus, she put the significance of the norm of a nuclear family somewhat in perspective and, crucially, also urged the party and legislature to do so. By calling for the equal treatment of mothers, irrespective of their marital status, the state was to effectively accept the legitimacy of families that did not fit the nuclear family model.

Female politicians such as Lucy Lameck were vital to the effort to create equal conditions for female workers.[131] In February 1972, parliament voted against a motion by Said Ng'wanang'walu to extend paid maternity leave to all working mothers. Only presidential support for an amendment to alter the current law would have caused parliament to support it.[132] After parliament's inaction, the debates in the *Daily News* soon skyrocketed. One of the first articles written by Jenerali Ulimwengu was highly critical of parliament's decision. By not taking action, he argued, parliament allowed acts of cruelty against unmarried mothers to continue. Furthermore, their innocent children were punished even though they were potentially in greater need than those children of married mothers.[133] Other readers embraced the decision of parliament by arguing from a point of Christian morality, while others pointed to the inequality the law would produce: As a majority of women in the countryside were not employed, and as such would not be eligible for any paid

---

130   See: Swantz and Bryceson, "Women Workers in," 27.
131   See: Marjorie Mbilinyi, interview by Harald Barre.
132   See: *Daily News*, "MPs may debate maternity leave," February 20, 1973, No. 258, *Daily News*, "House drops 'maternity' motion," February 23, 1974, 261.
133   See: Jenerali Ulimwengu, "The maternal question," *Daily News*, March 2, 1974, No. 267.

maternity leave.[134] While the former opinion against paid maternity leave for all can be seen as the perpetuation of missionary, and by extension, colonial viewpoints, while the latter position argued with an interpretation of socialist equality. However, a number of readers were quick to rebuke such arguments by calling for maternity leave for peasants and regulation in the private sector, where mothers could only rely on marginal support.[135] Such opinions rested on the argument that socialism did not only stand for the equality of women, but that it should encompass men and women alike.

Readers were also quick to point out that the matter of unmarried mothers and birth control were related – a "concerned" reader reiterated that mothers were stuck with caring for their children while a child's father can deny his responsibilities. The author denounced readers calling for no maternity leave or no extension of maternity leave for all working mothers as "inhuman." "Concerned" went on to write:

> "To the authorities I would like to tell them that if this can not [SIC] be avoided we should have contraceptives legalised to girls from the age of 19. This is for the safety of the nation. How much money is going to be spent to look after thousands and thousands of these children every year? Surely the Government must do something now but to stop paying maternity leave to unmarried women will not solve anything."[136]

The letter not only connected the arguments for birth control with the topic of unmarried mothers, but also outlined the dramatic consequences of the government's inaction. Even though there were no immediate repercussions in the legislature and executive branch, the arguments for maternity leave became sharper, and the pressure on the government accordingly increased.

The spectrum of published opinions points to the diversity of socio-economic problems with which the Tanzanian state and society were confronted. On the one hand, many opined for hierarchal gender relations and regulations that emerged out of the colonial era. On the other hand, the party newspaper

---

134 See e.g.: A. D. Rugakingira, "Public money should not be wasted on unwed mothers," *Daily News*, March 6, 1974, No. 270; Subilagalyimo, "Abolish paid maternity leave," *Daily News*, March 8, 1973, No. 272.

135 See e.g.: H. R. Kassambala, "Maternity Leave: Some don't get it," *The Nationalist*, September 18, 1971, No. 2301; Mghamba, "Relax pressure on" Rosa Mistika, "How about maternity leave for peasant mothers!," *Sunday News*, March 18, 1973, No. 1055.

136 Concerned, "Problems faced by unmarried mothers," *Sunday News*, July 1, 1973, No. 1070.

increasingly pinpointed gender discrimination as a large problem, as it not only published readers' differing positions, but also articles, which pointed to the injustices in the regulation of men and women's roles. The former position suggests that the society was to a significant degree strongly shaped by values from the colonial era. The party newspaper's willingness to publish and occasionally support the latter position clearly indicates a determination to challenge and transform these views. However, the party and the government were not united in this view, as the vote against an extension of the paid maternity leave for all demonstrates. Yet, the opposition to the law could also be explained with the country's increasingly dire financial outlook and not necessarily the continued defense of values from the colonial era.

Through the lens of gender concerns, the state's administration was questioned. This was true in legal matters, such as paid maternity leave for all mothers, but also in the matter of infrastructure and transportation, a topic for which the administration was actively criticized. The Dar es Salaam Motor Transport Company (D.M.T.) was founded as a private company in 1949 and nationalized in 1970. In 1974, it was renamed Usafiri Dar es Salaam (UDA). While some believed the low fares set by the government led to the decline of UDA's services in 1975,[137] letters to the editor instead addressed high fares, mismanagement, and inefficiency soon after the company's nationalization. Under the pseudonym "weeping student," a reader lamented:

> "I have seen big cars coming to take my friends to their homes – most of them in your cars – not OUR cars! I begin to weep now, because you (my country) have betrayed me. Where is that equality? Why should my friends (V.I.P's [SIC] children) enjoy the privilege of using our ST, GT,-cars? [government cars] [...] I don't want a car. I want a FREEEEEEEEEEEEE RIDE TO SCHOOL as well."[138]

As the reader, presumably a student from Jangwani Girl's Secondary School, pointed not only to the absence of adequate public transportation, but also to the privileges family members of administration officials received at public expense. For her letter dramatically illustrated the gap between the socialist ideals promised by the government and the increasing inequality between

---

137 See: A. Kanyama et al., "An Analysis of the Situation in Dar-es-Salaam in Tanzania from an Institutional Coordination Perspective," in *Urban Transport Development: A Complex Issue*, ed. G. Jönson and E. Tengström (Berlin Heidelberg: Springer, 2006), 68–70.
138 Weeping student, "Give us equal opportunities," *Daily News*, July 5, 1972, No. 61.

civil servants and a broader public. Such a critique became even more forceful once readers connected it to sexual harassment. One irritated reader complained about the bureaucracy and inefficiency of the state-run bus services of D.M.T. School girls were asked to provide a birth certificate for a reduced fare, even though the age limit was eighteen years:

> "bus fare to school children is a big burden. Those who cannot get bus fare from their poor families do not go to school or else they find other means of getting it, by stealing, begging or prostitution on part of girls, etc."[139]

The reader identified the implications of the inadequate infrastructure and its inefficient administration for school girls, even though he appears to have struggled to articulate the aspect of sexual exploitation. Nonetheless, the reader explicitly connected prostitution with the failure of the state to provide mobility for all citizens. Towards the late 1970s, the problem remained. In her interview, Fatma Alloo, who would then proceed to target the issue in an information campaign, and co-founded Tanzania Media Women's Association (TAMWA) in the 1980s, described the devastating relationship between poor public transportation services and teenage pregnancies:

> "[T]he girls had to walk for miles to go to school. And there were many atrocities being done. Girls from poor households would leave home to go to school by bus. On the way back they would not have eaten anything, they wouldn't have any money. While they are waiting for the bus, a Mercedes Benz would pull up and offer her a lift. And as you can see, our [...] weather is very hot. And she'll take the ride and the person who is giving it usually [...] was a government official. And would take her, give her chicken and chips and coca cola to drink and she would relax. And the next thing you know she is pregnant. When she gets pregnant, she would be chucked out of school. Nothing would happen to the man."[140]

Fatma Alloo's description explained the dramatic consequences of insufficient and mismanaged public transportation for school-going children. Car owners exploited the students' dependency and sexually abused them. Fatma Alloo's comment, "and the next thing you know she is pregnant," suggests that these girls had no family or organization to confide in, making the discussion in

---

139   F.P.J. Shayo, "School girl's plight." *Sunday News*, April 30, 1972, No. 1010.
140   Fatma Alloo, interview by Harald Barre.

the public sphere, where they had been stigmatized for years, even more crucial. The particular responsibility of members of the administration was also highlighted in an article by Daily News journalist Felix Kaiza. In the article, he reported about the pick-up and attempted sexual assault of a "house-wife" at the hands of a driver of a government car. Kaiza tied the attack directly with the crisis of the public transportation services DMT, as well as the enrichment of the government:

> "One would have tended to think that the 'gentleman' was one of those government drivers who decide to fill in the service gaps left by the Dar es Salaam Motor Transport Company. [...]
> The ST letters on number plates stand for "Serikall ya Tanzania." But as the misuse of government vehicles increased, some people came up with new names for them – Among them, "sex training," "sasa tule" (let's now eat) and "Serikali tajiri" (the Government is rich)!"[141]

His article provides a glimpse into the increasingly critical perception of the administration by a broader public. The fact that government vehicles had become the target of ridicule and disdain indicates that there was a significant degree of public awareness of the abuse of power at the hands of the administration. It is remarkable that the party newspaper provided space for articles that were highly critical of the government on the sensitive matter of sexual assault.

The low public regard for the administration is also reflected in the absence of published criticism for car-owning Asians. Deborah Bryceson recollected that "race" was a visible factor in urban mobility, as the majority of cars were owned by non-Africans.[142] Yet, despite the manifestations of economic differences between "races" in the social world, readers did not criticize Asians' affluence with regard to mobility and infrastructure, and "race" did not become part of the increasing criticism of the D.M.T. Considering the absence of "race" in the transportation debate, the published opinions' forceful criticism of the administration are all the more impressive. It constitutes a significant departure from the almost completely uncritical views toward the government in the mid-1960s, and from the extreme hostility toward Asians who were seen as the main cause for socio-economic inequality. Since "race" had not vanished from the reader debates in other fields, it seems improbable

---

141 Felix Kaiza, "Destroying Evidence," *Sunday News*, July 15, 1973, No. 1072.
142 See: Deborah Bryceson, interview by Harald Barre.

that all readers were unconcerned about "race" and dissatisfied with the government. It seems more likely that those readers who criticized the administration were not concerned with "race" in the first place and rather perturbed by the unfulfilled promise of equality for all citizens.

The willingness to criticize the government openly in its own newspaper also may have been aided by the publication of the new party guidelines, which encouraged open debate. These critiques often gave insight into public discontent, which was likely growing because of the deteriorating infrastructure and a growing awareness of transgressions at the hands of privileged members of the administration. Such critique and discontent in these articles and letters fuelled the outrage over infrastructural problems that made women vulnerable to sexual abuse. The *Daily News* published an increasing number of letters that regarded gender relations more in the realm of power relations and less related to of the norms of piety and morality. Even though marriage was questioned by few readers and journalists, many men and women regarded pre-marital pregnancies as acceptable and prostitution as a result of the dire socio-economic conditions women faced. This development may be explained by events in the social world, such as conferences, but possibly also because of the realization that women were hit hardest by the perpetuation of sexist norms and regulations from the colonial era as well as the strained economic conditions. In the face of the new party guidelines' renewed call for building an egalitarian socialist nation, the contrast between socialist ideals and experiences in the social world transformed the call for gender equality into a vehicle of government critique.

5.4 Conclusion: "Race" Demoted and Gender Transformed

The newspaper debates in the early 1970s were characterized by an increased willingness to engage and criticize the government vis-à-vis its efforts to achieve an independent African socialist nation. In light of the rising regional tensions against Uganda, the new party guidelines seemed to encourage this trend. The debates, which included readers, journalists, academics, and members of the party, transformed the meaning of gender for society and relegated "race" to an insignificant category in the socio-political debates.

The party did not react uniformly to these debates: At the UDSM, challenges by staff or students were met by strong antagonism by the university's administration, which was by now more TANU-controlled than ever. However, as was shown in chapter 5.2, students and teachers maintained critical debates, and were able to organize clandestinely. In contrast to parts of the administration, namely at the UDSM, TANU's own English-written newspapers published ardent criticism against various parts of the government, including readers' letters which criticized the publication style of the *Daily News* itself.

The air of protest and willingness to criticize may possibly be illustrated best by an example that lies outside the topics at hand. Rural Tanzania had been a prime topic of TANU's agenda. The newspaper regularly idealized the prospects and vision of rural life under TANU's villagization scheme. Yet, the scheme had in many ways and for many reasons fallen behind, and the party had begun to force the rural population to engage in the so-called Ujamaa Villages. Yet, this enforcement was publicly criticized in a letter to the editor in 1973.[143] The fact that readers dared to criticize the party's youth organization with regard to its handling of the prestigious villagization efforts reflects not only the reader's, but also the party newspaper's willingness to engage in a discussion about highly abusive action by the party.

In this tense setting, both research as well as publications in the press reflected a transformed understanding of gender roles. Both chapters 4 and 5 detailed how women faced oppression in everyday life, as well as scepticism from progressive colleagues who feared a division in the struggle. Overcoming the gaps in opportunity along gender lines appears to have held larger support in the party and the administration. Academics pursuing research on gender relations remembered the support of ministries and other parts of the administration. Their research detailed the discrimination against women in various places of the social world, and thereby provided substance to increasingly vociferous critiques of gender discrimination. *The Nationalist* as well as the *Daily* and *Sunday News* published articles and letters to the editor that challenged not only the social circumstances, but also the inaction or even active misconduct of government and party officials.

Similar to students' criticism of continued class division, the debate around gender roles often pointed explicitly to the roots of discriminatory practices and values from the colonial era, while bolstered their arguments for greater equality by contrasting Tanzania with the achievements of other socialist countries. The matter of maternity leave for all working women was an issue through which the interplay between social world and public sphere became highly visible. Some politicians, such as Lucy Lameck, pushed the

---

143 See: Lal 2015, 100.

matter on the agenda in parliament. The debate, which was an important topic in the newspaper, did not target the president. However, journalists and readers were quick to connect the inaction of parliament with administrative relics from the colonial era that discriminated against women in various ways. The poor infrastructure created a dependency which was abused by government employees. It also exacerbated the education gap between men and women, as school girls were expelled according to regulations emanating from the colonial era. Furthermore, females encountered numerous obstacles in gaining employment in urban areas, and were often faced with sexual abuse. As all these aspects of structural discrimination and exploitation were discussed, the refusal to include all women workers in the maternity leave law became a particularly delicate matter, which likely put pressure on parliament and the government by the public..

As the newspaper debates openly pointed out these various aspects of gender discrimination and moralistic opinions about women's' alleged indecency became increasingly marginalized. Gender equality had emerged to become a dominant, though not exclusive, demand. The lack of gender equality became the vehicle to pinpoint criticism of the administration in the newspaper; a significant departure from the first five years of publication where criticism of the administration was essentially absent. Gender norms were no longer paternalistically preached by the editor, but debated by a spectrum of agents in the public sphere.

While the significance of gender as a category was transformed in the society, the category of "race" further vanished from the published discourse. This dynamic was particularly obvious in relation to "racial" solidarity. Even though the new party guidelines promoted pan-Africanism, the concept and political discourse disconnected the "racial" component of pan-Africanism. On an international stage, the Sixth Pan African Congress (6PAC) explicitly ended the aspiration of some groups and activists to examine and include the significance of "race" in the independence struggles. As such, the 6PAC confirmed a development of Tanzanian politics which had been mirrored in *the Nationalist* since 1968. "Race" remained significant on cultural levels, as the ban on Soul music had illustrated, but as a category of political thought, it was neither officially sanctioned nor applied by local academics.

However, regarding "racial" tensions, the period displayed conflicting dynamics. The new party guidelines' tone encouraged freedom of expression, and may have also been a factor in the resurging of "race" in readers' opinions and the public sphere. Possibly spurred by Idi Amin's racist politics, some readers targeted Asians living in Tanzania. Yet, many readers actually articulated their critique in economic and not "racial" terms, which suggests that the explanatory significance of "race" faded from the *Daily News'* debates. Nyerere's vision to tackle Tanzania's problems in terms of class, and not "race," was apparently accepted at least by the small group of educated, English-speaking urban readers who had access to *the Nationalist* and *Daily News*.

This apparent change in conceptualizing the social world in published debates, however, had less of an impact than the nationalization of private property. Even though younger members of the Asian community remembered decreasing "racial" tensions, the larger society had not risen above these tensions which stemmed from the colonial era. Against the background of unresolved problems, the Buildings Acquisition Act spurred the mass emigration of Asians from Tanzania. Emigration was certainly aided by the preceding exodus of Asians from Kenya and Uganda and the existence of socio-religious networks, such as the Aga Khan's. These developments likely provided Tanzanian Asians with international contacts, and thereby decreased hesitations to leave the country. Therefore, decreasing "racial" tensions in the public sphere could not match the shifting conditions in the social world, much in contrast to gender relations, where continued debate culminated in an amendment of the maternity leave law in early 1975.

6 1975-1979: Finding New Arenas in which to Debate

The second half of the 1970s was in many ways a continuation of the trend of the early 1970s, where the party became more constrictive on campus, and the category "race" only had a marginal significance on the discourse in the *Daily News*. However, in 1976, a year into the international women's decade, the debate and portrayal of gender roles would see a major shift.

Since the 1960s, the significance of "race" in newspaper debates appears to have reflected international and regional developments. The increased interest in "racial" relations in the U.S. led to a peak of the expression for international "racial" solidarity and domestic antagonism towards Tanzanian Asians. In the same vein, the treatment of Asians in Kenya in the late 1960s, and Uganda in the early 1970s, reignited debates on "racial" relations. However, Nyerere's "non-racial" paradigm was also supported by international events. In speeches during the 6PAC and its coverage in the *Daily News*, the success stories of Liberation movements such as Mozambique's Frelimo had been explicitly interpreted as proof for the necessity of "non-racialism." This logic was given more credence with the independence of former Portuguese colonies in 1975. Intercontinental events, such as the end of the Vietnam War, were also signals of the success of resistance against both colonialism and domination by Cold War super powers. Even though these events were not explicitly portrayed as tales of success of "non-racialism" in the *Daily News*, they were likely implicitly seen as such.

Despite the success of the Liberation movements and the appraisal of Tanganyika African National Union (TANU), the Liberation movements continued to be viewed ambivalently within urban society, as the following excerpt from a letter to the editor from 1976 suggests:

> "The phase 'Aluta [SIC] Continua' [...] has been Frelimo's motto ever since they started their 10 years' liberation struggle [...]. [...] But, as I see it now, this motto might lose its meaning in the near future because some people are misusing it. Is one really serious (when he is in a bar boozing) when he yells 'Aluta [SIC] Continua' while holding up his full bottle of beer?"[1]

The quote indicates that the relationship between Tanzanian citizens and the Liberation movement was complicated. While the author of the letter clearly was consciously supportive of pan-African solidarity, he observed that some of his fellow citizens misused the rallying cry of Frelimo for trivial purposes. While this could imply that there was little respect for the Liberation movements, it could also reflect the formative impact of the Liberation movements on urban culture. In any case, political alliances and solidarity were no longer expressed in "racial" terms.

As a category of differentiation, however, "race" continued to play a perceptible role in Tanzania. Occasionally, "racially" coded political aversions even found their way into the *Daily News*' people forum, even albeit guised in different terms. For instance, the presence and problems around expatriate experts became a frequent topic which revealed some readers' "racial" biases. One unnamed reader was consternated about the influx of expatriates to the country and wondered if they could not be replaced by the local population. Even if many Tanzanians were not formally qualified, the reader argued that they could be trained for many jobs carried out by expatriates.[2] This aspect could have reflected Nyerere's call for localization, but the author went on:

> "As for expatriates from Asian countries, they have very limited technical knowledge as the countries they come from are themselves under-developed and technically [more] backward than the industrialised countries as USA., [SIC] Germany or Japan. Moreover, the remittances which they send overseas is [SIC] a heavy drain on our foreign exchange and cannot be justified in relation to the services offered by them."[3]

Curiously, the letter invoked many of the "racial" stereotypes that had evolved in the colonial era. While Asian superiority had been shattered by the experi-

---

1 Ibrahim H. Chimgege, "'Aluta [SIC] continua' misused," *Daily News*, August 18, 1976, No. 1349.
2 See: Aggrieved Tanzanian, "Expatriates: Poor country's burden or a luxury?," *Daily News*, May 14, 1976, No. 1266.
3 Ibid.

ence of extreme poverty in Asia during World War II, Europeans were less targeted, as the main social interactions and tensions predominantly took place between Asians and Africans.[4] The letter demonstrates that "racial" stereotypes remained part of the public sphere, and were even occasionally published. However, as in the early 1970s, these opinions were contested. In fact, among a number of responses that the *Daily News* published, one reader even pointed to the problem of referring to expatriate experts from India and Pakistan as Asians:

> "The Asian word was used by the colonialists in East Africa and the term is presently used [...] by those who still have some sort of correlation with their ex-rulers. The term erupts from a feeling of hatred towards a section of citizens and calling Indians and Pakistani Asians is quite insulting to them."[5]

Although the exchange illustrates the continued presence of "racial" stereotypes in Tanzanian society, the response demonstrated that "race" had been questioned thoroughly as a valid political category. Particularly exposing the colonial roots of thinking in terms of "race," delegitimized the question of paying for expatriate experts depending on their "racial" backgrounds. The exchange in the newspaper was followed by a few letters written by Asian expatriate experts who refuted the racist accusations.[6] The fact that both perspectives had been published may be explained as an attempt to ease "interracial" stereotypes and tensions.

Furthermore, "race" remained a factor even though experiences in the social world were different, as Najma Sachak's recollection illustrated:

> "Sometimes you had really good experiences and sometimes you had bad experiences. But I never felt fear [...] from... that I would be attacked or raped or whatever. Because I lived alone on the campus. So, I never felt fear that other Indians or [...] some members of my family felt for me. [...] They feared for me, but I did not fear anything. Because I was so sure of the friends I had, really human relationships I had formed. [...] [A]t the university, with your

---

4 See: Chapter 2-2.2.
5 Other Side, "Expatriates: The other side of the coin," *Daily News*, May 18, 1976, No. 1269.
6 See: An Expatriate, "Qualified Indian experts," *The Daily News*, May 25, 1975, No. 1275; Concerned Expatriate, "Expatriates are not to blame," *Daily News*, May 27, 1976, No. 1277.

friends, your colleagues, you were ok. Because you were somehow protected. It is probably not an appropriate microcosm to draw conclusions from."[7]

The quote suggests fears of racism and physical violence continued amongst Asian communities. However, at least in spaces such as the university, as Najma Sachak reiterates, "race" was not a matter of concern to her. While she implies that she had negative experiences, possibly based on her "racial" background, her social network ensured that she did not worry. Her experience contrasts with how she recollected her sister's perspective:

> "[…] [M]y sister would complain, when she came home, [a]nd said: 'How come somehow my stuff disappears', you know, and said 'the maid takes it.' […] But this niggling, you see. […] '[S]o nobody touched a hair of your head in National Service. But […], remember in Uganda and so on, girls got raped. In Zanzibar they got raped, remember how afraid we were?'"

Najma Sachak's recollection of exchanges with her sister illustrates the longevity of "racial" structures as well as the transnational experiences of "race." Even though it appears to have been marginal to experience "racial" violence in mainland Tanzania, the fear of violence enacted by the African majority was strong. The sentiment, which had already been observable in the end of the colonial era and the early independence era,[8] was reignited by events of hostility against Asians in other East African regions as well as by acts of racism in Tanzania. Furthermore, the fact that relatives of Najma Sachak pointed to the suffering of Asian communities beyond Tanzania's mainland indicates that at least some members of these communities retained a transnational group feeling which had been fostered in the colonial era. Therefore, even though the experience of racism in mainland Tanzania was apparently significantly less violent compared to other places in East Africa, "race" remained a crucial category for some Asians to make sense of their experiences in the social world. The party newspaper, it seems, did not portray the continued significance of "race" for both Asians and Africans. However, equally clearly, a new consciousness that discarded the significance of "race" in general had evolved among other people. This became manifest in many letters to the editor, but also in Najma Sachak's memories of life on campus.

---

7   Najma Sachak, interview by Harald Barre.
8   See chapters 2.1 and 3.1.

At the University of Dar es Salaam (UDSM), significant regulatory changes further increased the TANU administration's control over the student body. The 1974 Musoma Resolution changed the university's admission standards, leading to an older student body that had acquired more practical experiences, but not necessarily strong academic qualifications. The changes had been justified by TANU as an attempt to ensure the implementation of the Arusha Declaration on practical work, but academics saw it as an attempt to build up a more manageable student body.[9] In this sense, the reformed admission standards marked a substantial change in direction for an administration that had hitherto focused on bans of unwanted organization or repressive leaders.

Even though the reforms had the desired effect of producing a more compliant student body, the independent student organization DUSO remained a challenge to the party's goal of controlling potential political hazards. Similar to previous interventions against student autonomy, a 1978 demonstration of DUSO was used as an excuse to ban the organization and replace it with a party-controlled student organization. In contrast to the 1966 student demonstration which President Nyerere had previously condemned, he now admitted to students that he was wrong to ban their protest against raised salaries of members of parliament. Nonetheless, the decision of the state, led by the merged parties of Tanganyika and Zanzibar, CCM,[10] was not altered.[11] The president's contrasting behavior may raise the question of how far his policies regarding higher education were dominated by him or by other forces in TANU, and later CCM. However, regardless of his personal convictions, the ruling party had brought the hub of academic debate under its control.

Compared to violence against students in Kenya or Amin's Uganda, Melchiorre characterized the situation in Tanzania as exhibiting rare and mild repression.[12] However, as Deborah Bryceson recalled, the interventions against undesirable students potentially ruined their careers.[13] Beyond this sacrifice of academic and individual freedom, the accelerated repression of the mid to

---

9   See: Bulada Itandala, "University of Dar es Salaam's Immediate Response to Musoma Resolution," in Kimambo; Mapunda; Lawi, *In Search of Relevance*, 195-199.
10 In 1977, TANU and Zanzibar's Afro Shirazi Party merged to chama cha mapinduzi (CCM).
11 See: Melchiorre, "Building Nations," 216, 222-226.
12 Ibid. 198.
13 See: Deborah Bryceson, interview by Harald Barre.

late 1970s led to widespread political apathy among students.[14] This meant that an important arena which had debated and produced ideas to support Nyerere's national vision of African socialism ceased vitalizing the debates around nation building.

6.1 Gender Roles in the Newspaper

In its dedication to supporting gender equality, TANU appeared to be undeterred. In fact, when it became obvious that the Musoma Resolution excluded female students at disproportionately high rates from entering the university, the party exempted female students from the resolution's admission criteria in 1976.[15] Furthermore, international developments such as the International Women's Year in 1975 led to a boost in research on gender-related topics on campus, as Deborah Bryceson recalls.[16] However, this consistency was not reflected by the coverage of gender relations in the party newspaper *Daily News* where 1976 turned out to be a turning point.

The break in coverage would not have been predictable from the coverage and debates on gender roles in 1975. The year commenced with the introduction of paid maternity leave for all working mothers, irrespective of their marital status. Even though the passing of the law was met with skepticism,[17] it clearly constituted a victory to advocates against gender discrimination. Women gained claims to citizens' benefits in their own right, not through a husband. This constituted a departure from the value system which had dominated Tanzanian society since before national independence, and effectively seemed to support the positions proponents of gender equality voiced in the newspaper debates of the past years.

While the achievement of this milestone on the national level created no further debates in the newspapers, the commencement of the International Women's Year[18] sparked debates in newspapers and at local events. For instance, the *Daily News* covered a major rally in Dar es Salaam in a special

---

14 See: Itandala, "University of Dar," 202-203.
15 See: Itandala, "University of Dar," 199.
16 See: Deborah Bryceson, interview by Harald Barre.
17 See: Mike Sikawa, "Paid maternity leave: will it pay?," *Daily News*, January 27, 1975, 860.
18 See: Scholastica Kimaryo and Hilda Kokuhirwa, "1975: International Women's Year," *Daily News*, January 15, 1975, No. 850.

supplement. While a number of concerns were mentioned at the rally, the article repeatedly reiterated that the inadequate transportation infrastructure was the largest obstacle to working mothers taking on a greater role in society.[19] The event and its coverage extended to many of the topics that were part of the national narrative around gender inequality of the previous years, and entwined them with the international debates on gender discrimination. In the course of these events and their public debate, the image of the working woman, which had become a towering, but also contested image of Tanzania's national narrative, reached its peak.

The changed narrative, away from one that evaluated social dynamics on the basis of certain Christian values to one that emphasized equality and responsibility of all citizens, also manifested itself in the sensitive topic of abandoned infants. While courts held women accountable,[20] readers called for the state to offer greater support.[21] In contrast to previous years, on the issue of prostitution, for instance, not a single reader appears to have condemned mothers who abandoned their infants. A comprehensive article on the topic quoted a number of officials who emphasized social responsibility and the need for the state to improve and increase support for mothers. One commissioner was quoted as stating that world-wide inflation aggravated circumstances for young mothers, who were also stigmatized by society for having a child out of wedlock.[22] This example of the positions officials and readers suggests that the debates of the past years had left a lasting impression in the public sphere. However, a conversation with a "housewife," quoted in the article, shed a different light on the developments. While she also condemned fathers, she advocated for confining unmarried women's access to the city.[23] This strategy of limiting women's freedom of movement had been practiced in the colonial era. The quote suggests that while debates in the English-written party newspaper were overall progressive, they did not necessarily reflect the spectrum of opinions in the larger society.

---

19   See: Scholastica Kimaryo, "Tanzania women struggle for equality," *Daily News*, March 8, 1975, Women's Day Supplement.
20   See: Nestas Kageuka, "Girl jailed two years for dumping of her baby," *Daily News*, January 29, 1975, No. 862.
21   See: Brown Ngwilulupi, "The question of dumbed babies," *Daily News*, January 29, 1975, No. 862.
22   See: Scholastica Kimaryo, "Baby Murderers!," *Daily News*, February 14, 1975, No. 876.
23   Ibid.

In 1976, after the International Women's year, the coverage of gender related issues cooled and the narrative shifted. While the *Sunday News* maintained a page devoted to topics it considered relevant to women, it no longer questioned social hierarchies as it had up to 1975.[24] Rather, it took up topics such as health care and housekeeping, much as it had in the mid-1960s.[25] This was a drastic turn, as the women's page had pushed the critical assessment of gender relations since the late1960s. Its reports had included critiques of discriminatory structures, as well as administrative practices and laws. In 1976, this characteristic feature of the government newspaper was gone, and along with it, the perspectives of a spectrum of young and old women that had often been interviewed. The regression of the women's page to its mid-1960s format reduced critical perspectives on gender relations to rare letters to the editor,[26] and ended the public presence of advocates working women's rights and their crucial role to the nation, which had been a continued feature of the newspaper since the early post-Arusha years.

Yet, in contrast to some studies' reasoning, this chapter will show that it is unlikely that this sudden turn in coverage was caused by the economic decline in Tanzania beginning in 1974.[27] TANU's heterogeneous levels of support on gender equality rather point to individual agency as a factor. This is strongly supported by the fact that the *Daily News'* editor changed in 1974 from Benjamin Mkapa to Sammy Mdee, and then again in 1976 to Ferdinand Ruhinda.[28] While the steep socio-economic concerns may have been a factor, the abrupt change in coverage points to other factors. Having had three different editors in three years may have led to discontinuity of coverage on some fields, namely gender issues. Most likely, personal support for or opposition to gender equality was a factor in the decision, to disband the coverage. As pointed out in chapter 5.3 support for perspectives on gender equality was a personal concern of editor Mkapa, which may very well have been viewed completely differently by Ferdinand Ruhinda.

24　See e.g.: Scholastica Kimaryo, "Polygamy is an oppression of woman by man," *Sunday News*, July 13, 1975, No. 1175.
25　See e.g.: *Sunday News*, "What every Tanzanian woman should know…," March 28, 1976, No. 1212.
26　See e.g.: Daniro Mbeleza, "The problem of dowry is historical," *Sunday News*, August 1, 1976, No. 1230.
27　See e.g. Callaci, *Street Archives*, 99-100.
28　See: *Daily News*, "Mwalimu names new Press chiefs," June 30, 1976, No. 1306.

6.2 New Arenas for Debates on Gender Roles

The awareness for gender discrimination in the 1975 narrative of the *Daily News* was also tangible in Dar es Salaam's social world, where many women exhibited their support for equality and justice.[29] This indicates a high degree of consciousness and determination among urban women to tackle the injustices they faced. Therefore, it is not surprising that the turn in coverage in the *Daily News* and *Sunday News* did not immediately impede women from organizing. As mentioned above, research on gender roles flourished in the wake of the International Women's Year, and President Nyerere remained supportive of women's struggle against discrimination.[30] Furthermore, in 1979, a workshop discussed research findings on gender research as the nation approached the middle of the International Women's Decade. Deborah Bryceson recalled that reaching the broader public was one crucial goal of the workshop, and accordingly it included not only academics, but also journalists and people working in the field of creative arts.[31] The design points to the organizers' concern that the public sphere was not sufficiently debating women's situation in the nation.

The concern over women's presence in the public sphere also impacted the outcomes of the workshop. In their publication of the workshop's proceedings, Deborah Bryceson and Najma Sachak referred to Agnes Kyaruzi's paper on women in newspapers. The paper confirmed that by 1979, women were nearly absent from newspapers with the exception of women's pages, which actually portrayed women in a discriminatory way.[32] Edda Sanga, who was then working for Radio Tanzania, recalled the academic findings of the workshop as the basis for women working in media to expand their expertise in order to seize key positions within.[33] It is noteworthy that the university, which had banned the critical student organization DUSO just a year earlier,

---

29   See: Rose Haji, "TAMWA Reflections: Planting the Seed," in Alloo; Sanga; Singh, *30 years of Tanzania Media Women's Association (TAMWA)*, 31.
30   See: Marjorie Mbilinyi, interview by Harald Barre.
31   See: Deborah Bryceson, interview by Harald Barre.
32   See: Deborah F. Bryceson and Najma Sachak, eds., *Proceedings of the Workshop on Women's Studies and Development: 24-29 September 1979*, BRALUP Research Paper 60 (1979), 70.
33   See: Edda Sanga, "Editorial," in Alloo; Sanga; Singh, *30 years of Tanzania Media Women's Association (TAMWA)*, 27; Bryceson and Sachak, *Proceedings, Address List of Participants*.

turned out to be the main arena in which women could organize to identify problems in gender discrimination and discuss strategies to overcome them.

However, even research on gender discrimination was in danger of being overtaken or co-opted, as Marjorie Mbilinyi called to mind, when describing events of a women's group she led at the Institute of Development Studies (IDS). Marjorie Mbillinyi moved from the Department of Education to IDS in 1980:

> "[A]s soon as we got the funding promised and our partner was about to hand over the money, the IDS administration intervened. We held a joint meeting of all members of IDS Women Study Group and the administration. – they were a trio, the director and the two associate directors –insisting the grant belongs to IDS [Institute for Development Studies]: 'IDS Research and Publications Committee will decide how to allocate the research funds; the car will belong to the Institute, etc.' And then we had to say: 'here we have been studying cases in the village where women put together a bar, hall or a coffee-shop or shamba and then it's taken over [...]. My goodness it's happening to us.' [*laughing*] And we marched out of IDS, we told Ford [Foundation] to hold onto the funds until we have an independent location [...] And the university administration went along with that. Supported us and [...] the Women's Programme of the International Adult Education Association in Toronto, Canada facilitated the initial grant. So it was very internationalist with a great deal of local support as well. Eventually we created what was called the Women's Research Documentation Project (WRDP). WRDP was the shining light for a while with critical voices and we did really good work together. We kept that idea, participatory decision-making and practiced it as an organisation."[34]

This quote illustrates that there was a general tendency in some departments or institutes for higher levels of the administration, in this case the institute's leadership, to take over control of independently funded research. It also demonstrates that the university administration was a heterogeneous space, as it supported the independence of the group. Maintaining independence allowed the then-founded Women's Research Documentation Project (WRDP) to preserve critical research. Furthermore, WRDP gained prominence as the only Tanzanian non-governmental organization to officially lead

---

34   Marjorie Mbilinyi, interview by Harald Barre.

a workshop in the 1985 UN conference in Nairobi, which concluded the International Women's Decade. It was also at this point that WRDP was recognized by Umoja wa Wanawake (UWT) as a crucial group for identifying and finding strategies against the discrimination against women.[35] The history of WRDP highlights that independent research remained possible in Tanzania, and was eventually embraced by the party's women's section.

However, even before UWT recognized the importance of WRDP's research, the group reignited the debate on sexual harassment and discrimination of school girls. However, research depended on female journalists, as Fatma Alloo, who was going through training to become a journalist in the late 1970s, described:

> "So they gave us the research findings and we produced them into radio programs. [R]adio in Africa is the most effective. Then – even now. And we produced and the research was on (at that time there was a huge problem – there still is) pregnancy among school girls. [...] We produced four sets. And we asked the girls themselves to give solutions. [...] [I]t was like a wildfire. It really was very effective in terms of touching each and every household. [E]very household had this issue. Particularly in the rural areas. [...] When she [the school girl] gets pregnant, she would be checked out of school. Nothing would happen to the man. So that was the thing, to really expose who are the culprits. And [...] the program was very successful and UWT [...] was forced to call a national debate on this issue. This is how these debates went into [the newspapers] *Nation, Uhuru* and there was a huge national debate. And that's when the law was passed that the girl would have the child and then come back to school. And anybody found guilty, the man [would be for] fourteen years in jail. That's how we got this law."[36]

Her quote demonstrates how research reignited a national debate. Publishing the perspectives of affected school girls spurred the party's women's section to debate the matter. Eventually, the public debate led to legal changes, as it limited the discriminatory practices against pregnant school girls, and attempted to target the men responsible. However, as Fatma Alloo stated, the legal changes did not end the problem of sexual harassment of school girls.

---

35   See: Ruth Meena and Marjorie Mbilinyi, "Women's Research and Documentation Project (Tanzania)," *Signs* 16, no. 4 (1991): 854-855, accessed March 18, 2018, http://www.jstor.org/stable/3174577.
36   Fatma Alloo, interview by Harald Barre.

Furthermore, although female journalists' work was highly impactful, they were to soon experience how male decision makers could block their work:

> "[The set on school girl pregnancies] had such a powerful impact and results that we felt very encouraged. So we produced the next set which was on 'wife beating' [...] [W]e sent it to the head of the radio station, because those days [...] you had to pass through this channel. And when he saw it he said: 'you guys have to be kidding. I beat my wife, so what? She is my wife.' And threw our programs out. That's when [...] we got very disillusioned and very disheartened and we all went our ways. [...] [S]ome gave up, some got married, some went away [...]. [E]ven I went away. But then we regrouped in 1987 and that's when TAMWA [Tanzania Media Women's Association] was born. But the seeds were from the 1980s."[37]

Fatma Alloo's recollection strikingly highlights the rough shifts individual careers and political strategies could experience because of the power of key agents. Edda Sanga's memory of the strategy to get into key positions in the media merely through training and expertise also could have been thwarted by such experiences.

However, despite the degree of frustration and resignation that was expressed in Fatma Alloo's quote, women's activism in research and media did not subside. In order to systematically question women's roles and positions in Tanzanian society, Ophelia Mascarenhas and Marjorie Mbilinyi published an analytical bibliography of materials on the gender issue available in Tanzania.[38] As expressed by Fatma Alloo and Edda Sanga above, academic findings were an important foundation for women working in media, as they sought to address the discrimination and oppression of women in the nation.

Notably, the interrelation between academia and media was merely one aspect of the relationship between the public sphere and the social world: The activists, who regrouped as TAMWA in 1987, remembered that their determination and dedication to resist against women's oppression was crucially motivated and inspired by the African Liberation movements.[39] This points to the lasting impact of pan-African solidarity, as it was nurtured by the TANU

---

37 Ibid.
38 See: Ophelia Mascarenhas and Marjorie Mbilinyi, *Women in Tanzania: An Analytical Bibliography* (Uppsala, Scandinavian Institute of African Studies, 1983).
39 See: Fatma Alloo, "Editorial," in Alloo; Sanga; Singh, *30 years of Tanzania Media Women's Association (TAMWA)*, 23.

government in the 1960s and 1970s. The presence of the Liberation movements in Tanzania made the need and ability to combat injustice part of Tanzania's national narrative. Therefore, despite setbacks and frustration in the social world, activists were able to find common ground to reorganize and continue their struggle.

6.3 Conclusion: Uncertainty and Agency

In the second half of the 1970s, the debates in the *Daily News* and *Sunday News* were shaped by continuity with regard to the absence of "race," and by a dramatic turn in the emphasis on gender roles. "Race" either as a category of solidarity or difference only fleetingly appeared in readers' debates. On the occasion of the "racialized" critique of expatriate workers, other readers were quick to respond and denounce it as a viewpoint stemming from the colonial era. Thus, "race" continued to hold significance in the social world, but there was no tangible interplay with the public sphere, namely the English-written party newspaper, where it had been deconstructed as a meaningful category. Debates on gender, however, were shaped by letters to the editor, which were highly conscious of discrimination against women throughout 1975. However, in 1976, this trend, which had lasted since the late 1960s, broke off, and women were almost exclusively covered from male vantage points. Women's issues were usually confined to the role of the family care taker. Thus, in the party newspaper, the debates and articles that advocated for rights and opportunities for working women ceased.

This change in coverage, however, did not reflect a homogenous position of TANU. As TANU realized that its changed admission rules for the university disproportionately disadvantaged women, it scrapped those rules for women in 1976 – the very year when the *Daily News* abandoned its progressive coverage of gender equality. Furthermore, the university, which was increasingly under the control of the party, ended up being a crucial location for renewed debates on gender equality. This became particularly visible in the 1979 workshop which linked academia with various communicative institutions. Thus, despite, or maybe even because of TANU interventions, academics and activists supportive of gender equality were able to continue research on gender discrimination. Accordingly, the macro-economic decline in Tanzania cannot be identified as a factor in this shift of discourse from the newspaper to the arena of the university, but rather the agency and agenda of individuals in these arenas.

Scholars at the university who were concerned with gender equality were able to deal with the topic in a more stable setting. This was supported by the TANU-led university administration at least to some degree. This continuity turned out to be crucial, as it enabled the institutionalization of research on gender discrimination, as well as the networking between a spectrum of social agents, who were active in gender equality advocacy. Both the 1979 workshop as well as the foundation of WRDP enabled the establishment of links between academics and communicative institutions, namely women who worked in radio.

This epilogue's glimpse into the developments after 1974 illustrates the significance of the developments in the 1960s and early 1970s. In particular, the recollections of the female activists for women's rights point to the significance of a national narrative which was shaped by calls for justice and solidarity. This demonstrates that the debates around "race" and gender in the 1960s and 1970s had a lasting impact on Tanzanian society, as they structured the social world and categories of perception. Obstacles in the social world, such as growing poverty, the Ugandan invasion in 1979, the continued dominance of social key positions by men, and the structural adjustment programs in the mid-1980s do not appear to have shaken the foundation laid during these years.

7 Conclusion

This work's detailed analysis of developments in Tanzania's public sphere and its interrelations with developments in the social world contributes to understanding processes of social structuration. In particular, it highlights how the objective of building a nation was negotiated in the public sphere, and how these developments intersected with developments in the social world. By examining different arenas of the public sphere, this study was able to establish that the Tanganyika African National Union (TANU) heterogeneously perceived the significance of key components of its national project: "non-racialism" and (gender) equality. In contrast to studies that work with larger periodical frames, this study helps perceive TANU in a more differentiated manner and accordingly highlights the agency of individuals and smaller groups.

The first two decades after independence saw Tanzania struggle to imagine a nation independent of the structures that had shaped the society in the colonial era. While Schneider has pointed to the continuity in the administration's practice, this work's examination of debates in the public sphere has painted a different picture. In newspaper debates, research and retrospective testimonies, the continuity of values, laws and regulations from the colonial era was actively challenged, and at least partially changed. In the course of the 1960s and early 1970s, these debates reduced the significance of the category "race," and transformed the meaning of the category of gender. While social disparities were not nullified, they were perceived in new terms. Even though socialist ideas were discussed early on, it was particularly after the Arusha Declaration in 1967 that class was introduced as the decisive category of difference. Over the following years, the focus of the category "race" was replaced by class in many areas, and gender equality was advocated for on the grounds of socialism. By 1974, the national narrative had developed a strong current, which was distinct, but not detached from the colonial categories of perception. These outcomes support Bourdieu's assumption that structures and categories of perception, which had been shaped in the colonial era, had a long-lasting, but not continuous impact, on society well beyond formal independence.

Particularly chapter 6 illustrated that this discourse was not only bounded by the social world, but that it moreover impacted developments in the social world, as academics and media women began to organize against discrimination. The following concluding sections will reflect on how shifts and continuities brought about linked but uneven developments in the social world in addition to discourses in the public sphere.

7.1 A Contested National Narrative

In this sense, the categories "race" and gender, which had gravely defined social distinction during colonialism, slowly changed in their significance, as new ideas were taken up by agents who introduced them in various arenas of the public sphere. However, it was not a uniform or continuous development, but as Balibar's weft of a collective narrative illustrated, rather a struggle in which views were divided and contested. Breaks and turns in the narrative have become particularly visible through this long-term analysis of the English-written party newspapers. Furthermore, the discourse as it was manifested in the newspaper occasionally contrasted with other arenas within the public sphere. This can be said for both the discourse on "race" as well as gender.

Although "racial" solidarity in terms of politics, namely with African Americans, was no longer was an element of the newspaper discourse as of the late1960s, this cannot be said for "racial" solidarity, which was expressed in terms of culture. Outside the confines of political discourse, African American culture continued to be an important emotional reference point. In fact, this cultural affinity to prominent African Americans preceded the emerging explicit discourse of "racial" solidarity, as it can be seen in the highly popular figure of Muhammad Ali in 1964. The continued significance of "race" as a category to make sense of social divisions and imbalanced power was also visible in other arenas of the public sphere. For instance, conceptualizations of Black Power advocates, such as white power structures became part of official debates. Although Black Power hosted an umbrella of interpretations and approaches, it commonly regarded "race" as a crucial category which had to be included in analyses of social disparities. The fact that even high ranking members of the TANU government used it shows that "race" was a relevant category in leading government circles. However, these views were not conveyed in other arenas, such as the *Daily News* and its predecessor, *the Nationalist*.

The meaning of "Race" as a category of difference also changed over time in different communicative institutions in the public sphere. With the exception of a few months around the time of the Arusha Declaration, during which "race" was used to discriminate, Nyerere's ideal of "non-racialism" was defended almost throughout the entire period of coverage by the English-written government newspaper. In times of crises, such as the aftermath of the revolution in Zanzibar, commitment to "non-racial" pan-Africanism was almost ostentatious in the newspaper, as though the TANU newspaper attempted to reassure the readers. By the mid-1970s, "race" had been deconstructed by journalists and many readers, and therefore became meaningless for the political discourse as it manifested itself in the newspaper. However, this trend did not correspond with other arenas of the public sphere. For instance, in education, "race" was a crucial category at the end of colonialism. However, former students recollected that the efforts to integrate schools contributed to bridging the divide between Asian and African students. The same can be said for the experiences in National Service Camps. Even though students faced mutual stereotypes, the interaction in somewhat neutral spaces challenged this trend. Research and memories of witnesses from the time place this development in the mid-1960s, before *the Nationalist's* brief phase of "racially" coded coverage began.

In regard to the discourse on gender, this divergence was even more recognizable. While equality had been a crucial motivator for women to support TANU in the 1950's, the newspaper narrative up to the mid 1960's was dominated by men's ambivalent views on women and their role in the nation. After the Arusha Declaration, the newspaper discourse was sharply divided: On the one hand, conservative voices advocated Christian or "traditional" African values and particularly condemned urban women who attempted to lead a life independent of the constraints of family and matrimony. On the other hand, a spectrum of women and men struggled to create a greater degree of independence by advocating for laws and benefits in order to overcome gender discrimination, and by raising a social debate that questioned the status quo. However, the newspaper's coverage was volatile. Its support of opponents of gender discrimination appeared to depend on editor Benjamin Mkapa (1966-1974) and his successor Sammy Mdee (1974-1976).

In other arenas of the public sphere, namely the university, this dynamic was different. As it was visible in contemporary publications as well as interviews and memoirs, women were able to set foot and slowly expand their agency for gender equality at the university since the late 1960s. Through their own media networks as well as through interviews and memoirs, they continue to impact a national debate on gender discrimination and equality, whereas the English-written government newspaper abandoned its progressive coverage on gender issues in 1976.

In fact, these diverging perspectives in the public sphere seem to inform contemporary research as well: The topic of misogyny at the university campus was not debated in the English-written party newspaper. However, some former female students recalled it as a crucial and inhibiting aspect of life on campus. This was also reflected in Ivaska's work, who found evidence of sexism and misogyny in student newspapers in the early 1970s.[1] These views consider sexism to be a part of the culture that was nurtured by a scarcity of opportunities and the competition with older men who could rely on secure income. Conversely, according to Itandala, misogyny became only a characteristic of campus culture in the late 1970s, and was triggered by apathy and frustration of students when the Musoma Declaration was enacted and stricter university leadership depoliticized the campus. Thus, the imagination of a national community is a process which is characterized by heterogeneity and asynchrony. While the unfolding events were perceived, evaluated, and discussed from multiple angles at the time, they continued to have multiple meanings in hindsight, as seen in the contradictory characterization of the state of gender relations at the university portrayed in the research by Itandala and Ivaska.

7.2   Interrelation Between the Public Sphere and Social World

The existence of a national narrative that consists of converging and diverging strings of opinions has an important relationship with the social world. This is true for both the impact of the social world on the discourses in the

---

1   Ivaska's position is also supported by the study at hand, which showed that Tanzanian women protested in *the Nationalist* in the late 1960s against sexual harassment at the hands of men.

public sphere, and vice versa. As Alexander suggested, discourses in the public sphere would be bounded by entities in the social world, e.g. family and community. The dynamics in the interrelation between public sphere and social world, which were identified in this study, provide helpful answers to Bourdieu's assertion that structuring structures can be altered and changed. In essence, this analysis of the interrelation between public sphere and social world could illustrate the possibility of continuity and change as social groups evolved in their perception of the social world.

Looking at the government newspaper, the debates between readers appear to have fulfilled crucial civic and emotional functions. They established a counter-narrative to the occasionally domineering tone in articles and editorials of the newspaper. In this way, the readers' section helped to democratize the narrative. Furthermore, the spectrum of perspectives in the newspaper debates points to the relevance of a national narrative for a nation, as sketched by Vilashini Cooppan: As nations are composed of ambivalent, rather than harmonious forces, a national narrative has the potential to create a sense of belonging. The debates around "race" and gender were characterized be a great degree of tolerance. Only on very rare occasions did the party explicitly intervene in the debates. Therefore, a large spectrum of men and women of various backgrounds were able to voice their opinions, hopes, and fears for the nation. Even perspectives from abroad became very much part of a national narrative as they became part of national debates. The particular interest in the reader's section by the newspaper's customers had been confirmed in contemporary studies and underlines the public relevance of these published debates: This was a space where readers who imagined themselves as Tanzanians could come together and share their views and feelings for the new nation. They also shared their personal struggles as the country developed an identity. In this sense, the debates in the public sphere created the narrative and shaped the categories through which the social world would be understood.

Conversely, the social world, or in Alexander's words, 'non-civil spheres' such as state, family and community, framed the discourses in the public sphere. For example, as the observations in section 7.1 suggest, the discourse on "race" could only change in certain spaces under certain conditions. It was necessary that the old categories could be challenged by new categories introduced by the state – a social agent with formative power, as Bourdieu argued. Conversely, revisiting Alexander' argument, the category "race" could only be fundamentally challenged in those spaces that were less impacted by family or community, i.e. a school, a National Service Camp or a newspaper with a relatively open discussion. The constraints that family and community exerted on the public discourse regarding "race" can be seen in recollections as well as letters to the editor in *the Nationalist*, which blamed the older generation for continued "racial" thinking.

While the letters to the editor in the late 1960s addressed the older generation's racism across "racial" lines, Najma Sachak and Karim Hirji's recollections illustrate the problem in more detail from the perspective of Asian communities. This was evidenced by the concern about integrated spaces, namely schools. In this context, parents feared the lowering of standards. This reflected stereotypes and competitive "racial" relations, which had been introduced in the colonial era. These family-promoted stereotypes certainly made unprejudiced interaction across "racial" lines harder, albeit not impossible. However, Asian experiences of threats and violence, such as in Zanzibar or Uganda, increased a common group sentiment in these communities. These experiences reaffirmed the importance of "race" as a divisive category among Asians, and certainly inhibited those individuals affected by it from contributing to a discourse in the public sphere. In this sense, they were largely excluded from the discussion.

Similarly, the dialogue on the meaning of gender roles was bounded by the social world. This changed dramatically once women began to contribute to the newspaper. While gender equality was an important aspect of the mid-1960s coverage of *the Nationalist*, many articles portrayed them in confined roles as mothers and wives. This changed in the months surrounding the Arusha Declaration, as women began contributing to the readers' section, and as journalists began reporting in depth about the various forms of discrimination women faced. This development was also aided by research from the UDSM, which in turn had been requested by the TANU-led state. Thus, the discourse in the public sphere was shaped significantly by the affected group's ability to contribute to the newspaper, the state's capability to see gender discrimination as a problem, and the availability of qualified academics and journalists to explore it.

While the discourse was restricted by such factors in the social world, the debate evidently evolved in its own right in the newspaper, and up to 1975, the discourse on women's rights and opportunities not only uncovered numerous new aspects of discrimination, but also discussed new values. It could not be conclusively established in this work in how far the newspaper discourse of the late 1960s and early 1970s impacted the social world. The introduction and eventual amendment of the maternity leave law followed the public debate over it, but it is likely that the mounting pressure exerted in the newspaper was merely one factor. It is clear, however, that the discourse that evolved in the newspaper was a manifestation of a larger public conversation among women and probably some men.[2] This public discourse was interlinked with other debates on justice and solidarity, which were interrelated with the presence of the African Liberation movements in Tanzania, as well as the political positions of the TANU government. These debates provided the agents who organized themselves at the university and in the media with the skills to analyze and address gender discrimination, as well as with the inspiration to advocate and struggle for justice.

Even though it is not possible to pinpoint the moments of interrelation, i.e. when articles were read, debated, and led to action, it is possible to demonstrate the evolution of the interrelation between the social world and the public sphere. In independent Tanzania, public and published debates were shaped by the social world and the history it was embedded in, but, in turn, the debates also restructured the social world and the way it was perceived. The resilience of the new structures can be seen in the continuation of women's research and activism against gender discrimination despite the setback in the newspaper coverage starting in 1976.

7.3 Formative Obscurities

Many aspects that revolved around the categories "race" and gender were made explicit in the newspaper debates or in research. Therefore, the way in which the public sphere was influenced by the social world was relatively discernible, e.g. as values and ideas were discussed. However, one element which restructured the social world fundamentally and certainly influenced the dynamics in the public sphere was not verbalized in the newspaper debates, but only in retrospective testimonies. That was the element of fear and uncertainty.

One area, where this fear was pivotal for the experience of the social world, but completely obscure from the post-colonial newspaper discourse, was the

---

2   For instance, the list of participants of the 1979 workshop on women's studies organized by Najma Sachak and Deborah Bryceson also lists Walter Bgoya.

fear among the Asian community of violence at the hands of the African majority. This topic had been part of published debates in the colonial era, where educated urbanites, particularly Asians, complained about crimes committed by Africans. As independence dawned, this fear continued, as the recollections of Karim Hirji and Najma Sachak have demonstrated. However, the government newspaper did not address them in any way, even as the repercussions of the revolution in Zanzibar still loomed over the society when *the Nationalist* was first published. And while Asian mass emigration from Kenya or the persecution of Asians in Uganda were considered problematic for the nation, only a few articles expressed sympathy for Asians in light of their emotional distress. The fact that there were no Asians expressing such feelings themselves in the newspaper certainly exacerbated the obscurity of this aspect of the social world in public debates. As a consequence, an important key factor in this social dynamic was absent and could not become part of the discussion about the national narrative.

Fear and concern also appear to have been a crucial factor in the relationship between the TANU government and politically organized students. From the perspective of Nyerere's government, the young nation was threatened from abroad, namely by the armed forces of colonial and white minority regimes. Internally, it feared division along "racial" and socio-cultural lines. These concerns overlapped, as Bjerk was able to show. In the early 1960s, Nyerere observed the situation in Congo and became aware of the link between the intervention of Cold War super powers and former colonizers on the one side, and internal division in the nation on the other side. Against this background, his government regarded unity as an existential necessity.

In the same sense, concerns over Tanzania's internal security seem to have been closely interlinked with the government's repression against politically organized students, even though the political direction of organized students varied significantly between the mid-1960s and early1970s. In 1966, the student union, which was targeted after a demonstration, was motivated by its members' concerns over individual careers and lack of privileges – demands, which were visibly in contrast with the socialist vision of TANU. However, the students, whose organization USARF was banned in 1970, were motivated by and dedicated to many aspects of that socialist vision. It is striking that those very different organizations prompted such stern governmental reaction. This strongly suggests that TANU viewed organized student groups outside of its control as a serious threat.

Looking at the internal and external politics in Tanzania at the time helps to contextualize these concerns. The confrontation and ultimate expulsion of a significant number of Tanzanian students occurred in the aftermath of heightened tensions between Great Britain and Tanzania over the consolidation of the white minority regime in Rhodesia. The events not only heightened consciousness over the strong dependency with a potential adversary such as Great Britain. The events also led to a relative isolation of Tanzania vis-à-vis a majority of other British Commonwealth states, who had not followed suit to sever their diplomatic ties with Great Britain. Faced with politically active and organized students whose demands not only conflicted with TANU's socialist politics, but also appeared to align with British values of individual competitiveness, TANU appears to have felt a high level of concern over the potential of a social uprising, even though it merely opposed the students in matters of politics.

These concerns may have been somewhat dissipated by the relatively strong public support for the Arusha Declaration. However, as the allegations over an attempted coup by former TANU leader Oscar Kambona surfaced in 1969, the feeling of insecurity must have risen again in TANU's leadership. It was during these months when an article in which Walter Rodney discussed revolutionary overthrow was firmly repudiated in an editorial in *the Nationalist*. Likewise, the ban of USARF and its magazine *Cheche* occurred in the aftermath of the alleged conspiracy. Whatever veracity was in those allegations, they certainly added fears of infiltration, subversion, and overthrow. Politically active students who were independently organized and critical in their analysis of the socio-political conditions appear to have been seen as a dangerous threat by TANU's leadership.

The government's repression sparked fear among students, as Hirji and Shivji's recollections show, but neither the government's concern nor the intimidation of students was publicly discussed. The events in the social world, i.e. the bans and expulsions, effectively thwarted those public debates which Chambi Chachage considers to be Nyerere's legacy. A critical, independent in-depth analysis of the society could only take place to a limited degree in some arenas of the public sphere, namely the university. Even though criticism of the administration flourished in *the Nationalist's* successor, the *Daily News*, this criticism mostly focused on symbolic and obvious acts of mismanaged politics, such as complaints about misuse of government cars or sexual harassment, for example. Moreover, the topic of gender discrimination continued to be critically discussed at greater length because the government evidently did not fear the unorganized younger women, and because the older generation was organized in TANU's women's section.

Section 7.2 pointed to the rather directly observable interrelation between the development of a multi-directional discourse in the public sphere and the trajectories of agents participating in it. In contrast hereto, this section illustrated that fear was a crucial element in the social world, which is noteworthy due to its absence from published discourse. Merely those testimonies which were narrated from the safety of temporal distance made the significance of fear explicit.

7.4 Limitations and Prospects

This study of the development of the discourse on "race" and gender in some specific arenas of the public sphere was able to exemplify how the TANU government implemented its power through public debates, and how categories of perception from the colonial era were altered. The findings also raise new questions and invite further research both by contrasting spaces as well as periods of time with the outcomes at hand.

This study identified a slow but discernible shift in the discourse on "race." The younger generation which experienced integrated schools and National Service camps seemed less affected by "racial" stereotypes. This outcome leads to the question of how "racial" relations evolved in the following decades. How did the generation that grew up in the 1960s and 1970s experience "race" in Tanzania as they grew older, and how did the generations that grew up in the years after Nyerere's politics of determined "non-racialism" perceive the social disparities in Tanzanian society?

The heterogeneity in attitudes and actions of agents from the party and the administration, which is identified in this work, and which Aminzade and Callaci attributed to socialization in different education systems, raises the question of the impact of the developments in the interrelation between the public sphere and the social world during the 1960s and 1970s had on subsequent decades. Many of the future administrators, academics, journalists, teachers and politicians were to emerge out of the debates in the first two decades after independence. How did these agents, who were exposed to a spectrum of world views, reconcile these with their professional work, and how did these positions interfere with crucial developments in the social world, such as the structural adjustment programs in the 1980s.

In a similar vein, the focus on activism against gender discrimination warrants further investigation. Both the academic debate and the engagement against gender inequality came to be under unique conditions. While agents faced highly biased gender ideals that had emanated from the colonial era, they also seized upon TANU's socialist and political stance as well as the ideals of national Liberation movements in order to challenge these structures. It would be highly insightful to research the evolution of this struggle as Tanzania went through significant changes in the following years. How did the increasingly organized female cohort reach and affect the larger society? And how did their relationship to the government and the administration evolve in the light of the end of Nyerere's presidency and the shrinking public sector under the structural adjustment programs? And lastly, how did the media coverage of gender roles evolve in the years and decades after the end of the women's decade in 1985 and the formation of TAMWA in 1987?

As projected in the introduction, the national narrative that was woven in the English-written government newspaper and the university only reached a small section of the entire Tanzanian society. The scope of this study has proven to be valid, as many of the key agents, such as students, academics, and journalists interacted in these communicative institutions. However, female radio journalists claim to have triggered a national debate over the sexual harassment of school girls, which raises a two-fold question: Didn't the gender discourse that manifested itself in the newspapers of 1960s and 1970s also extend to the countryside? Or were rural populations equally aware of the sexual harassment of schoolgirls, but merely unable to articulate their concerns, as the topic remained absent from published debates until it became part of the national radio coverage? Future interview-based studies on those groups who were excluded from the written English discourse could help to shed light on the society at large.

This work also helped discern the connection between the dynamics of public discourse and the creation of a national society. Even though Chachage's claim that Nyerere's legacy was the creation of debate about issues of importance to society has to be put into perspective to some degree, this work argues that Tanzania was a special case in its handling of the public sphere and empirically supports his assertion. Tanzania's remarkably tolerant history of dealing with critique is further validated by Melchiorre's comparison of the relation between state and academia in Kenya and Tanzania, respectively. This raises the question of how societies fared, where public discourse was steered by the government, or where private media enjoyed less interference by the state. Research on such cases should identify crucial debates and in which arenas they took place. It should include foci on the very categories of "race" and gender that were used in this study.

Such analyses can add perspective to the complex process of nation formation which was explored and explained in this study. It can show the effect and importance of how a national narrative is shaped by agents with different ideas about what society should look like. In Tanzania, this narrative has integrated a broad spectrum of socio-political perspectives and arguably fostered changes in the social world. This included the TANU government, which enabled and influenced debates, but which also responded and reacted to the public discourse. In light of this, Tanzania's national narrative in the 1960s and early 1970s is one of contented optimism, which may be best summarized up by Marjorie Mbilinyi:

> "At the time we were quite critical of what was going on, later we had to defend what was going on, because regardless of what mistakes had been made, there were real achievements."[3]

---

3   Marjorie Mbilinyi, interview by Harald Barre.

8 Bibliography

8.1 Secondary Literature

Adi, Hakim. "The African Diaspora, 'Development' & Modern African Political Theory." *Review of African Political Economy* 29, no. 92 (2002): 237–51. Accessed September 9, 2019. https://www.jstor.org/stable/4006813.

Aiyar, Sana. *Indians in Kenya: The Politics of Diaspora*. Cambridge, Massachusetts: Harvard University Press, 2015. Accessed October 26, 2017. http://search.ebscohost.com/login.aspx?direct=true&scope=site&db=nlebk&AN=970803.

Alexander, Jeffrey C. *The Civil Sphere*. Oxford: Oxford Univ. Press, 2006.

Aminzade, Ronald. *Race, Nation, and Citizenship in Postcolonial Africa: The Case of Tanzania*. Cambridge Studies in Contentious Politics. Cambridge: Cambridge University Press, 2013.
https://doi.org/10.1017/CBO9781107360259.

Anderson, Benedict. *Imagined Communities: Reflections on the Origin and Spread of Nationalism*. Rev. and extended ed., 13. impression. London: Verso, 2003.

Askew, Kelly. *Performing the Nation: Swahili Music and Cultural Politics in Tanzania* (Chicago, The University of Chicago Press, 2003).

Balibar, Étienne, and Immanuel Maurice Wallerstein. *Race, Nation, Class: Ambiguous Identities*. 1. publ. London et al.: Verso, 1991.

"Benjamin Mkapa." Accessed June 19, 2019. http://www.clubmadrid.org/miembro/benjamin-mkapa/.

Berman, Bruce J., and John M. Lonsdale. "Nationalism in Colonial and Post-Colonial Africa." In *The Oxford Handbook of the History of Nationalism*. Edited by John Breuilly. 1. ed., 308–17. Oxford: Oxford Univ. Press, 2013.

Bertz, Ned. "Indian Ocean World Cinema: Viewing the History of Race, Diaspora and Nationalism in Urban Tanzania." *Africa* 81, no. 01 (2011): 68–88. https://doi.org/10.1017/S0001972010000045.

Bertz, Ned. *Diaspora and Nation in the Indian Ocean: Transnational Histories of Race and Urban Space in Tanzania*. Honolulu: University of Hawai'i Press, 2015.

Bienen, Henry. "National Security in Tanganyika after the Mutiny." *Transition*, no. 21 (1965): 39. https://doi.org/10.2307/2934101.

Birmingham, David. *A Concise History of Portugal*. Cambridge Concise Histories. Cambridge: Univ. Press, 1993.

Bjerk, Paul. "African Files in Portuguese Archives." *History in Africa* 31 (2004): 463–68. Accessed July 14, 2015. http://www.jstor.org/stable/4128541.

Bjerk, Paul. "Postcolonial Realism: Tanganyika's Foreign Policy under Nyerere 1960-1963." *The International Journal of African Historical Studies* 44, no. 2 (2011): 215–47. Accessed July 14, 2015. http://www.jstor.org/stable/23046879.

Bjerk, Paul. *Building a Peaceful Nation: Julius Nyerere and the Establishment of Sovereignty in Tanzania, 1960-1964*. Rochester Studies in African History and the Diaspora v. 63. Rochester: University of Rochester Press, 2015.

Borstelmann, Thomas. *The Cold War and the Color Line: American Race Relations in the Global Arena*. 1. Harvard Univ. Press paperback ed. 2003.

Bourdieu, Pierre. "The Social Space and the Genesis of Groups." *Theory and Society* 14, no. 6 (1985): 723–44. Accessed March 29, 2018. http://www.jstor.org/stable/657373.

Bourdieu, Pierre. "The Forms of Capital." In *Handbook of Theory and Research for the Sociology of Education*. Edited by John G. Richardson, 241-258. New York: Greenwood Press, 1986.

Bourdieu, Pierre. "Die biographische Illusion." *BIOS*, no. 1 (1990): 75–81.

Bourdieu, Pierre, Loïc J. D. Wacquant, and Samar Farage. "Rethinking the State: Genesis and Structure of the Bureaucratic Field." *Sociological Theory* 12, no. 1 (1994): 1. https://doi.org/10.2307/202032.

Brennan, James R. "Democratizing Cinema and Censorship in Tanzania, 1920-1980." *The International Journal of African Historical Studies* 38, no. 3 (2005): 481–511. Accessed March 18, 2018. http://www.jstor.org/stable/40033967.

Brennan, James R. "Between Segregation and Gentrification: Africans, Indians, and the Struggle for Housing in Dar es Salaam, 1920-1950." In Brennan; Burton; Lawi, *Dar es Salaam*, 118-135.

Brennan, James R. "Politics and Business in the Indian Newspapers of Colonial Tanganyika." *Africa: Journal of the International African Institute* 81, no. 1

(2011): 42–67. Accessed July 26, 2017UTC. http://www.jstor.org/stable/414 84965.

Brennan, James R. *Taifa: Making Nation and Race in Urban Tanzania.*. Athens, Ohio: Ohio University Press, 2012.

Brennan, James R. "Constructing Arguments and Institutions of Islamic Belonging: M. O. Abbasi, Colonial Tanzania, and the Western Indian Ocean World, 1925-61." *The Journal of African History* 55, no. 02 (2014): 211–28. https://doi.org/10.1017/S0021853714000012.

Brennan, James R., and Andrew Burton. "The Emerging Metropolis: A History of Dar es Salaam, circa 1862-2000." In Brennan; Burton; Lawi, *Dar es Salaam*, 13–75.

Brennan, James R., Andrew Burton, and Yusufu Qwaray Lawi, eds. *Dar es Salaam: Histories from an Emerging African Metropolis*. Dar es Salaam, East Lansing, MI, USA: Mkuki na Nyota Publishers, in association with the Britsih Institute in Eastern Africa, Nairobi; Distributed in North America by Michigan State University Press, 2007.

Brennan, James R. "Youth, The TANU Youth League and Managed Vigilantilism in Dar es Salaam, Tanzania, 1925-73." *Africa: Journal of the International African Institute* 76, no. 2 (2006): 221–46. Accessed July 14, 2015. http://www.jstor.org/stable/40027110.

Bromber, Katrin. *Imperiale Propaganda: Die ostafrikanische Militärpresse im Zweiten Weltkrieg*. 1. Aufl. ZMO-Studien 28. Berlin: Schwarz, 2009. Zugl.: Wien, Univ., Habil.-Schr., 2009.

Burton, Andrew. *African Underclass: Urbanisation, Crime & Colonial Order in Dar es Salaam*. Eastern African Studies. Oxford: Currey, 2005.

Callaci, Emily. "Dancehall Politics: Mobility, Sexuality, and Spectacles of Racial Respectability in Late Colonial Tanganyika, 1930s–1961." *The Journal of African History* 52, no. 03 (2011): 365–84. https://doi.org/10.1017/S0021853 711000478.

Callaci, Emily. *Street Archives and City Life: Popular Intellectuals in Postcolonial Tanzania*. Radical Perspectives. Durham: Duke University Press, 2017. Accessed February 16, 2018: http://ebookcentral.proquest.com/lib/tib-hann over/detail.action?docID=5116557.

Carthew, John. "Life Imitates Art: The Student Expulsion in Dar es Salaam, October 1966, as a Dramatic Ritual." *The Journal of Modern African Studies* 18, no. 3 (1980): 541–49. Accessed February 6, 2019. https://www.jstor.org/sta ble/160370.

Chachage, Chambi. "Mwalimu in our popular imagination: The relevance of Nyerere today | Pambazuka News." Accessed July 15, 2019. https://www.pambazuka.org/pan-africanism/mwalimu-our-popular-imagination-relevance-nyerere-today.

Chatterjee, Partha. "The nation in heterogeneous time." *Futures* 37, no. 9 (2005): 925–42. https://doi.org/10.1016/j.futures.2005.01.011.

Chung, Clairmont, ed. *Walter A. Rodney: A Promise of Revolution*. New York: Monthly Review Press, 2012. Accessed May 2, 2018, http://site.ebrary.com/lib/alltitles/docDetail.action?docID=10659285.

Cooppan, Vilashini. *Worlds Within: National Narratives and Global Connections in Postcolonial Writing*. Stanford: Stanford University Press, 2009. Accessed: August 16, 2017. http://search.ebscohost.com/login.aspx?direct=true&scope=site&db=nlebk&AN=395793.

Decker, Alicia. "Idi Amin's Dirty War: Subversion, Sabotage, and the Battle to Keep Uganda Clean, 1971-1979." *The International Journal of African Historical Studies* 43, no. 3 (2010): 489–513. Accessed February 28, 2019. https://www.jstor.org/stable/23046822.

Engel, Ulf. ""I will not recognise East Germany just because Bonn is stupid".: Anerkennungsdiplomatie in Tansania, 1964 bis 1965." In *Kalter Krieg in Ostafrika: Die Beziehungen der DDR zu Sansibar und Tansania*. Edited by Ulrich van der Heyden, 9-29. Die DDR und die Dritte Welt 8. Berlin, Münster: Lit, 2009.

Feierman, Steven. *Peasant Intellectuals: Anthropology and History in Tanzania*. Madison Wis. a.o.: Univ. of Wisconsin Press, 1990.

Fouéré, Marie-Aude. "Recasting Julius Nyerere in Zanzibar: The Revolution, the Union and the Enemy of the Nation." *Journal of Eastern African Studies* 8, no. 3 (2014): 478–96. Accessed January 25, 2019. https://doi.org/10.1080/17531055.2014.918313.

Frazier, Robeson Taj. *The East is Black: Cold war China in the Black Radical Imagination*. Durham, NC, London: Duke University Press, 2015.

Füllberg-Stolberg, Katja. "Amerika in Afrika: Die Rolle der Afroamerikaner in den Beziehungen zwischen den USA und Afrika, 1880 - 1910." ZMO-Studien 17. Berlin: Schwarz, 2003

Geiger, Susan. *TANU Women: Gender and Culture in the Making of Tanganyikan Nationalism, 1955-1965*. Social history of Africa Series. Portsmouth, NH, Oxford, Nairobi, Dar es Salaam: Heinemann; James Currey; E.A.E.P; Mkuki Na Nyota, 1997.

Geiger, Susan. "Engendering & Gendering African Nationalism: Rethinking the Case of Tanganyika (Tanzania)." In Maddox; Giblin, *In Search of a Nation*, 278–89.

Ghodsee, Kristen. "Revisiting the United Nations Decade for Women: Brief Reflections on Feminism, Capitalism and Cold War Politics in the Early Years of the International Women's Movement." *Women's Studies International Forum* 33, no. 1 (2010): 3–12. https://doi.org/10.1016/j.wsif.2009.11.008.

Giblin, James Leonard. "Some Complexities of Family & State in Colonial Njombe." In Maddox; Giblin, *In Search of a Nation*, 128–48.

Glassman, Jonathon. "Slower Than a Massacre: The Multiple Sources of Racial Thought in Colonial Africa." *The American Historical Review* 109, no. 3 (2004): 720–54. Accessed May 8, 2018. http://www.jstor.org/stable/10.1086/530553.

Glassman, Jonathon. *War of Words, War of Stones: Racial Thought and Violence in Colonial Zanzibar*. Bloomington: Indiana University Press, 2011. Accessed August 5, 2018. http://site.ebrary.com/lib/alltitles/docDetail.action?docID=10448616.

Glentworth, Garth, and Ian Hancock. "Obote and Amin: Change and Continuity in Modern Uganda Politics." *African Affairs* 72, no. 28 (1973): 237–55. Accessed February 28, 2019. https://www.jstor.org/stable/719846.

Go, Julian. "Decolonizing Bourdieu." *Sociological Theory* 31, no. 1 (2013): 49–74. Accessed August 9, 2018. https://doi.org/10.1177/0735275113477082.

Hall, Budd L. "Revolution in Rural Education; Health Education in Tanzania." *Community Development Journal* 9, no. 2 (1974): 133–39. Accessed March 19, 2019. https://www.jstor.org/stable/44255658.

Hall, Simon. "The NAACP, Black Power, and the African American Freedom Struggle, 1966? 1969." *The Historian* 69, no. 1 (2007): 49–82. https://doi.org/10.1111/j.1540-6563.2007.00174.x.

Hunter, Emma. *Political Thought and the Public Sphere in Tanzania: Freedom, Democracy and Citizenship in the Era of Decolonization*. African Studies v.133. New York: Cambridge University Press, 2015.

Hunter, Emma. "*Komkya* and the Convening of a Chagga Public, 1953-1961." In Peterson; Hunter; Newell, *African Print Cultures*, 283-305.

Iliffe, John. *A Modern History of Tanganyika*. African Studies Series 25. Cambridge u.a.: Cambridge Univ. Press, 1979.

Ivaska, Andrew M. "'Anti-Mini Militants Meet Modern Misses': Urban Style, Gender and the Politics of 'National Culture.'" *Gender & History* 14, no. 3 (2002): 584–607.

Ivaska, Andrew M. "Of Students, '"Nizers," and a Struggle over Youth: Tanzania's 1966 National Service Crisis." *Africa Today* 51, no. 3 (2005): 83–107. https://doi.org/10.1353/at.2005.0022.

Ivaska, Andrew Michael. *Cultured States: Youth, Gender, and Modern Style in 1960s Dar es Salaam*. Durham NC u.a.: Duke Univ. Press, 2011.

Jacobs, Sylvia M. "James Emman Kwegyir Aggrey: An African Intellectual in the United States." *The Journal of Negro History* 81, no. 1 (1996): 47–61. Accessed January 6, 2018. http://www.jstor.org/stable/2717607.

Kanyama, A., A. Carlsson-Kanyama, A-L. Lindén, and J. Lupala. "An Analysis of the Situation in Dar-es-Salaam in Tanzania from an Institutional Coordination Perspective." In *Urban Transport Development: A Complex Issue*. Edited by G. Jönson and E. Tengström, 67–85. Berlin Heidelberg: Springer, 2006.

Killingray, David, and Martin Plaut. *Fighting for Britain: African Soldiers in the Second World War*. Rochester: James Currey, 2010.

Kimambo, Isaria N. "Evolution of the Administrative Structure." In Kimambo; Mapunda; Lawi, *In Search of Relevance*, 83–106.

Kimambo, Isaria N., Bertram Baltasar Mapunda, and Yusufu Qwaray Lawi, eds. *In Search of Relevance: A History of the University of Dar es Salaam*. Dar es Salaam, Tanzania: Dar es Salaam University Press, 2008.

Lal, Priya. *African Socialism in Postcolonial Tanzania: Between the Village and the World*. Cambridge: Cambridge University Press, 2015. https://doi.org/10.1017/CBO9781316221679.

Larson, Lorne Erling. "A History of the Mahenge (Ulanga) District: c 1860-1957." University of Dar es Salaam, 1976.

Lewis, R. *Walter Rodney's Intellectual and Political Thought*. Kingston: Press University of the West Indies, 1998. Accessed May 20, 2019. https://books.google.de/books?id=1XkCzBiP7NoC.

Leys, Colin. "Letter." *London Review of Books*, August 2, 2018. 15. Accessed February 19, 2019. https://www.lrb.co.uk/v40/n14/mahmood-mamdani/the-african-university.

Lovett, Margot. "On Power and Powerlessness: Marriage and Political Metaphor in Colonial Western Tanzania." *The International Journal of African Historical Studies* 27, no. 2 (1994): 273–301. Accessed April 6, 2018. http://www.jstor.org/stable/221026.

Lovett, Margot. "She Thinks She's like a Man": Marriage and (De)Constructing Gender Identity in Colonial Buha, Western Tanzania, 1943-1960." *Canadian Journal of African Studies* 30, no. 1 (1996): 52–68. Accessed April 6, 2018. http://www.jstor.org/stable/486040.

Maddox, Gregory, and James Leonard Giblin, eds. *In Search of a Nation: Histories of Authority & Dissidence in Tanzania*. Eastern African Studies. Oxford, Dar Es Salaam, Athens: James Currey; Kapsel Educational Publications; Ohio University Press, 2005.

Mamdani, Mahmood. "The African University." *The London Review of Books* 40, no. 14 (2018): 29–32. Accessed November 19, 2018. https://www.lrb.co.uk/v40/n14/mahmood-mamdani/the-african-university.

Mapunda, Bertram B.B. "University of Dar es Salaam's immediate response to Arusha Declaration." In Kimambo; Mapunda; Lawi, *In Search of Relevance*, 170–92.

Mapunda, Bertram Baltasar. "Infrastructure." In Kimambo; Mapunda; Lawi, *In Search of Relevance*, 60–82.

Markle, Seth M. "'Book Publishers for a Pan-African World:' Drum and Spear Press and Tanzania's 'Ujamaa' Ideology." *The Black Scholar* 37, no. 4 (2008): 16–26.

Markle, Seth M. *'We Are Not Tourists': The Black Power Movement and the Making of Socialist Tanzania 1960-1974*. New York, 2011. A dissertation submitted in partial fulfillment of the requirement for the degree of Doctor of Philosophy.

Markle, Seth M. *A Motorcycle on Hell Run: Tanzania, Black Power, and the Uncertain Future of Pan-Africanism, 1964-1974*. Ruth Simms Hamilton African Diaspora Series. East Lansing: Michigan State University Press, 2017.

Mascarenhas, Ophelia, and Marjorie Mbilinyi. *Women in Tanzania: An Analytical Bibliography*. Uppsala, Scandinavian Institute of African Studies, 1983.

Mbilinyi, Marjorie J. "The 'New Woman' and Traditional Norms in Tanzania." *The Journal of Modern African Studies* 10, no. 1 (1972): 57–72. Accessed March 18, 2018. http://www.jstor.org/stable/159821.

Mbilinyi, Marjorie J. "The State of Women in Tanzania." *Canadian Journal of African Studies* 6, no. 2 (1972): 371–77. Accessed March 18, 2018.

Mbilinyi, Marjorie J. "Struggles Concerning Sexuality among Female Youth." *Journal of Eastern African Research & Development* 15 (1985): 111–23.

Mbilinyi, Marjorie J. "Women's Resistance in 'Customary' Marriage: Tanzania's Runaway Wives." In *Forced Labour and Migration: Patterns of Movement within Africa*. Edited by Abebe Zegeye, 211–54. African Discourse Series 1. London: Zell, 1989.

Mbughuni, Azaria. "Tanzania and the Pan African Quest for Unity, Freedom, and Independence in East, Central, and Southern Africa: The Case of the Pan African Freedom Movement for East and the Central Africa/Pan African Freedom Movement for East Central and South Africa." *The Journal of Pan African Studies* 7, no. 4 (2014): 211–38.

Melchiorre, Jonathan Luke. "Building Nations, Making Youth: Institutional Choice, Nation-State Building and the Politics of Youth Activism in Postcolonial Kenya and Tanzania." University of Toronto, 2018.

Miller, Charlotte Lee. "Who are the "permanent inhabitants" of the state? citizenship policies and border controls in Tanzania, 1920-1980." PhD (Doctor of Philosophy) thesis, University of Iowa, 2011. Accessed: September 20, 2018. https://ir.uiowa.edu/etd/4877/.

Molony, Thomas. *Nyerere: The Early Years*. Rochester: James Currey, 2014.

Newell, Stephanie. "Afterword." In Peterson; Hunter; Newell, *African Print Cultures*, 425–33.

Oanda, Ibrahim. "The Evolving Nature of Student Participation in University Governance in Africa: An Overview of Policies, Trends and Emerging Issues." In *Student Politics in Africa: Representation and Activism*. Edited by Thierry M. Luescher, 61–84. s.l.: African Minds, 2016.

Peterson, Derek R., Emma Hunter, and Stephanie Newell, eds. *African Print Cultures: Newspapers and Their Publics in the Twentieth Century*. African Perspectives. Ann Arbor: University of Michigan Press, 2016.

Portelli, Alessandro. "What makes oral history different." In *The Oral History Reader*. Edited by Robert Perks and Alistair Thomson. 2nd ed., 32–42. New York: Routledge, 2006.

Provini, Olivier. "The University of Dar es Salaam: A Post-Nyerere Institution of Higher Education? Legacies, Continuities and Changes in an Institutional Space (1961-2012)." In *Remembering Julius Nyerere in Tanzania: History, Memory, Legacy*. Edited by Marie-Aude Fouéré, 279-304. Dar es Salaam, Tanzania: Mkuki Na Nyota, 2015.

Roberts, George. "The Uganda–Tanzania War, the Fall of Idi Amin, and the Failure of African Diplomacy, 1978–1979." *Journal of Eastern African Studies* 8, no. 4 (2014): 692–709. Accessed March 4, 2019. https://doi.org/10.1080/17531055.2014.946236.

Schneider, Leander. "Colonial Legacies and Postcolonial Authoritarianism in Tanzania: Connects and Disconnects." *African Studies Review* 49, no. 1

(2006): 93–118. Accessed March 18, 2018. http://www.jstor.org/stable/200 65195.

Scotton, James F. "Tanganyika's African Press, 1937-1960: A Nearly Forgotten Pre-Independence Forum." *African Studies Review* 21, no. 1 (1978): 1–18. Accessed March 18, 2018. http://www.jstor.org/stable/523760.

Sieder, Reinhard. "Erzählungen analysieren – Analysen erzählen: Praxeologisches Paradigma, Narrativ biografisches Interview, Textanalyse und Falldarstellung." In *Ethnohistorie: Rekonstruktion, Kulturkritik und Repräsentation; eine Einführung*. Edited by Karl R. Wernhart. 4., gänzlich überarb. und erw. Aufl., 150–80. Forschung. Wien: Promedia-Verl., 2014.

Sturmer, Martin. *The Media History of Tanzania*. Ndanda via Mtwara: Ndanda Mission Press, 1998. Zugl.: Wien, Univ., Diss., 1998.

Tenga, Nakazael, and Chris Maina Peter. "The Right to Organise as Mother of All Rights: The Experience of Women in Tanzania." *The Journal of Modern African Studies* 34, no. 1 (1996): 143–62. Accessed March 26, 2019. https://www.jstor.org/stable/161742.

Tordoff, William, and Ali A. Mazrui. "The Left and the Super-Left in Tanzania." *The Journal of Modern African Studies* 10, no. 3 (1972): 427–45. Accessed March 18, 2018. http://www.jstor.org/stable/160129.

Ture, Kwame. *Ready for Revolution: The Life and Times of Stokely Carmichael*. With the assistance of Ekwueme Michael Thelwell. New York, NY: Charles Scribner's Sons, 2003.

Ture, Kwame, (formerly known as Stokely Carmichael), and Charles V. Hamilton. *Black Power: The Politics of Liberation*. New York: Vintage Books, 1992.

Westcott, Nicholas. "The Impact of the Second World War on Tanganyika, 1939-49." In *Africa and the Second World War*, 143–59, edited by David Killingray Richard Rathbone. Basingstoke: Macmillan, 1986.

Wilkins, Fanon Che. "The Making of Black Internationalists: SNCC and Africa before the Launching of Black Power, 1960-1965." *The Journal of African American History* 92, 4, New Black Power Studies: National, International, and Transnational Perspectives (2007): 467–90.

Willis, Justin. "Unpretentious Bars: Municipal monopoly and independent drinking in colonial Dar es Salaam." In Brennan; Burton; Lawi, *Dar es Salaam*, 157–73.

Yahya-Othman, Saida, ed. *Yes, In My Lifetime: Selected works of Haroub Othman*. Dakar: Mkuki Na Nyoka, 2013. Accessed June 15, 2015. https://books.google.de/books?id=SdwWAgAAQBAJ.

Zachernuk, Philip Serge. *Colonial Subjects: An African Intelligentsia and Atlantic ideas.* Charlottesville, Va.: University Press of Virginia, 2000.

8.2 Sources

Newspapers

The Long Island Traveler, 1974, 1975.
The Times, 1970.
The Nationalist, 1964-1971.
The Daily News, 1972-1976.

Interviews and Autobiographic Accounts

Interviews Conducted by the Author
Alloo, Fatma. Interview by Harald Barre. March 19, 2018. Her residence in Dar es Salaam.
Bgoya, Walter. Interview by Harald Barre. March 8, 2018. His office, Dar es Salaam.
Bryceson, Deborah. Interview by Harald Barre. February 13, 2018. Oxford.
Hamdani, Salha, and George G. Hajivayanis. Interview by Harald Barre. February 14, 2018. Cafeteria of School of Oriental and African Studies, London.
Mbilinyi, Marjorie. Interview by Harald Barre. March 12, 2018. Café, Dar es Salaam.
Sachak, Najma. Interview by Harald Barre. September 1, 2018. Her apartment in Lyon.
Tandon, Yash. Interview by Harald Barre. February 13, 2018. Oxford.

Published Interviews and Biographic Accounts
Alloo, Fatma, Edda Sanga, and Gurnam Ajit Singh, eds. *30 years of Tanzania Media Women's Association (TAMWA).* Dar es Salaam, Tanzania: Tanzania Media Women's Association (TAMWA), 2017.
Alloo, Fatma. "Editorial." In Alloo; Sanga; Singh, *30 years of Tanzania Media Women's Association (TAMWA),* 23–24.

Babu, A. M. "Introduction." In *The Debate*. Edited by Yash Tandon. 1. print, 1–12. Dar es Salaam: Tanzania Publ. House, 1982.

Bgoya, Walter. "Walter Bgoya. From Tanzania to Kansas and Back Again." In *No Easy Victories: African Liberation and American Activists Over a Half Century, 1950-2000*. Edited by William Minter, Gail Hovey and Charles E. Cobb, 103–6. Trenton, NJ: Africa World Press, 2008.

Bhikhabhai, Rama. "Life at National Service camp." Accessed March 5, 2019. https://michuzi-matukio.blogspot.com/2014/12/life-at-national-service-camp-by-rama.html#links.

Bujra, Janet. "Gender and Politics in Africa: an Interview with Marjorie Mbilinyi - ROAPE." Accessed March 1, 2019. http://roape.net/2017/08/24/gender-politics-change-africa-interview-marjorie-mbilinyi/.

Burgess, Jan, Lionel Cliffe, Martin Doornbos, Bereket Habte Selassie, Issa Shivji, Paul Puritt, Tajudeen Abdul-Raheem, and Mahmood Mamdani. "A Tribute to A. M. Babu." *Review of African Political Economy* 23, no. 69 (1996): 321–48. Accessed March 18, 2018. http://www.jstor.org/stable/4006376.

Claude, Judy. "Some Personal Reflections on the Sixth Pan-African Congress." *The Black Scholar* 37, no. 4 (2008): 48–49. Accessed September 19, 2014. http://www.jstor.org/stable/41069283.

Haji, Rose. "TAMWA Reflections: Planting the Seed." In Alloo; Sanga; Singh, *30 years of Tanzania Media Women's Association (TAMWA)*, 31–35.

Hajivayanis, George G. "Night-Shift Comrades." In Hirji, *Cheche*, 83–98.

Hall, Budd L. "Surf On Paulino - Poem for Paulo Freire." Accessed March 19, 2019. https://www.academia.edu/5712588/Surf_On_Paulino_-_Poem_for_Paulo_Freire.

Hamdani Meghji, Zakia. "Sisterly Activism." In Hirji, *Cheche*, 77–82.

Hamilton, Marybeth. "Terence Ranger: Life as Historiography." Accessed January 28, 2019. http://www.historyworkshop.org.uk/terence-ranger-life-as-historiography/.

Hirji, Karim F. "From Cheche to MajiMaji." In Hirji, *Cheche*, 109–22.

Hirji, Karim F. "Not So Silent a Spark." In Hirji, *Cheche*, 53–63.

Hirji, Karim F. "The African University: A critical comment." Accessed February 19, 2019. https://www.pambazuka.org/education/african-university-critical-comment.

Hirji, Karim F. "The Spark is Kindled." In Hirji, *Cheche*, 17-34.

Hirji, Karim F. "Tribulations of An Independent Magazine." In Hirji, *Cheche*, 35–51.

Hirji, Karim F. *Growing up with Tanzania: Memories, Musings and Maths*. Dar es Salaam: Mkuki na Nyota Publishers, 2014. Accessed August 2, 2018. http://search.ebscohost.com/login.aspx?direct=true&scope=site&db=e000xat&AN=839171.

Hirji, Karim F., ed. *Cheche: Reminiscences of a Radical Magazine*. Dar es Salaam: Mkuki Na Nyota Publishers, 2010. Accessed September 11, 2015. http://site.ebrary.com/lib/academiccompletetitles/home.action.

Joseph, May. *Nomadic Identities: The Performance of Citizenship*. Public worlds v. 5. Minneapolis: University of Minnesota Press, 1999. https://doi.org/10.5749/j.ctttvc1p.

Kassum, Al Noor. *Africa's Winds of Change: Memoirs of an International Tanzanian*. London, New York: I. B. Tauris & Co Ltd, 2007. Accessed December 13, 2016. http://search.ebscohost.com/login.aspx?direct=true&scope=site&db=e000xat&AN=216712.

Levy, LaTasha. "Remembering Sixth-PAC: Interviews with Sylvia Hill and Judy Claude, Organizers of the Sixth Pan-African Congress." *The Black Scholar* 37, no. 4 (2008): 39–47. Accessed September 19, 2014. http://www.jstor.org/stable/41069282.

McCracken, John. "Terry Ranger: A Personal Appreciation." *Journal of Southern African Studies* 23, no. 2 (1997): 175–85. Accessed January 21, 2019. https://www.jstor.org/stable/2637616.

Meena, Ruth, and Marjorie Mbilinyi. "Women's Research and Documentation Project (Tanzania)." *Signs* 16, no. 4 (1991): 852–59. Accessed March 18, 2018. http://www.jstor.org/stable/3174577.

Mtei, Edwin. *From Goatherd to Governor: The Autobiography of Edwin Mtei*. Dar es Salaam: Mkuki Na Nyota Publishers, 2009. Accessed December 13, 2016. http://site.ebrary.com/lib/academiccompletetitles/home.action.

Mwakikagile, Godfrey. *Life in Tanganyika in the Fifties*. 3rd ed. Dar es Salaam, Tanzania: New Africa Press, 2009.

Mwakikagile, Godfrey. *Life under Nyerere*. 2. ed. Dar es Salaam: New Africa Press, 2006.

Mwakikagile, Godfrey. *My Life as an African: Autobiographical Writings*. 1st ed. Dar es Salaam: New Africa Press, 2009.

Mwakikagile, Godfrey. *Tanzania Under Mwalimu Nyerere: Reflections on an African Statesman*. Dar es Salaam: New Africa Press, 2006.

Ochieng, Philip. "Nostalgia and when to be on first name terms." Accessed June 20, 2019. https://mobile.nation.co.ke/blogs/Nostalgia-and-when-to-be-on-first-name-terms/1949942-4995042-item-1-hfpdsgz/index.html.

Rodney, Walter. "The Black Scholar Interviews: Walter Rodney." *The Black Scholar* 6, no. 3 (1974): 38–47. Accessed September 19, 2014. http://www.jstor.org/stable/41066348.

Sanga, Edda. "Editorial." In Alloo; Sanga; Singh, *30 years of Tanzania Media Women's Association (TAMWA)*, 25–27.

Shivji, Issa G. "Lionel Cliffe, 1936–2013: A comradely scholar in Nyerere's nationalist Tanzania." *Review of African Political Economy* 41, no. 140 (2014): 284–87. Accessed January 25, 2019. https://doi.org/10.1080/03056244.2014.873162.

Shivji, Issa G. "Remembering Walter Rodney." Accessed February 19, 2019. monthlyreview.org/2012/12/01/remembering-walter-rodney/.

Shivji, Issa G. "The Life & Times of Babu: The Age of Liberation and Revolution." *Review of African Political Economy* 95, no. 95 (2003): 109–18. Accessed March 20, 2019. https://www.jstor.org/stable/4006743.

Swift, C. R. *Dar Days: The Early Years in Tanzania*. University Press of America, 2002.

UONGOZI Institute. "Meet the Leader: Interview with H.E. Benjamin Mkapa Former President of Tanzania." Accessed June 20, 2019. https://www.youtube.com/watch?v=BKlpQyeV1_k.

Documents, Diplomatic Correspondences, Historical Studies

"T.A.N.U. Guidelines on Guarding Consolidating and Advancing the Revolution of Tanzania, and of Africa." *The African Review* 1, no. 4 (1972): 1–8. Accessed February 28, 2019. https://hdl.handle.net/10520/AJA00020117_2.

Arusha Declaration. TANU, Publicity Section 1. 1967. Accessed November 26, 2018. https://www.fes.de/suche/?id=84&q=arusha.

Bryceson, Deborah Fahy, and Najma Sachak, eds. *Proceedings of the Workshop on Women's Studies and Development: 24-29 September 1979*. BRALUP Research Paper 60. 1979.

Condon, John C. "Nation Building and Image Building in the Tanzanian Press." *The Journal of Modern African Studies* 5, no. 3 (1967): 335–54. Accessed October 18, 2018. https://www.jstor.org/stable/158728.

Embassy Dar es Salaam. *Sixth Pan African Congress*. 3 vols. 1974; Electronic Telegram, DAR ES SALAAM 1958; STATE 129503.

Hirji, Karim F., and Naijuka Kasihwaki. "Appendix E: Our Last Stand." In Hirji, *Cheche*, 207–12.

Leslie, J. A. K. *A Survey of Dar es Salaam*. London, New York, Nairobi: Oxford University Press, 1963.

Mazrui, Ali. "Tanzaphilia." *Transition*, no. 31 (1967): 20. https://doi.org/10.2307/2934403.

Museveni, Yoweri. "Activism at the Hill." In Hirji, *Cheche*, 11–16.

Mytton, G. L. "Tanzania: The Problems of Mass Media Development." *International Communication Gazette* 14, no. 2 (1968): 89–100. https://doi.org/10.1177/001654926801400204.

Nyerere, Julius K. "Inauguration of the University of East Africa." In Nyerere, *Freedom and Unity*, 218–21.

Nyerere, Julius K. "Oral Hearing at the Trusteeship Council, 1955." In Nyerere, *Freedom and Unity*, 35–39.

Nyerere, Julius K., ed. *Freedom and Unity: A Selection from Writings and Speeches, 1952-1965*. Dar es Salaam: Oxford University Press, 1973.

Ranger, Terrance, ed. *Emerging Themes of African History: Proceedings of the International Congress of African Historians held at University College, Dar es Salaam, October 1965*. London: Heinemann, 1968.

Resolutions and Selected Speeches from the Sixth Pan African Congress. Dar es Salaam: Tanzania Publishing House, 1976.

Rodney, Walter. "Towards the Sixth Pan African Congress: Aspects of the International Class Struggle in Africa, the Caribbean and America." In *Resolutions and Selected Speeches from the Sixth Pan African Congress*, 21–34. Dar es Salaam: Tanzania Publishing House, 1976.

Swantz, Marji-Liisa, and Deborah Fahy Bryceson. "Women Workers in Dar es Salaam: 1973/74 Survey of Female Minimum Wage Earners and Self-Employed." Research Paper No. 43, University of Dar es Salaam, Dar es Salaam, 1975.

Twining. "The Last Nine Years in Tanganyika." *African Affairs* 58, no. 230 (1959): 15–24. Accessed April 6, 2018. http://www.jstor.org/stable/718045.

Historical Sciences

Federico Buccellati, Sebastian Hageneuer,
Sylva van der Heyden, Felix Levenson (eds.)
**Size Matters –
Understanding Monumentality
Across Ancient Civilizations**

2019, 350 p., pb., col. ill.
44,99 € (DE), 978-3-8376-4538-5
E-Book: available as free open access publication
PDF: ISBN 978-3-8394-4538-9

Sebastian Haumann, Martin Knoll, Detlev Mares (eds.)
Concepts of Urban-Environmental History

2020, 294 p., pb., ill.
29,99 € (DE), 978-3-8376-4375-6
E-Book:
PDF: 26,99 € (DE), ISBN 978-3-8394-4375-0

Jesús Muñoz Morcillo, Caroline Y. Robertson-von Trotha (eds.)
Genealogy of Popular Science
From Ancient Ecphrasis to Virtual Reality

2020, 586 p., pb., col. ill.
49,00 € (DE), 978-3-8376-4835-5
E-Book:
PDF: 48,99 € (DE), ISBN 978-3-8394-4835-9

**All print, e-book and open access versions of the titles in our list
are available in our online shop www.transcript-verlag.de/en!**

Historical Sciences

Monika Ankele, Benoît Majerus (eds.)
Material Cultures of Psychiatry

2020, 416 p., pb., col. ill.
40,00 € (DE), 978-3-8376-4788-4
E-Book: available as free open access publication
PDF: ISBN 978-3-8394-4788-8

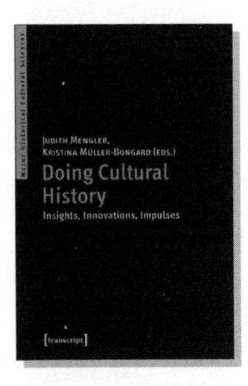

Judith Mengler, Kristina Müller-Bongard (eds.)
Doing Cultural History
Insights, Innovations, Impulses

2018, 198 p., pb., col. ill.
34,99 € (DE), 978-3-8376-4535-4
E-Book:
PDF: 34,99 € (DE), ISBN 978-3-8394-4535-8

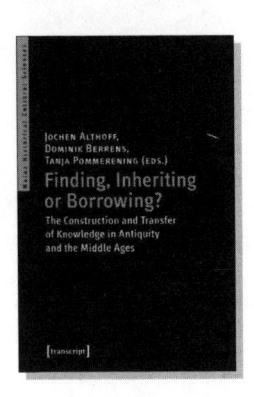

Jochen Althoff, Dominik Berrens, Tanja Pommerening (eds.)
Finding, Inheriting or Borrowing?
The Construction and Transfer of Knowledge
in Antiquity and the Middle Ages

2019, 408 p., pb., ill.
54,99 € (DE), 978-3-8376-4236-0
E-Book: available as free open access publication
PDF: ISBN 978-3-8394-4236-4

**All print, e-book and open access versions of the titles in our list
are available in our online shop www.transcript-verlag.de/en!**